WORKING WITH VULNERABLE CHILDREN, YOUNG PEOPLE AND FAMILIES

Edited by
Graham Brotherton and Mark Cronin

Routledge
Taylor & Francis Group

LONDON AND NEW YORK

First published 2013
by Routledge
2 Park Square, Milton Park, Abingdon, Oxon, OX14 4RN

Simultaneously published in the USA and Canada
by Routledge
711 Third Avenue, New York, NY 10017

Routledge is an imprint of the Taylor & Francis Group, an informa business

British Library Cataloguing in Publication Data
A catalogue record for this book is available from the British Library

Library of Congress Cataloging in Publication Data
Working with vulnerable children, young people and families / edited by Graham Brotherton and Mark Cronin.
pages cm
Includes bibliographical references.
1. Problem children--Services for--Great Britain. 2. Problem youth--Services for--Great Britain. 3. Families--Services for--Great Britain. 4. Social work with children--Great Britain. 5. Social work with youth--Great Britain. 6. Family social work--Great Britain. I. Brotherton, Graham. II. Cronin, Terence Mark.
HV751.A6W695 2013
362.74'50941--dc23
2012050605

ISBN: 978-0-415-53472-7 (hbk)
ISBN: 978-0-415-53473-4 (pbk)
ISBN: 978-0-203-11314-1 (ebk)

Typeset in Bembo
by Taylor & Francis Books

MIX
Paper from
responsible sources
FSC
www.fsc.org   FSC® C013056

Printed and bound in Great Britain by
TJ International Ltd, Padstow, Cornwall

WORKING WITH VULNERABLE CHILDREN, YOUNG PEOPLE AND FAMILIES

The potential for early intervention to prevent social problems later in life has become the focus of much debate in recent years and finds itself at the centre of contemporary social policy. The meaning of 'vulnerability' – one of the key concepts in this drive – is examined in this book, as well as the relationship between vulnerability and the individual, communities and society.

This book introduces students to a broad debate around what constitutes vulnerability and related concepts such as risk and resilience, and examines how vulnerability has been conceptualised by policy makers with a clear focus on early intervention. Adopting a case study approach, it opens with chapters examining the concept of vulnerability from sociological, psychological and social policy perspectives before looking at examples around disability, homelessness, leaving care, victims of violence, sexual abuse, prison, the internet and drug use.

Supporting students in engaging with and evaluating the conceptualisation and application of vulnerability in professional practice, this book is suitable for anyone either preparing for or currently working within the children's workforce, from social work and health care to education and youth work.

Graham Brotherton is Head of Working with Children Young People and Families at Newman University, UK.

Mark Cronin is Senior Lecturer in Early Childhood Education and Care at Newman University, UK.

Irene Barrow (1925–2008) A woman who
knew how to triumph through adversity – love you Nan

TABLE OF CONTENTS

LIST OF CONTRIBUTORS

Karen Argent has been a senior lecturer in Early Childhood Education and Care at Newman University since 2001. Prior to this, she taught in a wide range of educational settings, including special, nursery and primary schools and a further education college. She has also worked in the voluntary sector as an inclusion worker on one of the first Sure Start Programmes. Her research interests include working with the families of prisoners and other socially excluded groups, children's literature, disability awareness and children's rights.

Graham Brotherton is head of Working with Children Young People and Families at Newman University. Prior to working in higher education he worked in a number of roles within both the voluntary and statutory sectors, encompassing looked-after children, supported housing and disability. His particular interest is the relationship between social policy and practice, especially in the context of 'family' policy.

Chris Collett is a senior lecturer in Early Childhood Education and Care at Newman University. She has taught in a range of special schools, working with children with moderate to profound disabilities, from nursery age to young adults. After a short time teaching adults with learning and mental health difficulties she moved to the Birmingham Special Educational Needs advisory service, and Area SENCO Team. Chris's academic interests are inclusion, SEN and disability and equality and human rights.

Mark Cronin is a senior lecturer in Early Childhood Education and Care at Newman University. Prior to entering higher education he worked as a Children and Families social worker in both the statutory sector as part of a local authority care management team and the voluntary sector in a community-based family centre. He has also worked for a number of other voluntary organisations involved in family support and direct work with children. His particular interests are safeguarding, social policy and working with children and families.

Stephen Dixon is a senior lecturer in Education Studies at Newman University and teaches on a range of courses, including the BA (Hons) in Education Studies, BA Media and Creative Arts modules and the MA programme. Previously a senior lecturer in ICT, Stephen specialises in E-learning and the use of multimedia in learning and teaching, with particular focus on web-based materials, web design and film making. He also runs modules on the social, political and ethical considerations of using technology. He has acted as external consultant for other universities, and is a Fellow of the Higher Education Academy.

Dr Sharon Hall lectures in Working with Children Young People and Families at Newman University. She completed ESRC-sponsored doctoral research into working holistically with young people who had sexually harmed others, building on her background as an integrative therapist with this group. Prior to this, Sharon worked as a dramatherapist and with young people in local authority care.

Terry Potter has extensive experience of working in the statutory, voluntary and trade union sectors with families and individuals in poverty and has published a number of studies relating to the impact of low pay and unemployment. In 2001 he became Director of Research for Birmingham Voluntary Service Council and in 2006 he founded the Centre for Community Research. He has been a senior lecturer in Working with Children Young People and Families at Newman University for five years, specialising in community development, social class and participatory research.

Mike Seal is head of Youth and Community Work at Newman University. He has worked in and around the housing and homeless sector for 20 years as a worker, researcher and academic. He was elected to the Royal Society of Arts for his work in this area. He has written four previous books about working in the sector and published numerous articles on issues relevant to it.

Roger Willoughby is a senior lecturer in Education Studies at Newman University. He has a background in clinical psychology, counselling and psychotherapy and his interests include the development of interdisciplinary perspectives on psychoanalytic and psychological theory and practice and lifespan developmental psychology – in particular, child and adolescent development.

1

WHAT DO WE MEAN WHEN WE TALK ABOUT 'VULNERABILITY'?

Terry Potter and Graham Brotherton

Introduction

The idea that individuals or groups of people who share certain common characteristics can be categorised as 'vulnerable' has become an established part of the debate about the development of effective social policy interventions. In a time of limited resources, the argument runs, it is sensible to focus time, expertise and taxpayers' money in the form of benefit payments on those people most at risk of harm. This is not, of course, a new idea. As Samantha Williams (2011) has pointed out in her study of the English poor laws of the eighteenth and nineteenth centuries, if it is possible to describe the key attributes that make a person, family or whole community 'vulnerable', it becomes easier to make more resources available to them and, crucially, easier to withdraw such support if their behaviour or actions transgress the boundaries of what is deemed to be socially acceptable.

Reflective Activity

Think about your own understanding of the word 'vulnerable': who do you think is vulnerable, and why? Where do you think your ideas have come from?

However, the concept of vulnerable individuals or vulnerable social groups is often easier to talk about than to define. Historically, the debate about what constitutes vulnerability has been ideologically polarised: either the focus is on structural explanations which locate the cause of potential risk or harm in social and/or economic circumstances that are largely beyond the control of the individual (poverty, high levels of crime, unemployment, poor public health, housing shortages, etc.); or, alternatively, responsibility for vulnerability and its attendant risks (both to the person and to the wider social good) is seen to rest with the frailty and failure of the individual (low educational attainment, drug or alcohol dependency, susceptibility to abuse, etc.). However, although these two positions are associated with very different ideological approaches, it is often the case that the popular discourse freely mixes these different explanations together and this has served to obscure the fact that discussions about who gets labelled as 'vulnerable' are in fact debates about competing ideological and political ideas over what we really think about issues of personal and collective responsibility.

One of the results of this hybridisation of the causes of vulnerability is that it has encouraged policy makers to depoliticise the notion of vulnerability and see it as something with common characteristics that is located in the outside world and which can be identified and measured. By using a combination of known structural barriers to well-being in conjunction with the personal characteristics and qualities of the individual, policy analysts are encouraged to produce a set of measurable indicators (both qualitative and quantitative) that allow funds to be allocated and interventions deployed to lessen or overcome the perceived levels of vulnerability experienced by individuals or groups. However, Mary Anderson (1994, p.327) points out that, 'when vulnerability is seen only as a criterion for selecting bene-ficiary groups', its value as a policy concept becomes extremely limited. This chapter will argue that to properly understand the concept of vulnerability it is necessary to re-establish the idea of it as a political discourse and go back to the fundamental ideological schism that set social and economic structure against indi-vidual agency. Who is identified as vulnerable, why and who decides that such a label is merited is not simply an argument about how we redistribute wealth to alleviate risk but a much wider battle between competing political ideas about the kind of society we wish to live in. Constantly changing ideas of what constitutes social and economic vulnerability clearly reflect this political battleground and has driven the ongoing debate about the role and structure of welfare.

In many ways the key manifestation of the argument that vulnerability is created by structural barriers in society has been the 'classic' model of the British welfare state (Lowe 2005). Seen as the quintessential Liberal/Left response to vulnerability it captures the idea that what is at issue is the absence or unfair application of economic and social power. Individuals and groups become vulnerable and at risk when they are not equipped to deal with the vicissitudes of the social or economic marketplace. Those with economic or political power exercise that power to the disadvantage and peril of those who do not have the same levels of 'insurance' and, as a result, society as a whole needs a system of collective welfare that ensures the well-being of those who may come to harm without help and support. This idea of providing those at risk with an insurance underwritten by the wider community is at the heart of what became known as the British post-war consensus on the state's role in welfare provision.

However, for the Right, this focus on the structural causes of vulnerability has always been problematic because it depersonalises the debate. The role of personal decision-making and individual responsibility becomes marginalised when it is possible to blame outside forces for the risks run by individuals and their families. Vulnerability is, as a consequence, frequently cast by those on the right of the political debate either as a deficit or a weakness that describes the shortcomings of individuals from both a skill/accomplishment perspective *and* from a moral and ethical viewpoint. The idea that the individual is in some way responsible for their vulnerability and the consequent risk they place themselves and their family or community in is as much a moral and ethical concern as it is an economic one. Charles Murray (1990), in his conceptualisation of the 'underclass', articulates this link between social circumstances and personal morality. He differentiates the deserving poor from the undeserving poor – those who are at risk through no fault of their own (the truly vulnerable) and those who select risky situations as a calculated lifestyle choice, expecting wider society to act as a welfare guarantor.

Identifying who is vulnerable is, clearly, not something which can be done through the simple application of a set of objective criteria. The concept of the vulnerable individual or group is, and has always been, shaped and influenced by the dominant political ideology of the day and tells us a lot about the type of society that is being crafted. The principles underlying the introduction of the British welfare state in 1948 provide a useful case study of how the liberal Left interpreted the idea of vulnerability and the role the state would play in supporting its citizens. By contrast, the views of Charles Murray and his conceptualisation of the 'underclass' prefigures the emergence of a very different, more critical right-wing interpretation of the value of state-based welfare and the perceptions of vulnerability it embodies.

The chapter continues with an examination of these two positions with a view to establishing the way in which notions of vulnerability were influenced by the dominant political discourses at the heart of each model.

Vulnerability and the 'classic' model of the British welfare state

Asa Briggs (2000, p.18) refers to the welfare state as the use of 'organised power' to 'modify the play of market forces'. He postulates the view that this is done at three different levels: to ensure a minimum income regardless of the market value of work and/or property; to meet social unexpected or unwelcome contingencies such as unemployment or sickness; to guarantee fair and equal access to all services regardless of social status.

Ann Oakley (1994, p.6), in referring to the classic phase of the welfare state, 1945–76, identifies social class as the key issue that shaped both thinking about vulnerability and the responses to those risks:

> Class divisions, seen in a unidimensional light, provided the raw material for welfare intervention: in this sense, both the existence of class inequalities and the motive for eradicating these were intrinsic to post war conceptions of welfare.

What is clear from both these statements is that those who are vulnerable and hence in need of, or potentially in need of, welfare are those people in society who are seen to be disadvantaged in terms of the accumulation of material wealth, access to services and the ability to control or influence power and decision-making. In essence, vulnerability in this model springs from fundamental structural inequalities that arise from the way in which society is organised and may have nothing to do with the economic or moral worth of the individual. Indeed, such structural inequalities within the capitalist system may be seen to make whole groups of people vulnerable because they all share the lack of economic and political power that ensures well-being. In this way the welfare state and the services it offers is predicated on a belief that whole groups of people – women, black and minority ethnic groups, the disabled, the very elderly and the very young – are always, at some level, vulnerable because they are excluded in a variety of ways from power and influence.

It is easy to see how this characterisation of vulnerability could be used to justify the role of direct state intervention in wealth creation and distribution through the creation of a bureaucracy. Indeed, Esping-Anderson (1990, p.13) notes that it has been argued that the welfare state is enabled by 'the rise of modern bureaucracy as a rational, universalist and efficient form of organisation'. However, it is also important to see the development of the British welfare state at this time in its contemporary political context, and here it is possible to see its creation as a manifestation of class politics. The Labour Party's conceptualisation of a universal welfare state had a clear *political* goal which had at its heart partisan class interest, made clear in Aneurin Bevan's extended meditation on the political backdrop to the creation of the welfare state, *In Place of Fear* (1952, p.37):

> [A]nti-Socialists shudder at the very name of planning and … planners and planning are the daily butt of reactionary newspapers. Nor is this difficult to understand. Their principal proprietors made their fortunes not by owning newspapers, but by successful speculation in industry and finance … . For the great mass of the people the case is wholly different. They are the victims who are preyed upon. It is they who are stalked and waylaid, harried and tormented, their lives made a nightmare of uncertainty.

Esping-Anderson refers to this as the class-mobilisation theory, which 'assumes that welfare states do more than simply alleviate the current ills of the system: a social democratic welfare state will, in its own right, establish critical power resources for wage-earners and thus strengthen labor movements' (1990, p.16).

It is possible to see the era of the classic welfare state, 1945–76, as a period in which the role of welfare in helping deal with vulnerability found some common political ground – at least within the confines of parliamentary politics – despite the adversarial nature of the British political party system. This consensus was built upon a shared or common characterisation of what vulnerability was and, albeit in largely coded language, an acceptance that vulnerability arose because of the unfair workings of the capitalist system. Those most vulnerable and most at risk were in that state because of social structures which unfairly denied opportunity or significantly undervalued the contributions of certain groups of people. As a result of this it was the legitimate role of the state to intervene in that process, take the side of the vulnerable and create ways of equalising or at least redressing their comparative lack of power.

Recasting the post-war consensus on welfare

Powell and Hewitt (2002, pp.52–3) note the widely held view amongst many sociologists that the mid-1970s marks 'the end-point of nearly 100 years of welfare state growth' but also highlight the range of different reasons given for citing that date. However, what is undeniable is that, by the time of the Conservative general election victory of 1979, a very different set of ideas about what constitutes vulnerability had begun to emerge that would reshape dominant ideas about what the role and nature of a welfare state should be. Powell and Hewitt also marshal evidence to suggest that, throughout the 1980s, 'the welfare state was chipped away rather than rolled back' (p. 48), but this failure to make wholesale organisational or bureaucratic change did not prevent the emergence of a new discourse around welfare and vulnerability that moved significantly away from a structural political explanation towards an analysis that gave a much more dominant role to the notion of individual agency. Oakley (1994, p.7) notes that:

> Over the period since the 1970s, the traditional structural paradigm of welfare came to be seen to be providing an inadequate explanation of the origins of differences between people in health and welfare outcomes ... . It was argued that the search for the explanation of these differences had to include some notion of individual coping strategies – some idea of humans being capable of constructing their own lives creatively, even in 'objectively' difficult conditions.

This focus on the *responsibility* of the individual to minimise risk to themselves, their family and their community was, in political dialogue, often contrasted with the suggested exploitation by welfare claimants of their 'rights' to a wrap-around support system which would protect them from the consequences of their actions no matter how feckless their behaviour. The emergence of this populist debate has been characterised by the Left as part of the liberal 'backlash' and the emergence of a critique of the welfare state articulated by the New Right and constructed to make clear links with the associated doctrine of neo-liberalism (Harvey 2005, pp.55–63).

In this construct of vulnerability it is not just the individual who is at risk but society itself. The behaviour of the individual not only puts them and their families at risk but threatens the well-being of civil society and the body politic. A range of social and economic problems – unemployment, educational failure, marital breakdown, homelessness, drug dependency, poor health – are not seen as being brought about by inequality or power differentials but are recast as individual failings and the outcome of poor choices. The role of the state is not to pander to these supposed vulnerabilities but to help the individual find a personal path to their own salvation. This is not only good for them but good for society because it moves people from dependency to self-sufficiency and, at the same time, cuts the long-term cost of welfare provision. But this is not simply a pragmatic response to need. Ensuring that the state pulls back from assuming responsibility for those who have previously been seen as vulnerable is a morally and ethically necessary thing to do (Hayek 1944) and has the added bonus of allowing increasing scarce resources to be focussed on those who are 'genuinely' vulnerable. What emerges from this, as a result, is a modern-day revisiting of the Victorian notion of the deserving and the undeserving poor.

As the reference to Frederick Hayek suggests, this discourse has a significant historical heritage and a distinctly colourful lineage, taking in the likes of Keith Joseph and Margaret Thatcher in the UK and Ronald Reagan in the US (and most subsequent Republican presidents). Indeed, the Trans-Atlantic cross-fertilisation of ideas around the restructuring of the state's relationship to welfare has been a key part of the development of the core ideas. The work of Charles Murray provides a useful case study and illustrates the way in which global economies now generate global social policy trends. Murray's reputation in the UK is largely built on two papers he published in 1990 and 1994 and which deal with the notion of an emerging 'underclass' – a term he uses to describe and explain what he sees as the growing numbers of poor working-class people who display undesirable, reckless or even criminal behaviour. Murray did not himself invent the tern 'underclass' but, according to Ruth Lister (1996), adopted it from the journalism of Ken Auletta who 'emphasised the behaviour and values of those deemed to be members of the underclass' (p.2). Christopher Jencks (1989), analysing the debate in the US, said:

> The term underclass, with its echoes of the underworld, conjures up sin, or at least unorthodox behaviour. Low income may be a necessary condition for membership in such a class, but it isn't sufficient.
>
> *(p.14)*

Murray effectively took these ideas forward and emphasised three key characteristics of 'underclass' identity – economic (especially those of working age unable or unwilling to get a job); educational (those unable or unprepared to get appropriate qualifications); moral (those who display a disregard for social norms and displaying anti-social or deviant behaviour). In his 1990 essay, 'The emerging British underclass', Murray's starting position is to challenge what he sees as a wrong-headed social consensus about the structural nature of poverty. He claims that, as the result of an 'intellectual reformation' (p.25) that took place in the 1960s, all individual blame for poverty was removed, leading to 'poor people, *all* poor people' being seen as 'victims [who] would be equally successful if only society gave them a fair shake' (p.25). His rejection of what he sees as a homogenisation of the poor leads him to postulate the view that we have developed a welfare state that effectively rewards behaviour that is fundamentally damaging to society. In seeking to explain why there is this growing 'underclass' he cites three key drivers of the process: the breakdown of traditional family structure, the prevalence and acceptance of low-level criminal activity and the decline of the work ethic. Society, he claims, has become too tolerant of the idea that the poor are victims and fails to apportion blame to them for their failure to contribute to society. The young (especially those who lack good role models), he claims, are quick to pick up the messages society offers: if crime isn't seen to be adequately punished, a proportion of young people will turn to crime. Similarly, if a life on benefits is available then, for some low-skilled and poorly educated young people, this will seem like a good option, especially if society does not force them to behave differently. When it comes to choices about family life, he says, young women are being privileged by the benefit and housing system for making socially bad decisions but economically understandable ones:

> I'm not saying that single young women get pregnant for the money. I'm not chiding them for immorality. I'm not saying they don't love their babies ... Rather a series of changes in benefit rates and collateral housing benefits lifted a large proportion of low-income young women above the threshold where having and keeping a baby became economically feasible.
>
> *(p.49)*

Murray's work has been both controversial and hugely influential in social and political terms. Whatever the merits of his hypothesis, Murray's work became a kind of legitimate rallying point for the New Right which was seeking to fundamentally challenge the long-term consensus on the role of the state in welfare provision. By cherry-picking some key sound bites from the likes of Charles Murray, those on the right were able to reshape and reform ideas about vulnerability. Here was 'evidence' that there were deserving and undeserving poor – those who were vulnerable through no fault of their own and those who were vulnerable as a result of their own choices and their own behaviour.

It is clear that the policies of both the Labour government between 1997 and 2010 and the subsequent Coalition government have bought into this analysis in a substantial way. Ideas about who can and cannot work and how benefits should be limited or redirected have been heavily influenced by this idea that there are groups of people and individuals in society who need to be seen not as vulnerable but as the architects of their own disadvantage. The legitimate role of the state, it is argued, is not to increase their dependency but to help them to self-sufficiency, and sometimes this is more about the use of the stick than the carrot. However, this is not just about behaviour but about the mentality behind the behaviour – it is a moral crusade as much as an economic one. Ideas about vulnerability and the role of the state in helping the vulnerable can only bring about effective social change if people's attitudes regarding the inter-relationship between welfare, work, family cohesion and personal responsibility can be changed. Welfare must be harnessed therefore to directly and explicitly support those behaviours seen as desirable against those seen to foster unacceptable personal decisions.

This section has focussed on the concept of vulnerability as a political idea. It has not tried to find a definitive set of characteristics that everyone would acknowledge as demonstrating vulnerability but has come to the issue from the other end of the debate. It argues that who is seen as vulnerable and how that vulnerability is catered for is a concept that depends on a shifting balance between competing political ideologies constantly redrawing the discourse on the nature of vulnerability and the state.

Neo-liberalism welfare and vulnerability

As has been argued in the previous section, key shifts in understanding, or at least operationalising, the concept of vulnerability can be traced to a number of key ideological debates which emerged during the second half of the twentieth century. First, the growing influence of neo-liberalism as a significant discourse on social policy, and second, the emergence of an influential strand of sociological thinking which emphasises individualisation and risk. These issues are discussed from a policy perspective in Chapter 3 but are considered here in a more theoretical way.

As previously highlighted, neo-liberalism emerged as a set of ideas with the capacity to influence policy during the 1970s (through the Thatcher administration in the UK and the Reagan administration in the United States), although its history is rather longer than this, with an intellectual lineage particularly in the United States and Austria/Germany that dates back to the aftermath of the Second World War. Central to the tenets of neo-liberalism are a series of assumptions about the appropriate role of the state which can be summarised as:

- the complete acceptance of free market capitalism as the only appropriate form of social organisation;
- the market is morally superior to the state in that it gives primacy to the values of self-reliance and individual resilience;
- the role of the state should be limited to areas where individuals cannot make their own arrangements.

David Harvey (2005) further suggests that neo-liberalism is a system of 'accumulation by dispossession', which has four main pillars:

First, the 'privatization and commodification' of public goods: in other words the removal of a range of goods and services from the public sphere and their sale or contracting out to private companies. This includes 'utilities' (things we all need to use, such as water or electricity) and services such as education or social care. The process of privatisation and commodification in the UK started in the 1980s with the utilities and has continued through to the present through the increasing privatisation of health, social care and education.

Second, Harvey talks about 'financialization', which incorporates a number of features but particularly addresses the liberalisation or deregulation of financial regimes and institutions during the 1970s and in subsequent years. Harvey argues that this approach leads to greater risks being taken which, he argues, can be very damaging to global economic structures when those risks don't pay off. The size of the problem that can be created is exemplified in the depth of the financial crisis that erupted in 2007/8 and which has been linked directly to speculative economic activity by large corporations in which short-term financial gain was prioritised over any other considerations.

He also talks about the 'management and manipulation of crises', in which moments of crisis, such as those witnessed in the financial sector and referred to previously, become seen as an opportunity to consolidate or develop neo-liberal interests. This process is also described by Naomi Klein (2007) as 'disaster capitalism', which, she argues, is where financial meltdown or military action create sufficient fear amongst the population to enable wholesale political change to occur where under more stable conditions change would be much more difficult to achieve. An example of this might be the widespread tendency to 'solve' the current 'problem' of public spending through ever greater privatisation or by transferring services from paid workers to volunteers. For Harvey this is 'state redistribution', in which the state becomes an agent of the upward redistribution of wealth through tax policy and the cutting of 'costly' public services.

Risk vulnerability and individualisation

Taken overall, the emergence of neo-liberalism as a dominant economic and social model can be summed up as a move towards greater individualisation, the commodification of those services previously associated with the state and, as a result, greater inequality. All of this has significant implications for how we conceptualise vulnerability. This has been reinforced by the emergence of sociological perspectives which also foreground processes of individualisation and which can be exemplified by considering the work of Ulrich Beck and Anthony Giddens.

Whilst there are significant overlaps – and indeed Beck and Giddens have worked collaboratively – we will turn first to Beck and the concept of the 'Risk Society'. For Beck, ever since the shift in social organisation started by industrialisation individuals have been less and less in control of their own circumstances and, he suggests, are consequently at greater risk. This may be because of factors over which they have little or no control, an example of which might be environmental pollution or industrialised food production. However, these risks are not evenly distributed but relate to economic status, though not necessarily to traditional notions of social class. Greater wealth brings with it more choice, though this is not sufficient for us to be free from exposure to certain categories of risk – everyone, regardless of income, may still be put at risk by global pollutants, for example. However, that is not to say money has no value in protecting us from such risks – if we have sufficient income we can choose to live in a 'desirable' neighbourhood or purchase organic produce which we believe is 'good' for us. The fact that some people can make such choices and can, at least to some degree, limit their risk while others can't underscores the basic truism that it is often poverty that puts us at risk rather than poor decision-making, and as a consequence it is poverty that makes many individuals and whole communities vulnerable.

It is important to note that Beck's thesis is not without its critics, who argue that the notion of a changing risk environment is overly simplistic. These critics would point to something like the role of infectious disease in previous generations. In this situation everyone was to some extent at risk, although it is still the case that risk was not evenly distributed because different groups had differing access to adequate housing, sanitation and clean drinking water. Furthermore Beck is criticised for not considering the uneven way in which power is distributed (see, for example, Elliott 2002). Beck argues, however, that it is not possible to make comparisons across different time periods because in pre-modern societies people saw the world in a different way, relying on fatalistic or supernatural explanations rather than seeing events as a consequence of human action.

In short, Beck's argument that modern, advanced societies have risk hard-wired into them and that it is the job of the individual to enhance their skills and resources in a way that will protect them from these risks presupposes that each individual has equal capacity to put such protections in place. Indeed, Beck's conception of risk raises some key issues for this book. We are arguing that vulnerability is created by a complex interconnection of social circumstances and should not be seen as arising from mistaken or misplaced individual behaviour, decisions or fecklessness. Indeed, it can be argued that some of the behaviour of vulnerable groups which is often perceived as problematic can also be constructed as a rational response to very difficult circumstances The practical consequences of this are discussed in Chapter 3, but here we need to focus on the way in which vulnerability is constructed by policy makers, practitioners and by those labelled as vulnerable.

'Reflexive modernization'

In order to do this we need to detour briefly into the concept of 'reflexive modernization', a concept deployed in slightly differing ways by Beck, Giddens and others. This is a complex idea and the subject of dispute and disagreement even amongst those who propose it (Beck 2009). There is not space here to explore it in detail, but the dispute relates to the ways in which we make sense of or gain knowledge of the world around us and whether this happens in a linear or non-linear way.

The first model – which Beck characterises as being found in the work of Giddens – sees reflexivity as rational: we construct and reconstruct our story of ourselves in response to changes in our personal circumstances. This view, it is suggested, prioritises scientific and linear understandings about the world and how it functions which allows us to predict and anticipate outcomes.

However, the alternative view of reflexive knowledge sees it as always contingent and uncertain – there is always the potential for new circumstances to arise and for unexpected knowledge to emerge which has the potential to upset, challenge or transform our understanding of a situation. This may seem a rather obscure and abstract distinction, but when we link it to notions of risk and vulnerability we can begin to see its practical importance for policy makers and for understanding the life worlds of those deemed to be vulnerable. In order to do this we now need to return to Giddens.

The role of reflexivity

Giddens is interested in notions of risk from a political as well as a sociological perspective. For example, in *The Third Way* (1998) he argues that one of the consequences of this pervasive notion of risk is that those who feel they can do least to 'control' the risks they face are liable to develop a sense of hopelessness and hence respond passively to those risks. The neo-liberal construct of Individualisation, according to Giddens, creates pressure on individuals to 'make sense' of the world around them through creating and recreating the story of their own lives. This process of reflexive narration is central to our sense of identity and we can only function effectively if we are able to master this process of taking responsibility for our subjective relationship with the external world. For Giddens, a primary manifestation of this is the growth of techniques and resources which purport to support this process; for example, 'self-help' books or job roles, such as counsellors, which are explicitly focussed on supporting individual adjustment. Being vulnerable can therefore be seen as a failure to take ownership of our lives and the opportunities available to us. In policy terms the logical conclusion of Giddens' construct of reflexivity is to develop policy initiatives which assume that reflexive individuals are rational actors who can be 'pushed' or 'nudged' by particular initiatives to act in particular ways. The 'New Labour' approach to Welfare to Work (discussed in Chapter 3) provides an illustration of this.

In this context reflexivity needs to be considered on two levels; first, as an element within the policy-making process which seeks to 'activate' those in receipt of support, but also as the way in which those who are on the 'receiving end' of policy make sense of it. This may seem an esoteric point but it has important practical consequences because it invites us to ask whether those who make and implement policy around so-called vulnerable groups are seeing or defining vulnerability in the same way as those they are defining as vulnerable. The financial crash of 2007/8 provides us with a good example to illustrate this point. The emergence of an analysis that located the cause of the financial crash as a problem of public spending rather than a problem of the banking system has created a new group of Europeans who had not previously seen themselves as 'at risk' but who certainly now are. Many people in Greece, for example, who, prior to the financial crash, saw themselves as professional or middle class suddenly found themselves perceived as vulnerable or marginalised. This had important consequences for the choices available to them in an environment where political and financial decisions were effectively in the hands of international financiers and politicians not accountable to the people of Greece. Beck's version of reflexivity provides a useful way of thinking about this through his notion of a 'world risk society' (Beck 1999) which highlights that the challenges and risks are globalised and need to be acknowledged as such.

This raises another element of Beck's thesis, the notion of organised irresponsibility. Beck argues, through the use of a number of case studies, that law and policy consistently fail to acknowledge either the causes or nature of risk in terms of compensating or responding to 'victims' and in terms of the accountability of key social actors. In particular he argues that notions of corporate responsibility tend to be either limited or absent. Whilst Beck is talking here mainly about risk in the environmental sense, it can be argued that it can also be applied to thinking about economic risk – especially in the light of the 2007/8 financial crisis. Most analysts accept that the major causal factor for the global financial crash was badly judged speculative lending by large banks, especially, but not exclusively, in the United States. However, over the course of the intervening period this has been recast as a crisis of the state and in particular of state spending. As Farnsworth and Irving (2010) highlight, this is at least in part because the money that sovereign governments were forced to borrow in order to support failing banks was itself borrowed from more stable banks; so in supporting banks that were seen as too big to fail, governments in fact became more dependent on money borrowed from the financial sector that had caused the crisis. Thus, money borrowed to bail out failing banks becomes debt that can only be paid by reducing spending on public services. In this sense the state itself has become more vulnerable to the market and less able to respond to the needs of vulnerable citizens.

A different perspective on risk has been elaborated by Zygmunt Bauman in a series of books published from the early 1990s onwards. Bauman has developed and explored the concept of 'liquidity', which can be best conceived of as the idea that in complex modern societies, personal relationships, including family relationships, as well as broader social structures have become more fluid, shifting and complex. A number of factors have been cited for this – mostly stemming from globalisation, with its massive flows of people, resources and information. Linked to it is the process of urbanisation and the greater mixing of diverse groups of people which is leading to a breaking down or challenging of 'traditional' beliefs and attitudes. For Bauman this increased complexity has very significant consequences for how we experience the world and specifically our need to acknowledge the contingent and uncertain nature of many aspects of our lives.

Bauman is particularly interested in how we respond to the need to make 'moral' choices when faced with strangers or 'the other' – a common facet of life in complex modern societies. Bauman draws on the work of Max Weber to try and explain the way in which emotional or potentially irrational responses have been replaced by what could be called a bureaucratic system of classification and processing which dehumanises the relationship between the practitioner and those in receipt of services. This provides distance between the professional and the subject so that the interaction becomes a technical rather than a moral encounter. Bauman (2000) used this idea of bureaucratisation as a way to explain why so many ordinary people became involved in the 'processing' of the victims of the Holocaust. Whilst it can of course be argued that this is an extreme example of making particular groups vulnerable, it provides a useful way of reflecting upon the debate about 'troubled families' or the controversial 'work capacity assessment' process and the way in which vulnerable groups are first constructed and then processed through policy discourses.

It is difficult to summarise a complex and nuanced body of work like Bauman's in a short summary like this, but the notion of life as contingent and linked to a subjective understanding of both the personal and the specific context provides a vital counterpoint to the determinist approach which underpins both neo-liberal thinking and Giddens' conceptualisation of the 'Third Way' with its very specific attempt to link a model of risk to policy prescriptions.

Vulnerability – a European perspective

No book which seeks to discuss vulnerability can fail to acknowledge that conceptions of vulnerability at both UK and European level have been profoundly affected by the impact of the financial crisis that has already been referred to several times in this chapter. Across the European Union there has been a widespread claim that existing models of social provision are unsustainable and that as a result there has been a move towards reducing spending on 'vulnerable' groups. Whilst this has been most pronounced in Ireland, Greece, Spain and Italy, in the UK the Coalition government has used the 'deficit' as a justification for its social policy agenda. As highlighted previously, neo-liberal politics, and the work of Charles Murray which has become so closely associated with it, has foregrounded a discourse of vulnerability which arises as a result of individual limitations or failure and this has also played a key role in justifying this shift.

However, a comparative approach sheds some useful light on some of these claims. There have been a number of attempts to develop comparative models of welfare regimes, of which perhaps the best known is the work of Gosta Esping-Anderson (1990). While there is not space here to explore the limitations of this model, it is important to note that there is a significant literature which seeks to evaluate and critique the model. However, Esping-Anderson's work can still provide some useful insights and his idea of three key models of welfare regimes – social democratic, conservative-corporatist and liberal-residual – can help us understand the extent to which welfare services have become commodified (the degree to which they are bought and sold), as well as the extent to which middle-class people remain users of welfare services.

TABLE 1.1 Summary of Esping-Anderson's model

	Social Democratic	Conservative-corporatist	Liberal-residual
Overview of welfare provision	State is primary provider of services; very limited private provision	Services seen as a partnership between state and individual, often mediated through third party, e.g. employer-based insurance	Seen as an individual responsibility, often private insurance-based. Public welfare is 'safety net'
Examples	Finland	Germany	United States
Perception of vulnerability	Emphasis on shared risks, vulnerability as social	Intermediate model, often with emphasis on family as mediator	Vulnerability as individual failure

Whilst it has to be acknowledged that the literature exploring which 'types' of welfare regime are likely to cope best with the financial crisis is limited, such evidence as does exist (for example, Farnsworth and Irving 2010) seems to suggest that, perhaps unsurprisingly, inequality has grown most quickly in the liberal regimes of the US and UK and some notion of inclusivity has been most effectively maintained in social democratic ones such as Denmark. As highlighted previously, this has real significance for the debate on vulnerability in terms of the debate about who is vulnerable and how they are defined as such.

Conclusion

The main intention of this chapter has been to explore how current ideas about vulnerability emerged historically and then to explore some of the ways in which sociological thinking has sought to explore the notion of vulnerability. Key to this is understanding that vulnerability is complex and contested and that it is constructed in different ways in different contexts. The next two chapters develop this theme by considering how vulnerability can be analysed from first a psychological and then a policy perspective

The intersecting nature of factors affecting vulnerability requires policy makers, practitioners to find ways of thinking which acknowledge this complexity and this is explored in a range of contexts in the remaining chapters: disability, homelessness, care leavers, the families of prisoners, young people who sexually harm, violence and online safety.

References

Anderson, M.B. (1994) 'The concept of vulnerability: beyond the focus on vulnerable groups', *International Review of the Red Cross*, 34, pp.327–332

Bauman, Z. (2000) *Modernity and the Holocaust*. Cambridge: Polity Press

Beck, U. (1999) *World risk society*. Cambridge: Polity

——(2009) *World at risk*. Cambridge: Polity Press

Bevan, A. (1952) *In place of fear*. Kingswood: Windmill Press

Briggs, A. (2000) 'The welfare state in historical perspective' in Pierson, C. and Castles, F.G. (eds) *The welfare state reader*. Cambridge: Polity Press, pp.18–32

Elliott, A. (2002) 'Beck's sociology of risk: a critical assessment', *Sociology*, 36(2), pp.293–315

Esping-Anderson, G. (1990) *The three worlds of welfare capitalism*. Cambridge: Polity Press

Farnsworth, K. and Irving, Z. (2010) *Varieties of crisis within variable capitalisms: Contemplating the implications of economic crisis for social policy*. Paper presented at the Social Policy Association Annual Conference, University of Lincoln, 5–7 July 2010. Available online at www.social-policy.org.uk/lincoln/Farnsworth%20and%20Irving.pdf (accessed on 12 September 2012)

Giddens, A. (1998) *The third way: the renewal of social democracy*. Cambridge: Polity

Harvey, D. (2005) *A brief history of neoliberalism*. Oxford: OUP

Hayek, F. (1944) *The road to serfdom*. London: Routledge

Jencks, C. (1989) 'What is the underclass – and is it growing?' *Focus*, 12(1), p.14

Klein, N. (2007) *The shock doctrine*. London: Allen Lane

Lister, R. (ed.) (1996) *Charles Murray and the underclass: the developing debate*. London: IEA Health and Welfare Unit/Sunday Times

Lowe, R. (2005) *The welfare state in Britain since 1945*. Basingstoke: Palgrave Macmillan

Murray, C. (1990) 'The emerging British underclass' in IEA Health and Welfare Unit (1996) *Charles Murray and the underclass*. Choice in Welfare No. 33. London: IEA/Sunday Times, pp.24–53

——(1994) 'Underclass: the crisis deepens' in IEA Health and Welfare Unit (1996) *Charles Murray and the underclass*. Choice in Welfare No. 33. London: IEA/Sunday Times, pp.100–136

Oakley, A. (1994) 'Introduction' in Oakley, A. and Williams, A.S. (eds) *The politics of the welfare state*. London: UCL Press

Powell, M. and Hewitt, M. (2002) *Welfare state and welfare change*. Buckingham: Open University Press

Williams, S. (2011) *Poverty, gender and life-cycle under the English Poor Law, 1760–1834*. Woodbridge: Royal Historical Society

2

NOTES ON PSYCHOLOGIES OF VULNERABILITY

Roger Willoughby

Introduction

Years ago, the psychoanalyst Roger Money-Kyrle (1971) drew attention to three uncomfortable basic facts of life: (1) we are all dependent on other people for our survival, (2) we are not the centre of the universe and consequently our exclusion is inevitable, and (3) the passage of time and ultimately death are inevitable. Such facts about human dependency and vulnerability in ourselves and others can evoke strong feelings, ranging for example from shame, fear, hatred, contempt, derision, depression and pity to concern, empathy and fellow-understanding. Behavioural responses may be similarly variegated, from the hostile and potentially lethal to the protective.

Vulnerability can thus be a very uncomfortable reality, particularly when it is our own. One common way of dealing with such psychological discomfort is to utilise processes of psychological splitting in order to disown or disavow it in ourselves and to then defensively localise it by projecting it into others (Segal, 1986). Such externalisation, when extreme, can lead to the dehumanisation and stereotyping of others and the concomitant impoverishment of the self (due to losing touch with core elements of our humanity). Such projective processes occur not only on an individual level but also in groups of all sizes: families, organisations, communities and nations.

It is important to emphasise these dynamic processes at the outset because in studying vulnerability it can be all too easy to identify individuals or populations that are supposedly at risk while overlooking our own inescapable individual human vulnerability. Thus, for example, people from ethnic minority groups, or who are very young, elderly, poor, homeless, female, or have disabilities or mental health problems are commonly clustered together as vulnerable or potentially vulnerable groups. They are seen as vulnerable *to* something, typically some negative health, social, economic or moral risk. Seeking to define the characteristics of such groups based on their relative risk of harm, while relevant for policy making and service planning, potentially entails an unhelpful deficit model that stereotypes and essentialises such groups under that banner (Liamputtong, 2007). Strengths and experiential qualities of those identified as vulnerable may be overlooked, as may dynamic and wider systemic social factors, and the baseline fact that – for any and all of us – to be alive is to be vulnerable. We all face distress and ultimately death.

With this as an important caution, the present chapter outlines several classic contributions to the biopsychosocial approach to vulnerability, to psychopathology (and to a lesser extent to the wider experience of distress), offers a conceptualisation of these factors in relation to development and help-seeking, and outlines associated vulnerability-stress models.

In considering different types of psychopathology (e.g. depression, anxiety, personality disorder, schizophrenia, etc), key vulnerability factors are typically seen as a necessary though not sufficient precursor to the emergence of a particular disorder, the emergence itself being triggered by other factors such as stress (for a review of the latter concept see Grant and McMahon, 2005). *Vulnerabilities are thus typically regarded as predispositional causal factors that may together with other factors catalyse distress and disorder.* These factors may be observed on many different though potentially interrelated levels: genetic, biological, cognitive, affective, interpersonal, attachment, etc (Hankin and Abela, 2005).

Working definitions of vulnerability as a concept frequently suggest it is a relatively stable, latent trait within individuals that confers a relative susceptibility to a disorder (Zubin and Spring, 1977; Ingram and Luxton, 2005). Where relatively immutable factors (such as genetic or other constitutional variables) are less significant as sources of vulnerability, other factors – such as psycho-social vulnerabilities – may be more plastic and thus more amenable to fluctuation within and between individuals over the life course, as well as more auspicious targets for intervention.

Notions of vulnerability or *diathesis* (the terms are interchangeable) have a long history dating back to ancient Graeco-Roman medicine, where the latter term related to the doctrine of the humours expounded by Hippocrates (*c*.460–*c*.370 BC) and Galen (AD 129–*c*.201). By the nineteenth century, the concept was part of the emergent psychiatric nosology and theories of aetiology. During the twentieth century, notions of vulnerability *and* stress were increasingly prominent in emerging conceptualisations of schizophrenia (Bleuler, 1963), as well as other forms of psychopathology. It is to a consideration of these concepts that we now turn.

Vulnerability, distress and help-seeking

The precipitants of human distress are many and varied, as are the factors that prompt individuals to seek help. In the health services, the demand for care is often said to be elastic and to constantly outstrip whatever provision is made (O'Donnell *et al.*, 1992). Given finite resources, difficult political and managerial decisions are required in their allocation. Some people become patients and some do not in this process. Some needs go unmet. This situation causes further distress for those untreated, guilt in some of those treated, anxiety for the health service workers and agendas for planners and politicians. It is well established, however, that those people who succeed in being considered potential patients are only a small proportion of those who at any one time have similar needs. This phenomenon, the clinical iceberg (Scambler and Scambler, 1984; Elliott *et al.*, 2011), posits that the majority of symptoms do not result in demands on the health services, instead being self or informally treated or untreated. This pattern exits for all symptoms and all levels of pathology (Wadsworth *et al.*, 1971; Wilkinson, 2007).

The work by Goldberg and Huxley (1992; Goldberg, 1995; Goldberg and Goodyer, 2005), looking more specifically at psychological and emotional disorders, has recapitulated this pattern. They found a one year community prevalence rate of between 26 and 31 per cent for such disorders. Only a proportion of these people are identified in primary care as having conspicuous psychiatric morbidity and fewer still are referred on to specialist mental health services (10 per cent and 3 per cent of the general population respectively). Their epidemiological work on pathways to psychiatric care predicted an average rate of 20.8 adults per 1,000 of the population would utilise specialist mental health services per year. More recent studies in Edinburgh found referral rates of between 23 and 24.6 per 1,000 (O'Sullivan *et al.*, 2005, 2007). For people with 'severe mental disorders', such as schizophrenia and bi-polar affective disorder, health service utilisation is markedly higher than those with 'common' varieties (Goldberg and Huxley, 1980, 1992). This distinction Goldberg and Huxley relate to the very marked social disability produced by the 'severe' disorders and their much lower spontaneous remission rates. A similar pattern pertains with somatic medical conditions. However, the general trend with 'common mental disorders' is clearly towards non-consultation with the appropriate health services. This is in spite of many of the disorders' being debilitating, chronic and sources of marked suffering. It is also in spite of their being responsive to treatment.

Considered from a naïve realist perspective, this picture might be regarded as counter-intuitive: people who are distressed would be expected (from utilitarian assumptions) to seek to minimise this. An alternative reading of the picture, however, might suggest that people who are distressed or who have an increased vulnerability to distress and disorder (where these are seen as points on a dimensional construct, moving from less to more severe) are also impaired in seeking help, and that perhaps the two phenomena have some common aetiological factors.

In considering this speculation in more depth, it is important to do so in the light of existing studies in two major areas: (a) common vulnerability and stress factors predisposing individuals to psychological distress and disorder, and (b) factors associated with health service help-seeking. The review will be largely limited to what Goldberg and Huxley (1992) term 'common mental disorders', particularly less severe depression and anxiety disorders. The plausibility of there being certain common factors will then be reconsidered.

Common vulnerability factors to psychological distress and disorder

When people encounter psycho-social adversity (variously termed as stressors, problems, life events, etc) they respond differently. For some the encounter is the precipitant of psychological disorder, others continue to function in a healthy manner and some grow or develop as persons, depending on their relative under-lying levels of vulnerability. This section considers three specimen potential sources of such different levels of vulnerability: inherited genetic factors, recent interpersonal factors and remote interpersonal factors.

Genetic factors

With severe mental disorders, such as bi-polar affective disorder, there is persuasive evidence for a significant specific genetic contribution (e.g. McGuffin and Katz, 1989; Hankin and Abela, 2005). The same, however, cannot be said for common mental disorders. Considering less severe (or 'non-endogenous') forms of depression, McGuffin and Katz (1989) conclude that, although heritability appears to be a factor, non-genetic influences seem to be more important. Kendler *et al.* (1987), in a large twin study, showed that, while genetic factors influenced the propensity to both depression and anxiety, the effect was not specific. It was non-genetic (environmental) factors that appeared to have more specific effects in determining a person's vulnerability to develop one or other variety of distress or disorder. Given the high incidence of such disorders (e.g. nearly 60 per cent of adults by the age of 65 will have had one or more episodes of clinically significant depression: Bebbington *et al.*, 1989), and the lack of specificity between genetic factors and particular disorders, it appears that such factors (while clearly contributory) are less relevant explanatory variables.

Recent interpersonal factors

Epidemiological studies have highlighted a number of factors that increase a person's vulnerability to stressors. The classic work of George Brown and his team has been of seminal importance in this area. Brown and Harris (1978) pointed to the centrality of social support in mediating the impact of stressful life events on working-class women, a group with a particularly high incidence of depression. Their emphasis on the lack of a close confiding relationship, the presence of three or more children under 14 and unemployment as vulnerability factors can each be seen as contributing to impaired support. The other vulnerability factor, death of one's mother before the age of 11, will be further discussed in the next section. The most crucial and subsequently most replicated element within this social support matrix has been the importance of a positive confiding relationship, a core tie (e.g. Campbell *et al.*, 1983; Bebbington *et al.*, 1984; and Harris, 1988). The lack of such a relationship conferred a markedly higher vulnerability to depression on people when experiencing stressful life events.

Brown *et al.* (1986) elaborated the earlier vulnerability picture. They found that in order to be protective against depression a confiding relationship needed to be associated with active unambivalent emotional support, i.e. without a negative response from the core tie. The quality of these central relationships was highly correlated with self-esteem. Being 'let down' by the core tie in the face of adversity increased the risk of depression, whilst crisis support for those with markedly low self-esteem was found to be very helpful. This susceptibility to the behaviour of the core tie supports Brown *et al.*'s (1986, 1990a) contention that people have few, and frequently only one, such core relationship.

Self-esteem was seen as a crucial intermediary in this research. Brown *et al.* (1986) argue that self-esteem is at least 'in part the internal representation of social support' (p. 827). Brown *et al.* (1990a) discuss this latter point in relation to their finding that a high correlation existed between 'objective' and 'subjective' ratings of the core tie, i.e. between the actual and the perceived support. They concluded that this correlation is due to the external environment having been internalised and so rendered potent.

The specific findings relating to core ties are supported by a number of studies looking at the prophylactic effect of more general social support (e.g. Power, 1988; Cramer, 1991; and Cresswell *et al.*, 1992). Cramer's (1990, 2001, 2006) studies of the utility of a close personal relationship for a person's psychological adjustment offers a similar conclusion. Nils Cochrane (1990) has lent further empirical support by showing a strong association between depression and unsatisfactory physical contact experience. He also demonstrates an independent association between depression and the experience of not being loved. He argues positively that good physical contact importantly contributes to a person's inner resources for coping with adversity. This echoes Brown *et al.*'s (1986; and see Brown, 2002) assertion that, when facing a crisis, it is the derivatives of the person's history of support, the subjective sense of having received 'unconditional love [that prevents] the subject from despairing of a better future' (p. 826).

These studies highlight the vital significance of current relationships in people's lives (Crocker, 2002; Tew, 2011). Such relationships confer meaning and purpose. In seeking to understand vulnerability and distress, this area has clear explanatory potential, which will be considered further below.

Remote interpersonal factors

The influence of early childhood experience on the later adult mind in general and on coping resources in particular (self-esteem, in Brown and Harris's [1978] terminology) has been the subject of an increasing number of studies from a variety of theoretical perspectives. A certain consensus appears to be emerging from these studies. The epidemiological studies by Brown and Harris (1978, 1989) indicated a correlation between loss of one's mother through death (before age 11) or long-term separation and adult depression. Bebbington *et al.* (1991) found that separation (particularly between age five and ten) was the one significant predictor of subsequent psychiatric difficulties. Brown *et al.* (1990a) reported that it was the lack of care consequent to such early experiences that increased later vulnerability, and that even without maternal loss, lack of early care was a significant predictor of increased adult vulnerability (via low self-esteem) to depression (Bifulco *et al.*, 1987). While this effect was independent of poorer quality adult core ties in accounting for part of the variance in vulnerability, it increased people's risk of such adult core ties. The combined effect of both poor adult and child relationships was unsurprisingly the severest, participants with both being five times more likely to have low self-esteem than those with neither (Brown *et al.*, 1990 a, b). Nils Cochrane (1990), in investigating childhood and adult physical contact and feeling loved, found a similar pattern: unsatisfactory early experience of these phenomena (particularly physical contact) increased later vulnerability to depression; however, adult experience was again the more powerful predictor.

Subsequently, Brown and his colleagues (Brown and Harris, 1993; Brown *et al.*, 1993; Brown, 2002; Oatley, 2007) expanded their earlier investigations into early experiences as precursors of adult depression, this time also considering adult anxiety disorders. They reconfirmed the role of both early and recent adversity (particularly lack of parental care, and abuse) in increasing the risk of adult depression. The experiences of loss and lack of hope were here the main differential influences in the development of depression. Adult anxiety disorders (excepting mild agoraphobia and simple phobias) were only found to be related to childhood adversity as a vulnerability factor. Danger and lack of security were the differential influences for such anxiety disorders. Given the high likelihood of negative life events producing apprehension of both danger and loss, the significant co-morbidity of the two conditions is unsurprising.

Developmental psychologists have also proposed that early experience has a significant influence on a person's later self. Taking one example from the extensive literature with this area, Newson (1978) argued that it is the infant's experience of 'unreasonable care', the sense the infant has that her parent (or special caregiver) considers her *especially* valuable, that is important to the child's development of a positive sense of self. Newson thus argued that 'partiality' is a necessary characteristic of the caregiving role for the child, an important point to emphasise, particularly in the context of social care services.

Attachment theorists, drawing frequently on Bowlby's (e.g. 1969, 1973, 1980, 1988; and see Davila *et al.*, 2005; Pearce, 2009) work, are paying increasing attention to links between insecure childhood attachment and later adult vulnerability to depression and distress. Healthy child and adult functioning, according to the theory, follows early parenting that is both supportive when necessary and encouraging of autonomy (Bretherton, 1992; Kennedy and Kennedy, 2004). This fosters the development of reciprocally influenced 'internal working models' of both self and others. A healthy working model would be one internalised or derived from an attachment figure experienced as accessible, trustworthy and ready to help if called on. The mother is usually the most significant and earliest attachment figure, although infants do form attachments to a hierarchy of other figures (Bretherton, 1992; Van der Horst, 2011).

Various researchers (e.g. Heard, 1987; Kennedy and Kennedy, 2004; Davila et al., 2005), in reviewing a number of attachment studies, have emphasised the correspondence between parent and child attachment classifications and that less secure infant attachment predicted adjustment difficulties in primary school. Further research by Fonagy (2001; Fonagy et al., 1991) using the Adult Attachment Interview (George et al., 1985) demonstrated a significant intergenerational correlation in attachment security: for example, early insecure attachment was thus associated with subsequent adult vulnerability. Adult psychopathology is not, however, the inevitable consequence of an insecure childhood attachment. Later experience, such as a good marriage, can powerfully mitigate the effects of early difficulties (Fonagy et al., 1991; Quinton and Rutter, 1988; Shaver, 2011). Pound (1987) corroborates these finding in her discussion of the NEWPIN project, a befriending project for vulnerable women. She highlights the self-perpetuating tendency for those with early childhood histories of adversity and related insecure attachment to have poorer adult relationships, which 'manifested themselves in a generalised withdrawal from or ambivalent attitude to people at large' (Pound, 1987, p. 10).

The development by Parker and his colleagues of the Parental Bonding Instrument (hereafter PBI) (Parker et al., 1979) provided one example of a straightforward measure of recalled parental behaviour, conceptualised here as a potential vulnerability factor. Research (e.g. Parker, 1981, 1989; Mackinnon et al., 1991) suggested the PBI was also a reliable and valid measure of actual parental characteristics. The measure incorporated two dimensions, care and overprotection, which were thought to be important components of such attachment experience. The poles of each dimension were caring and empathic versus rejecting or indifferent behaviour and behaviour that was overprotective, intrusive and fostering dependency versus encouraging independence and autonomy respectively. Parker's original research (Parker et al., 1979) found an association between a perceived lack of care and overprotection. This pattern appeared connected with adult distress in a number of subsequent studies with both psychiatric outpatients and non-patient groups. It characterised the early experience of those with neurotic disorders (e.g. Alnaes and Torgersen, 1990; Parker, 1983a, 1984) in general and non-endogenous depression (e.g. Birtchnell, 1988; Parker, 1983b, 1984; Parker et al., 1987; Plantes et al., 1988; Davila et al., 2005) in particular.

Gotlib et al. (1988), with a clinical sample, argued for the primacy of PBI care scores as the major predictor of distress (subsequently supported by Mackinnon et al., 1993) but suggested from their study that overprotection as a vulnerability factor was linked with more chronic distress. Richman and Flaherty (1986) concluded that early overprotection was linked with more chronic distress and may be linked to adult depression through it fostering a dependent and fatalistic personality style. Congruent with this, Plantes *et al.* (1988) conclude that low care may be of prime aetiological significance in failure to develop 'good enough' self-esteem, thus leaving the person vulnerable to adversity and potential psychological distress. Overprotection they argue may impair normal socialisation and independence, thus depriving the person of potential resources useful when facing difficult life events. Flaherty and Richman (1986), using a broad measure of adult social support, failed to find a relationship with parental overprotection. Positive relationships were however found between childhood parental and particularly maternal care and adult social support levels, a finding subsequently replicated by Parker and Barnett (1988).

As argued above with regard to current relationships, people's early relationships also seem of considerable importance in trying to understand their current states, including their levels of vulnerability. The general trend of the studies quoted makes it clear that early adversity can become a lived experience, predisposing people to vulnerability and continued distress as adults. This will be discussed further below.

Vulnerability and health service use

A number of studies have sought to delineate those patient factors that determine who does and does not make use of health services; factors that are important in both identifying vulnerability and remediating it. Numerous factors have emerged from these studies (and some with particular consistency) that relate to such 'illness behaviour' (Mechanic, 1992).

The most significant finding is that the severity, duration and number of a person's current symptoms all positively predict their likelihood of seeking professional help (e.g. Barker *et al.*, 1990; Bebbington *et al.*, 1991; Fylkesnes *et al.*, 1992; Hannay, 1986; Olfson and Klerman, 1992; Verhaak and Tijhuis, 1992). This was found when distress was both self-rated and professionally diagnosed. Looking at depression in a large white-collar cohort, Dew *et al.* (1991) reconfirmed this finding, but noted soberingly that only 32 per cent of those with depression at clinical levels actually sought help (a phenomenon known as the illness 'iceberg').

A person's past history of service utilisation is also predictive of current use (Dew *et al.*, 1991; Hannay, 1986). Having obtained some satisfaction from past service use appears important. Murray and Corney (1990) found that among GP low attenders experiencing marked psychosocial difficulties the main stated reason for not attending was past unsatisfactory or disappointing consulting experience. Apart from those who might be regarded as disillusioned, Murray and Corney (1990) note a smaller group of low attenders with marked psychosocial difficulties who seemed to have extreme difficulty in confiding in anybody.

Sex differences are commonly reported in professional help-seeking, with women consulting more frequently than men (Scambler and Scambler, 1984; Briscoe, 1987; Fylkesnes *et al.*, 1992; Wilkinson, 2007; Elliott *et al.*, 2011). Looking specifically at GP consultations, Briscoe (1987) found women consulted nearly twice as often as men, although more recent research has failed to note any significant sex difference when just considering professional help-seeking (Barker et al., 1990; Elliott et al., 2011).

Findings on age differences are variable. Barker et al. (1990) found older adults were more likely to seek professional help, as did Fylkesnes et al. (1992). The latter noted however that, while younger people were less likely to seek initial professional help, they were more likely to be referred on to specialist services. In their large study on help-seeking for emotional problems, Tijhuis et al. (1990) found younger adults more willing to seek help.

Higher socio-economic status, Mechanic (1992) argues, increases people's likelihood of consultation, as people with this status are more able to accurately appraise their symptoms. Tijhuis et al.'s (1990) finding that higher income levels and more education are both associated with a higher willingness to consult supports this. Fylkesnes et al. (1992) found those with more education were less likely to visit their GP, although more likely to be referred on to specialist services. Bebbington et al. (1991) confirmed psychiatric referral was associated with a higher educational level.

Dew et al. (1991), in her white-collar group, found that both poor support from one's spouse and encouragement to consult from family and friends were linked with an increased likelihood of service use. The latter finding has been widely supported and is seen as an important 'trigger' for seeking help (Zola, 1973; Scambler and Scambler, 1984). This form of 'peer encouragement' can be seen as influencing pre-patients' perception of the controllability or treatability of their distress. When this perception is raised, people engage in more active problem-related coping (Schussler, 1992), which could reasonably be thought to include health service help-seeking.

Illness behaviour would seem to be in a constant state of change, being influenced by both the availability of and wider politico-cultural attitudes towards health care and prevailing social attitudes about illness and distress. Bearing this in mind and given that the studies outlined in this section were carried out in several countries, some variation is to be expected. Sociological models have largely influenced the investigation of help-seeking (see, for example, Gallagher, 1980; Sørgaard, et al., 1999; Tuckett, 1976; and Zola, 1973). While these have been productive insofar as they go, they have largely failed to connect with the psychological studies of distress and its aetiology (as detailed in previous sections, for example). Thus, a holistic conceptualisation is still needed. The next section offers a sketch of one possible dynamic model to incorporate the origins of vulnerability, distress and help-seeking.

A conceptual model of vulnerability, distress and help-seeking

Balint (1957) was one of the first to suggest a holistic approach when he advised doctors that in addition to (a) considering the symptoms they ought to understand

(b) why the patient presents these particular symptoms (c) at this particular time and (d) what they seek from the consultation. He suggests this is a process of negotiation within a relationship, and it is this that appears to be a major common thread to vulnerability, distress and help-seeking.

Given a certain inherited genetic endowment, constitution and temperament (Rutter, 1987), humans develop within an interactive social context. Through the caregiver–infant relationship, infants gradually elaborate a model of themselves and of the caregiver that becomes incorporated into the mind. The interpersonal becomes intrapsychic (e.g. Brown *et al.*, 1990a). This might be regarded variously as a type of early cognitive-affective schema, a working model of attachment relationship or an internal object relationship.

In Western culture, a single caregiver, typically the mother, has been the prime model. Other significant relationships developmentally come after this and are usually of somewhat lesser importance, particularly when the infant is disturbed and seeks care or comfort. Given a 'good enough' early relationship, the infant can develop a sense of herself as good, lovable, worthwhile, creative, giving and autonomous. Simultaneously, she will form a model of the caregiver as a 'good object': someone who is trustworthy, accessible, loving and helpful. Where the early experience is less than might be averagely expected – through, for example, a difficult temperament in the infant or psychological disturbance in the caregiver – the results impact on the infant's nascent sense of self and other. The infant might thus come to view herself as bad, naughty, harmful or unlovable and the caregiver as unloving, withholding, rejecting, seductive, hostile, incompetent, vulnerable, fragile or erratic. Object relations theorists (see, for example, Rayner, 1990) argue that it is the relationship that is internalised as dynamic process. Thus, some reciprocity would be expected between the internal sense of self and other (or 'object', in psychodynamic terminology). Apart from the prime attachment figure, others undoubtedly influence the child's development (Shaver, 2011). These other attachments or object relaionships, if good, could mitigate some of the negative effects of a poorer-quality one. If bad, the reverse is likely, as later experiences reinforce and compound earlier ones. Self-esteem (Brown and Harris, 1978, 1989; though see Baumeister, 2005) appears clearly to be an aspect of these internal object relationships.

Such factors contribute to the everyday experience of psychological states, identity, social relationships and mental health. The specifics of lived experience in these areas are clearly important to consider for both indivuals and groups. Certain phenomena, such as childhood abuse (e.g. Chu *et al.*, 2011) and racialised life events (Brugra and Ayonrinde, 2001), can be readily seen to assume prominence in conceptualising this area.

The studies outlined above strongly suggest that early experience influences adult states. Early object relations, whilst changeable and not inevitably predisposing to vulnerability to adult psychopathology (Quinton and Rutter, 1988; Tew, 2011), are models that filter and influence adult perceptions of people (both self and other) and events. They can affect the quality of core ties and wider social support (e.g. Flaherty and Richman, 1986; Richman and Flaherty, 1986). While the early internalised childhood relationships seem to predispose people to the repetition of similar quality ones in adulthood, the adult relationships (core ties) can be viewed as independent (or at least semi-independent) of them. The relationship between the quality of adult core ties and vulnerability seems clear from the previous discussion of the literature.

Poor early child combined with poor later adult relationships are likely to confer a significant adult vulnerability to distress, particularly in the face of adverse life events. Poor early combined with good adult and good early combined with poor adult relationships all generally raise a person's vulnerability level, with the latter constellation appearing to confer the higher probabilistic risk. By contrast, good early and good adult (internal) relationships will generally be a protective pattern, promoting resilience (Seery et al., 2010). It seems to be the quality of the internalised current adult experience (i.e. that which is more contemporaneous) that is most associated with one's level of vulnerability.

While poor object relations are a vulnerability factor and raise one's risk of disorder even in the absence of life events, when in conjunction with difficult life events a compound effect occurs. Such life events act as a multiplier, increasing the risk of psychological disorder. Goldberg and his colleagues (Goldberg and Huxley, 1992; Goldberg, 1995; Goldberg and Goodyer, 2005) have pointed out that vulnerability factors increase both the rate and impact of life events, thus further raising the prospects of distress.

Weiss (1986) has offered a typology of adult bonds as derived versions of early childhood attachment relations and include within this 'help-obtaining' bonds. He argues that these are 'transferences' as they 'often contain the security-seeking motivations that children bring to relationships of attachment' (Weiss, 1986, p. 108). From an object-relations perspective, Bollas (1987) has elegantly discussed people's search for transformation through a 'transformational object' as a search for the lost infantile experience of rapid change, development, satisfaction or 'transformation' by the prime object (the mother or main caregiver). Help-seeking would clearly be a species of this transformational quest. It (like other adult relationships) would however not be fully immune from the effects of the first internal working model, or object relation, and we might expect, for instance, that those with a lack of trust in their early caregiver would on that basis be more likely to be ambivalent about seeking help as adults.

In summary, a dynamic model of development is here highlighted in which identity is formed in and through human relationships (and their internalisation and consequent incorporation into mental structure). The results of this contribute to our level of vulnerability to psychological disorder, particularly when faced with difficult life events, and to our ability to seek or utilise help. The basic dynamic model is outlined in Figure 2.1 and we can now turn to consider vulnerability models at a micro level.

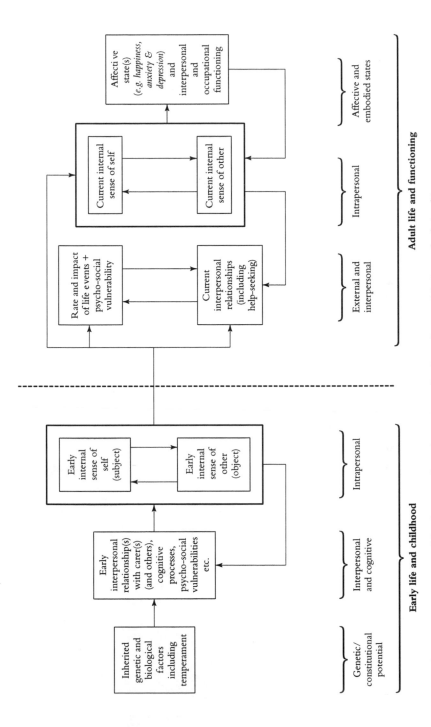

FIGURE 2.1 Schematic representation of development through a process of reciprocal external in internal relationships

Vulnerability-stress models

Most models that seek to conceptualise the role of vulnerability in combination with the experience of stressors in the development of distress and psychopathology contain a number of common principles (Ingram and Luxton, 2005; Tew, 2011). Chief among these are dose effects: essentially the greater the range and degree of vulnerabilities and the greater the number and severity of stressors the greater will be the level of distress and severity of psychopathology. This dose-response relationship is thus grounded on a view of quantified vulnerability and exposure as cumulative or arithmetic. The relative contributions of (1) particular vulnerability factors and (2) stressors needed to trigger distress or psychopathology may thus vary both within and between individuals and may vary across time. For instance, one person with high levels of vulnerability may thus succumb to a disorder in the face of modest stressors, while another with lower vulnerability loadings may be able to sustain far higher levels of stressors before negative outcomes are catalysed. Some models posit inverse (or ipsative) relationships between vulnerabilities and stressors, such that the greater the presence of one catalysing factor the less other factors are required to trigger a disorder (Monroe and Hadjiyannakis, 2002). Repeated experience of a disorder may over time increase the vulnerability to and likelihood of the disorder's reoccurrence in the face of diminishing stressors. Post (1992), for example, suggested this may be due to 'kindling', within which repeated experience produces heightened sensitivity to stressors, thus allowing similar disorders to be manifest when exposed in the future to lower levels of stressors.

These interactive factors are common to the majority of models of vulnerability-stress within the psychological literature (see Figure 2.2). Ingram and Luxton (2005) usefully delineate four types of vulnerability-stress model that, while sharing these features, vary in some degree: (1) interactive model with dichotomous vulnerabilities, (2) quasi-continuous vulnerability models, (3) threshold models, and (4) risk-resilience continuum models. The essential features of these are as follows:

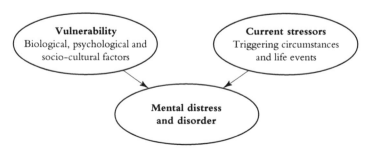

FIGURE 2.2 Basic Stress-Vulnerability model (adapted from Tew, 2011)

Interactive model with dichotomous vulnerabilities

The early models of schizophrenia developed by Meehl (1962) suggested that vulnerability to that condition was based on genetic factors that produced organic brain pathology, which in turn produced schizotypic personality. The latter when compounded with an environmental stressor could then trigger schizophrenia. The presence or absence of the supposed genetic vulnerability gave the model its *dichotomous* label; without the underlying vulnerability stressors would not induce a schizophrenic disorder. Similar models conceptualising Post Traumatic Stress Disorder (PTSD) by McKeever and Huff (2003) suggested two possible types of vulnerability: biological variations such as neurophysiological dysregulation and ecological variables such as childhood abuse and maltreatment and cognitive distortions. Among the large body of work on child abuse, that by Chu *et al.* (2011) usefully develops aspects of this.

Quasi-continuous vulnerability models

In contrast to the preceding model, following a threshold being passed, the vulnerability factors are here regarded as wholly or substantially continuous. Drawing on Aaron Beck's cognitive model of depression, Ingram and Luxton (2005) suggest his depressogenic schema theory could offer an example of this type of model within which differing degrees of cognitive schema toxicity would confer a continuous range of vulnerability, to be triggered by life events.

Threshold models

Here, vulnerability and stress are not merely seen as additive, but as having interactional effects rather like a multiplier, following a threshold being passed. Within Zubin and Spring's (1977) model of schizophrenia, for instance, they suggest vulnerability to the condition is universal: the disorder is manifest once rising life stressors precipitate an individual across their threshold for the development of the condition.

Risk-resilience continuum models

These models emphasise the opposite pole of the traditional vulnerability continuum: they thus focus instead on protective factors, resilience and competence, extending the basic threshold-type models in a positive direction. This allows for a more refined and extended continuum between health and disorder. In a large US longitudinal study, Seery *et al.* (2010) found typical linear relations between levels of lifetime adversity and measures of global distress, functional impairment, PTSD symptoms and lower life satisfaction. However, more interestingly, the study also found that – in contrast to no and high levels of adversity – a history of *some* lifetime adversity predicted lower levels of global distress, less functional impairment, lower PTSD symptomatology and higher life satisfaction scores. Such data suggest that, in moderation, the experience of adversity can have a positive impact on certain life outcomes, operating perhaps through a type of stress inoculation and the promotion of resilience.

Conclusions

The various models here presented suggest that vulnerability in itself (as a relative and dynamic concept) is a necessary though not sufficient precondition for disorder. Other environmental stressors in dynamic interactions with vulnerabilities are typically regarded as necessary to trigger states of distress and severer levels of disorder or psychopathology (Tew, 2011). Dose-response effects play an important role in this and in the key vulnerability-stress models. Research on and theorisation of vulnerability, however, has often utilised a positivist stance, which – when crudely deployed – can contribute to dominant discourses that essentialise the vulnerable as 'other'.

By contrast, it has been here argued that vulnerabilities exist in every human being as a basic fact of life (Money-Kyrle, 1971). The permeability of our psychological and social lives to the other (and thus to both vulnerability and growth) was earlier emphasised in the object-relations informed model of development (see Figure 2.1). Our own contextual and existential vulnerability is, however, so often concealed from everyday consciousness, with seductive notions of invulnerability (promoted by cultural archetypes such as super-heroes, armour and invulnerability, eternal life and deities, as well as psychological processes such as utopian fantasying, evasion of reality, and wish fulfillment) contributing to individual and collective denial of our own vulnerability. These ideas from psychoanalysis, which have certain commonalities with Foucault's (1974) discussion of dividing practices and the creation of binaries, offer an approach to vulnerability as a concept that eschews a strictly normative understanding in favour of a relational, dynamic and systemic approach.

Vulnerability is essentially being vulnerable *to* something, typically an environmental (whether biological or social) threat and this shift in focus is recognised within the biopsychosocial model. Modest experience of and engagement with adversity appears to confer some psychosocial benefit, impacting positively on quality-of-life scores, probably in part through promoting resilience (Seery *et al.*, 2010). Other modes of help-seeking, as previously discussed, importantly situate people within a dynamic matrix wherein self and other interrelate and these encounters contribute to the development and vicissitudes of mental life and our inner resources. The present psychologically and psychoanalytically informed reading of vulnerability thus situates the concept at the centre of human life, rather than othering it on the periphery.

References

Alnaes, R. and Torgersen, S. (1990) 'Parental representation in patients with major depression, anxiety disorder and mixed conditions', *Acta psychiatrica Scandinavica*, 81: 518–522.

Balint, M. (1957) *The doctor, his patient and the illness*, New York: International Universities Press.

Barker, C., Pistrang, N., Shapiro, D. A. and Shaw, I. (1990) 'Coping and help seeking in the UK adult population', *British journal of clinical psychology*, 29(3): 271–285.

Baumeister, R. (2005) 'Rethinking self-esteem: why nonprofits should stop pushing self-esteem and start endorsing self-control', *Stanford social innovation review*, Winter 2005: 34–41.

Bebbington, P. E., Hurry, J. and Tennant, C. (1991) 'The Camberwell community survey: a summary of results', *Social psychiatry and psychiatric epidemiology*, 26: 195–201.

Bebbington, P. E., Hurry, J., Tennant, C. and Sturt, E. (1984) 'Misfortune and resilience: a community study of women', *Psychological medicine*, 14: 347–363.

Bebbington, P. E., Katz, R., McGuffin, P., Tennant, C. and Hurry, J. (1989) 'The risk of minor depression before age 65: results from a community survey', *Psychological medicine*, 19: 393–400.

Bifulco, A., Brown, G .W. and Harris, T. O. (1987) 'Loss of parent, lack of parental care, and adult psychiatric disorder: The Islington Study', *Journal of affective disorders*, 12: 115–128.

Birtchnell, J. (1988) 'Depression and family relationships', *British journal of psychiatry*, 153: 758–769.

Bleuler, M. (1963) 'Conception of schizophrenia within the last fifty years and today', *Proceedings of the Royal Society of Medicine*, 56: 945–952.

Bollas, C. (1987). *The shadow of the object: psychoanalysis of the unthought known*, London: Free Association.

Bowlby, J. (1969) *Attachment and loss*: Volume 1. *Attachment*, London: Hogarth Press.

——(1973). *Attachment and loss*: Volume 2. *Separation*, London: Hogarth Press.

——(1980). *Attachment and loss*: Volume 3. *Loss, sadness and depression*, London: Hogarth Press.

——(1988) *A secure base: clinical applications of attachment theory*, London: Routledge.

Bretherton, T. (1992) 'The origins of attachment theory: John Bowlby and Mary Ainsworth', *Developmental psychology*, 28(5): 759–775.

Briscoe, M. E. (1987) 'Why do people go to the doctor? Sex differences in the correlates of GP consultants', *Social science and medicine*, 25(5): 507–513.

Brown, G. W. (2002) 'Social roles, context and evolution in the origins of depression', *Journal of health and social behaviour*, 43(3): 255–276.

Brown, G. W. and Harris, T. O. (1978) *The social origins of depression: a study of psychiatric disorder in women*, London: Tavistock.

——(1989) *Life events and illness*, New York: Guilford.

——(1993) 'Aetiology of anxiety and depressive disorders in the inner city population. I. Early adversity', *Psychological medicine*, 23: 143–154.

Brown, G. W., Andrews, B., Harris, T., Adler, Z. and Bridge, L. (1986) 'Social support, self esteem and depression', *Psychological medicine*, 16: 813–831.

Brown, G. W., Bifulco, A., Veiel, H. O. F. and Andrews, B (1990a) 'Self esteem and depression II: Social correlates of self esteem', *Social psychiatry and psychiatric epidemiology*, 25: 225–234.

——(1990b) 'Self esteem and depression III: Aetiological issues', *Social psychiatry and psychiatric epidemiology*, 25: 235-243.

Brown, G. W., Harris, T. O. and Elaes, M. J. (1993) 'Aetiology of anxiety and depressive disorders in an inner-city population. 2: Comorbidity and adversity', *Psychological medicine*, 23: 155–165.

Brugra, D. and Ayonrinde, O. (2001). 'Racism, racial life events and mental ill health', *Advances in psychiatric treatments*, 7: 343–349.

Campbell, E., Cope, S. and Teasdale, J. (1983). 'Social factors and affective disorders: an investigation of Brown and Harris's model', *British journal of psychiatry*, 143: 548–553.

Chu, A. T., Pineda, A. S., DePrince, A. P. and Freyd, J. (2011). 'Vulnerability and protective factors for child abuse and maltreatment', in J W White, M P Koss and A E Kazdin (Eds) *Violence against women and children, volume 1: mapping the terrain*, Washington, DC: American Psychological Association: 55–75.

Cochrane, N. (1990) 'Physical contact experience and depression', *Acta psychiatrica Scandinavica supplementum*, 357: 82.

Cramer, D. (1990) 'Psychological adjustment, close relationships and personality: a comment on McLennan and Omodei', *British journal of medical psychology*, 63(4): 341–344.

——(1991) 'Social support and psychological distress in women and men', *British journal of medical psychology*, 64: 147–158.

——(2001) 'Why I study ... close relationships', *Psychologist*, 14(1): 26–27.

——(2006) 'How a supportive partner may increase relationship satisfaction', *British journal of guidance and counselling*, 34(1): 117–131.

Cresswell, C. M., Kuipers, L. and Power, M. S. (1992) 'Social networks and support in long-term psychiatric patients', *Psychological medicine*, 22: 1019–1026.

Crocker, J. (2002) 'Contingencies of self-worth: implications for self-regulation and psychological vulnerability', *Self and identity*, 1: 143–149.

Davila, J., Ramsay, M., Stroud, C. B. and Steinberg, S. J. (2005) 'Attachment as vulnerability to the development of psychopathology', in B. L. Hankin and J. R. Z. Abela (Eds) *Development of psychopathology: a vulnerability-stress perspective*, London: Sage: 215–242.

Dew, M. A., Bromet, E. J., Schulberg, H. C., Parkinson, D. K. and Curtis, E. C. (1991) 'Factors affecting service utilisation for depression in a white collar population', *Social psychiatry and psychiatric epidemiology*, 26: 230–237.

Elliott, A. M., McAteer, A. and Hannaford, P. C. (2011) 'Revisiting the symptom iceberg in today's primary care: results from a UK population survey', *BMC Family Practice*, 12: 16.

Flaherty, J. A. and Richman, J. A. (1986). 'Effects of childhood relationships on the adult's capacity to form social supports', *American journal of psychiatry*, 143(7): 851–855.

Fonagy, P. (2001) *Attachment theory and psychoanalysis*, London: Karnac.

Fonagy, P., Steele, H. and Steele, M. (1991) 'Maternal representations of attachment during pregnancy predict the organisation of infant–mother attachment of one year of age', *Child development*, 62: 891–905.

Foucault, M. (1974) *The archaeology of knowledge*, London: Tavistock.

Fylkesnes, K., Johnsen, R. and Forde, O. H. (1992) 'The Tromso study: factors affecting patient-initiated and provider-initiated use of health care services', *Sociology of health and illness*, 14(2): 274–292.

Gallagher, B. J. (1980) *The sociology of mental illness*, New Jersey: Villanova University.

George, C., Kaplan, N. and Main, M. (1985) *The Adult Attachment Interview*. Unpublished manuscript, University of California at Berkeley, Department of Psychology.

Goldberg, D. (1995) 'Epidemiology of mental disorders in primary care settings', *Epidemiologic reviews*, 17: 182–190.

Goldberg, D. and Goodyer, I. M. (2005) *The origins of common mental disorders: vulnerability, destabilization and restitution*, London: Taylor and Francis.

Goldberg, D. and Huxley, P. (1980) *Mental illness in the community: the pathway to psychiatric care*, London: Tavistock.

Goldberg, D. and Huxley, P. (1992) *Common mental disorders: A bio-social model*, London: Tavistock/Routledge.

Gotlib, I. H., Mount, J. H., Cordy, N. I. and Whiffen, V. E. (1988) 'Depression and perceptions of early parenting: a longitudinal investigation', *British journal of psychiatry*, 152: 24–27.

Grant, K. E. and McMahon, S. D. (2005) 'Conceptualizing the role of stressors in the development of psychopathology', in B. L. Hankin and J. R. Z. Abela (Eds) *Development of psychopathology: a vulnerability-stress perspective*, London: Sage: 3–31.

Hankin, B. L. and Abela, J. R. Z. (2005) *Development of psychopathology: a vulnerability-stress perspective*, London: Sage.

Hannay, D. R. (1986) 'Referral behaviour of patients', *Update*, 15 September 1986: 489–496.

Harris, T. O. (1988) 'Psychosocial vulnerability to depression', in S Henderson and G Burrows (Eds) *Handbook of social psychiatry*, Amsterdam: Elsevier.

Heard, D. (1987) 'The relevance of attachment theory to child psychiatric practice: an update', *Journal of child psychology and psychiatry*, 28(1): 25–28.

Ingram, R. E. and Luxton, D. D. (2005) 'Vulnerability-stress models', in B. L. Hankin and J. R. Z. Abela (Eds) *Development of psychopathology: a vulnerability-stress perspective*, London: Sage: 32–46.

Kendler, K., Heath, A., Martin, N. and Eaves, L. (1987) 'Symptoms of anxiety and symptoms of depression', *Archives of general psychiatry*, 122: 451–457.

Kennedy, J. H. and Kennedy, C. E. (2004) 'Attachment theory: implications for school psychology', *Psychology in the schools*, 41(2): 247–259.

Liamputtong, P. (2007) *Researching the vulnerable: a guide to sensitive research methods*, London: Sage.

McGuffin, P. and Katz, R. (1989) 'The genetics of depression and manic depressive disorders', *British journal of psychiatry*, 155: 294–302.

McKeever, V. M. and Huff, M. E. (2003) 'A diathesis-stress model of posttraumatic stress disorder: ecological, biological, and residual stress pathways', *Review of genetic psychology*: 237–250.

Mackinnon, A. J., Henderson, A. S. and Andrews, G. (1991) 'The Parental Bonding Instrument: a measure of perceived or actual parental behaviour', *Acta psychiatrica Scandinavica*, 83: 153–159.

——(1993) 'Parental "affection less control" as an antecedent to adult depression: a risk factor refined', *Psychological medicine*, 23: 135–141.

Mechanic, D. (1992) 'Health and illness behaviour and patient–practitioner relationships', *Social science and medicine*, 34(12): 1345–1350.

Meehl, P. E. (1962) 'Schizotaxia, Schizotypy, Schizophrenia', *American Psychologist*, 17: 827–838.

Money-Kyrle, R. E. (1971) 'The aim of psycho-analysis', *International journal of psycho-analysis*, 52: 103–106.

Monroe, S. M. and Hadjiyannakis, H. (2002) 'The social environment and depression: Focussing on severe life-events', in I. H. Gotlib and C. L. Hammen (Eds) *Handbook of depression*, New York: Guilford Press: 314–340.

Murray, J. and Corney, R. (1990) 'Not a medical problem: an intensive study of the attitudes and illness behaviour of low attenders with psychosocial difficulties', *Social psychiatry and psychiatric epidemiology*, 25: 159–164.

Newson, E. (1978) 'Unreasonable care: the establishment of selfhood', in G. Vesey (Ed.) *Human values: lectures of the Royal Institute of Philosophy*, London: Harvester Press.

Oatley, K. (2007) 'Slings and arrows: depression and life events', *The psychologist*, 20(4): 228–230.

O'Donnell, O., Maynard, A. and Wright, K. (1992) 'Evaluating mental health care: the role of economics', *Journal of mental health*, 1(1): 39–51.

Olfson, M. and Klerman, G. L. (1992) 'Depressive symptoms and mental health service utilisation in a community sample', *Social psychiatry and psychiatric epidemiology*, 27: 161–167.

O'Sullivan, T., Cotton, A. and Scott, A. (2005) 'Goldberg and Huxley's model revisited', *Psychiatric bulletin*, 29: 116.

O'Sullivan, T., Batra, R., Nolan, M. and Scott, A. (2007) 'Goldberg and Huxley's model 27 years on', *The psychiatrist*, 31: 316

Parker, G. (1981) 'Parental reports of depressives: an investigation of several explanations', *Journal of affective disorders*, 3: 131–140.

——(1983a) *Parental overprotection: a risk factor in psychosocial development*, New York: Grune and Stratton.

——(1983b) 'Parental "affectionless control" as an antecedent to adult depression', *Archives of general psychiatry*, 40: 956–960.

——(1984) 'The measurement of pathogenic parental style and its relevance to psychiatric disorder', *Social psychiatry*, 19: 75–81.

——(1989) 'The Parental Bonding Instrument: psychometric properties reviewed', *Psychiatric developments*, 4: 317–335.

Parker, G. and Barnett, B. (1988) 'Perceptions of parenting in childhood and social support in adulthood', *American journal of psychiatry*, 145(4): 479–482.

Parker, G., Tupling, H. and Brown, L. B. (1979) 'A Parental Bonding Instrument', *British journal of medical psychology*, 52: 1–10.

Parker, G., Kinol, L. and Hayward, L. (1987) 'Parental representations of neurotic and endogenous depressives', *Journal of affective disorders*, 13: 75–82.

Pearce, C. (2009) *A short introduction to attachment and attachment disorder*, London: Jessica Kingsley.

Plantes, M. M., Prusoff, B. A., Brennan, J. and Parker, G. (1988) 'Parental representations of depressed outpatients from a USA sample', *Journal of affective disorders*, 15: 149–144.

Post, R. M. (1992) 'Transduction of psychosocial stress into the neurobiology of recurrent affective disorder', *American journal of psychiatry*, 149: 999–1010.

Pound, A. (1987) 'The development of attachment in adult life – the NEWPIN experiment', paper delivered at Association of Child Psychotherapy in London on John Bowlby's 80th birthday.

Power, M. J. (1988) 'Stress-buffering effects of social support: a longditudinal study', *Motivation and Emotion*, 12(2): 197–204.

Quinton, D. and Rutter, M. (1988) *Parenting breakdown: the making and breaking of inter-generational links*, Brookfield, VT: Gower.

Rayner, E. (1990) *The independent mind in British psychoanalysis*, London: Free Association.

Richman, J. A. and Flaherty, J. A. (1986) 'Childhood relationships, adult coping resources and depression', *Social science and medicine*, 23(7): 709–716.

Rutter, M. (1987) 'Temperament, personality and personality disorder', *British journal of psychiatry*, 150: 443–458.

Scambler, G. and Scambler, A. (1984) 'The illness iceberg and aspects of consulting behaviour', in R. Fitzpatrick, J. Hinton, S. Newman, G. Scambler and J. Thompson (Eds) *The experience of illness*, London: Tavistock.

Schussler, G. (1992) 'Coping strategies and individual meanings of illness', *Social science and medicine*, 34(4): 427–32.

Seery, M. D., Holman, E. A. and Silver, R. C. (2010) 'Whatever does not kill us: cumulative lifetime adversity, vulnerability and resilience', *Journal of personality and social psychology*, 99(6): 1025–1041.

Segal, H. (1986) *Introduction to the work of Melanie Klein*, London: Hogarth.

Shaver, P R (2011) 'New directions in attachment theory and research', *Journal of social and personal relationships*, 27(2): 163–172.

Sørgaard, K. W., Sandanger, I., Sørensen, T., Ingebrigtsen, G. and Dalgard, O. S. (1999) 'Mental disorders and referals to mental health specialists by general practitioners', *Social psychiatry and psychiatric epidemiology*, 34(3): 128–135.

Tew, J. (2011) *Social approaches to mental distress*, Basingstoke: Palgrave Macmillan.

Tijhuis, M. A. R., Peters, I. and Foets, M. (1990) 'An orientation towards help seeking for emotional problems', *Social science and medicine*, 31: 9: 989–995.

Tuckett, D. (1976) *An introduction to medical sociology*, London: Tavistock.

Van der Horst, F. C. P. (2011) *John Bowlby – From psychoanalysis to ethology. Unraveling the roots of attachment theory*, Oxford: Wiley-Blackwell.

Verhaak, P. F. M. and Tijhuis, M. A. R. (1992) 'Psychosocial problems in primary care: some results from the Dutch national study of morbidity and interventions in general practice', *Social science and medicine*, 35(2): 105–110.

Wadsworth, M., Butterfield, W. J. H. and Blaney, R. (1971) *Health and sickness: the choice of treatment*, London: Tavistock.

Weiss, R. (1986) 'Continuities and transformations in social relationships from childhood to adulthood', in W. W. Hartup and Z. Rubin (Eds) *Relationships and development*, Hillsdale, New Jersey: Lawrence Erlbaum.

Wilkinson, G. (2007) 'Psychiatry in general practice', in G. Stein and G. Wilkinson (Eds) *Seminars in general adult psychiatry*, 2nd edition, London: RCPsych Publications: 747–781.

Zola, I. R. (1973) 'Pathways to the doctor – from person to patient', *Social science and medicine*, 7: 677–689.

Zubin, J. and Spring, B. (1977) 'Vulnerability: a new view of schizophrenia', *Journal of abnormal psychology*, 86: 103–126.

3

THE LEGAL AND POLICY CONTEXT

Mark Cronin and Graham Brotherton

Introduction

As discussed earlier in Chapter 1, it is impossible to consider the concepts of individual vulnerability and vulnerable groups in social policy terms without understanding the political environment in which these ideas have been crafted. Historically there has been a shifting balance between explanations which outline vulnerability as a consequence of either the social or economic circumstances experienced by the individual which are largely out of their control or the failure of the individual to make the right moral choices and live a responsible life. In political terms the former, which was influential during the post-war consensus on the British welfare state, is associated with the left and the latter has to a considerable extent become the preferred explanation of vulnerability for those ideologically on the right and has become an increasing feature of contemporary social policy. This chapter will consider how these ideas have played out in recent social policy developments, as well as exploring the broad themes which have been influential in contemporary social policy reform.

Explanations for vulnerability which focus on individual choices and lifestyles re-emerged following the Conservative election victory in 1979. Those on the ideological right noted with interest the work of Charles Murray, who in 1984 published his now infamous *Losing Ground: Amercian Social Policy, 1950–1980*, a book that made reference to the role of social policy in contributing to the emergence of an underclass in the US through the provision of support which was seen to create dependency. Murray's ideas proved popular with Conservatives, especially those at the neo-liberal end of the spectrum, and he was subsequently invited by *The Sunday Times* to visit the UK in 1989 to explore whether similar social trends could be observed here. Later works 'confirmed' the emergence of a British underclass (Murray 1990, 1994) and contributed to debates aiming to justify a shift in how the poor were viewed and treated. These debates have contributed heavily to subsequent social policy reforms introduced during the Conservative government of 1979–1997, the New Labour government of 1997–2010 and continue to provide the rationale for recent Coalition social policy developments.

To a degree it could be argued that the Labour governments of the 1960s and 1970s continued to be influenced by the politics of solidarity which had emerged after the Second World War as part of the so-called 'post-war' settlement, as outlined by Wolfe and Klausen:

> The left demanded the creation and expansion of the welfare state. Public policy should redistribute income and subsidize, if not deliver directly, essential services such as education and health. The ideal was a society in which the inequalities associated with social class would fade away.
>
> *(2000, p.28)*

The growing influence of neo-liberalism within the Conservative party, though, created a significant policy shift after the general election of 1979, with the introduction of so-called 'Thatcherite' policies. The ideological context of these changes was discussed in the first chapter, so we turn here to the policy initiatives which turned ideas into practice. Thatcherism had a broad and ambitious agenda which encompassed significant change in many policy areas; from the privatisation of 'utilities' – gas, electricity, telephones and water – through to the selling off of previously nationalised companies, for example in the motor industry. However, for our purposes it is the policy agenda in social welfare which will now be addressed. This is where the story becomes a little complicated because there was often a gulf between rhetoric and action. In some areas – for example, benefit reform – action was swift and radical, whilst in other areas – for example, NHS reform – the Thatcher government was surprisingly pragmatic, especially in its earlier incarnation, fearing as it did the prospect of public disquiet over something as popular as the NHS. Most of the more radical reform therefore came in the later Thatcher years or during John Major's administration. There is not sufficient space here to address in detail the reforms or their timescale (for a full and fascinating review of this, see Timmins 2001) but the key features will be summarised in a reasonable amount of detail. They remain of genuine significance because they created the context in which the debate about vulnerability has been conducted ever since and it can be argued that the systems and structures created at this point remain the recognisable basis of existing services. In terms of the reform of the benefit system, they focused on reducing benefit levels in real terms and introducing much higher levels of conditionality and targeting, for example through the replacement of the relatively flexible supplementary benefit system with the much less flexible income support/social fund system which still remains. Other changes included the virtual abolition of the State Earnings Related Pension Scheme (SERPS) and the active promotion through financial incentives of switching out of (particularly public sector) employer pension schemes and into private schemes, a costly error which led to large-scale compensation having to be paid to workers who were badly advised.

In health and social care by the end of the 1980s the emphasis was on the creation of so-called 'internal markets', where responsibility for providing services was separated from responsibility for commissioning or paying for services. In the NHS this took the form of creating NHS trusts, local groupings of services usually based around one or more hospitals, providing services which would be commissioned (that is, the need both identified and paid for) by either 'fundholding' general practitioners or by health authorities. In social care, local authorities would commission and a range of private and voluntary organisations would provide any care required. Of course a significant difference was that whereas health care remained 'free', access to social care was means tested, with a contribution often expected from the service user. As suggested previously, both these systems have been subsequently amended (several times in the case of the NHS), and indeed the most recent round of NHS reform is in fact a return to a system that looks very like the system described above, though with more explicit and significant private sector involvement. This is discussed more fully later in this chapter.

As the Conservative administration became less and less popular in the mid-1990s, a debate was going on within the Labour party about the extent to which it needed to modernise its traditional social democratic values. By the time the New Labour government swept to power in 1997 it was driven by a new ideology referred to as the 'Third Way', signalling a shift away from traditional Labour values. Although there was reference to social justice, social policy during this era was driven by notions of developing a 'social investment state' where, in the words of Anthony Giddens:

> The guideline is investment in *human capital* wherever possible, rather than the direct provision of economic maintenance. In place of the welfare state we should put the *social investment state*, operating in the context of a positive welfare society.
>
> *(1998, p.117)*

This resulted in social policy which focused on social investment, with the primary aim of building an individual's capability to engage in the labour market. Influenced by (neo) liberal ideas which define freedom in terms of individual autonomy, the Third Way conceptualised freedom, in the words of Donald Sassoon, as 'the material ability to make more choices. The role of the state is to ensure that everyone possesses such material ability' (1996, p.738). Thus, social policy was to focus on tackling the social exclusion which got in the way of equal opportunity and access to the material ability to make choices. An example of such policy development was the 'welfare to work' programme, which talked of an individual's 'right' to receive support if they were unemployed provided they accepted their moral 'responsibility' to work towards re-entering the workforce. However, for Lavalette and Pratt what is significant about this arrangement is that:

The intent of much of the policy agenda suggested by the Third Way theory has been to fit workers for capital's purposes: not to modify capital so that its consequences no longer initially and ultimately rest on the shoulders of those made poor, vulnerable and unemployed by its operations.

(2006, p.39)

Therefore, what became clear to New Labour was that in order to enable society to prosper and to facilitate freedom, individuals were expected to adhere to a model of the ideal citizen which was defined by the needs of business and the economy, supported by state intervention/sanctions.

A case study – the strange case of Sure Start

At the heart of New Labour's agenda was the Sure Start initiative, which could be said to exemplify their broader policy approach. Initially targeted at the 20 per cent most 'disadvantaged' families, it was later given a broader remit in the context of the Every Child Matters approach. This approach was influenced in some senses by the Head Start and No Child Left Behind programmes in the United States. The very term, 'Sure Start', can be said to indicate the approach, which involved targeting families with children under the age of five with the expressed aim of ensuring that children were given the support they needed to benefit fully from the start of their formal education. It therefore encapsulated both the notion of social investment and the heavy emphasis on targeting identified 'vulnerable' groups with a view to making them more economically active and hence creating longer-term benefits for the economy. However, it also included an emphasis on early identification and an explicit acknowledgement of the role of the state in tackling inequality – as in the linked commitment to eradicate child poverty by the year 2020.

The impact of Sure Start in terms of improved 'outcomes' for vulnerable children and their parents has not proved straightforward to evaluate. The National Evaluation of Sure Start has sought to track the impact of the initiative but has encountered both methodological and political difficulties, though the most recent evaluation (2012) does suggest that Sure Start has had an impact in terms of approaches to parenting – with, in particular, parents in areas served by the Sure Start programme feeling more confident in creating a better learning environment at home and having effective strategies for disciplining their children. However, as is explored in a later section, the issue of evaluating parenting is both complex and contentious so these results need treating with some caution. The election of the Coalition government in 2010 has led to both a significant slimming down and a refocusing of Sure Start

An additional feature of New Labour social policy was an emphasis on 'what works' as a rationale for the introduction of new approaches to address social problems. In terms of its modernisation agenda this mantra indicated an intention to rationalise public finances and ensure cost-effective deployment of valuable resources. Although this focus has been correctly exposed as a lever to enable greater use of the private and voluntary sectors in the delivery of services, in line with New Labour's belief in a mixed market of provisions, it also led to an increasing focus on evidence-based initiatives. It was in this context that policy makers sought to provide solutions to social problems by utilising research evidence which supported their broader political motives. An example of this can be found in the use of ideas and theories relating to 'resilience' in children. It is unsurprising that children as recipients were at the heart of New Labour's social investment state. Very young children in particular were to receive special attention, as investment in their futures was seen as the best way to influence both the prosperity of individuals and most importantly that of society. In relation to children, the concept of resilience was defined by Fonagy *et al.* (1994, p.233) as 'Normal development under difficult conditions' and is concerned with understanding how and why some children appear to be able to manage and prosper in spite of adversity. There has been a great deal of interest in this concept but most writers agree (Rutter 1999; Fergusson and Lynskey 1994; Daniel and Wassell 2002) that resilience is affected by risk factors which increase a child's vulnerability and protective factors which increase the child's ability to cope with challenging and stressful life events. It is also widely acknowledged that these factors operate at three distinct levels. The first level focuses on the individual and considers the personal attributes of the child – their temperament and social skills. The second relates to the child's immediate environment and considers close personal relationships, family life and immediate sources of support. The third level looks at factors which relate to the wider community and social factors generally outside the individual's control, such as their socio-economic status. It is significant that particular aspects of this model, namely the influence of the first two levels – i.e. individual factors and close personal relationships (primarily family) – have come to play a key role in the emergence of what has become known as 'early intervention'.

Reflective Activity

- Why do you think these two aspects of the resilience model came to be influential in social policy terms?
- Why do you think the third level, which considered broader factors, did not receive the same social policy attention?
- What might this mean for people who the consequent social policy programmes were intended to serve?

In social policy terms, the concept of early intervention can be described in two main ways. First, providing support to and intervening in the lives of children and young people when there is evidence of problems which, if left unchecked, could result in serious harm or impairment of a child's well-being. This interpretation of early intervention was at the heart of the 'refocusing debate' which took place as a consequence of research (Audit Commission 1994; Department of Health 1995, 2001) and indicated that shifting resources from child protection interventions to family support interventions might promote children's welfare more effectively and prevent significant harm. The second interpretation advocates focusing resources and provision on younger children, based on the belief that this will provide the solid foundation necessary for an improvement in their future life chances. There is some evidence of social policy under the New Labour government being driven by the first of these interpretations in the general Every Child Matters agenda, the associated Common Assessment Framework and, to a certain extent, the Sure Start Children's Centres. However, it is clear that an enduring legacy of New Labour's social investment state, which has been enthusiastically embraced and taken further by the current Coalition government, is the notion that investment in the early years of a child's life is the best way to ensure their future success.

In seeking to explain this, Clarke (2004) argues that New Labour social policy, and particularly its emphasis on the centrality of 'modernisation', needs to be seen as a number of forms of privatisation, of which the two most significant were:

- Corporatisation – the privatising of service delivery through contracting out or by setting up quasi-public organisations (academy schools, foundation health trusts, etc.)
- Familialisation – the construction of idealised (for Clarke, hetero-normative) family structures which are then assumed to be able to take on a range of private caring responsibilities

Clarke goes on to suggest that the consequence of this is the creation of an idealised citizen-consumer who is hard-working, independent and morally upright. Furthermore, access to the public good of welfare in all its forms becomes conditional on meeting or seeking to meet the requirements of the 'ideal citizen'. Clarke also highlights the centrality of normative discourses in the process of constructing the ideal citizen. Parents are constructed as playing a central role through their responsibility for bringing up their children to be the next generation of responsible citizens. In this way vulnerability becomes associated with some form of failure and therefore as marginal, to be dealt with through the more coercive aspects of policy implementation.

Social policy under the Coalition

This section explores both continuities from the previous government and any significant changes. A useful place to start is the Coalition's plan for government. In the foreword to the Coalition agreement, the following claim is made:

> [W]hen you take Conservative plans to strengthen families and encourage social responsibility, and add to them the Liberal Democrat passion for

protecting our civil liberties and stopping the relentless incursion of the state into the lives of individuals, you create a Big Society matched by big citizens. This offers the potential to completely recast the relationship between people and the state: citizens empowered; individual opportunity extended; communities coming together to make lives better. We believe that the combination of our ideas will help us to create a much stronger society: one where those who can, do; and those who cannot, we always help.

There are several significant themes that can be drawn from the statement; first, the emphasis on shrinking the role of the state, second, the notion of individual responsibility being presented as a counterpoint to excessive intervention, and third, the emphasis on voluntary action as a key element of welfare, with only a safety net form of provision for those who 'cannot' help themselves. These principles clearly stem from an economically neo-liberal world view overlaid with a rhetoric of community empowerment, and we will now seek to explore this through looking in more detail at three specific examples: changes to benefits, parenting and Early Intervention and changes to health and social care.

Benefit reform

One of the most high-profile areas of reform has been the introduction of a new form of assessment for those seeking to claim disability benefits. The Department for Work and Pensions is planning to cut spending by around 20 per cent over three years, mainly through replacing the Disability Living Allowance with a new system called Personal Independence Payments, which builds upon changes to the Employment and Support Allowance. In order to do this it introduced a new assessment process for claimants and put the contract to undertake assessments out to tender. The bulk of the contracts were won by the French company ATOS, who will undertake the new 'Work Capability Assessments' – based on a model introduced by the previous government – at a cost of £400 million over four years. The new process has proved controversial, with widespread claims by those who have undergone assessment that the process is flawed and unfair. The government claims to have amended the process after an independent review, but disability groups, doctors and lawyers argue there are a range of ongoing issues.

A detailed analysis published by a group of UK charities (Disability Rights UK 2012) suggests that the overall impact will be that 500,000 people will lose entitlement, thus pushing many disabled people out of employment or into inappropriate employment and therefore into poverty. It also highlights that the removal of benefits is likely to mean that people are pushed into dependence on informal carers or health and social care services. The overall impact of the changes is therefore likely to be an increase in spending rather than a reduction and, in the context of this book, individuals who are currently able to maintain reasonably independent lives become vulnerable and dependent. In this sense it can be argued that the impact of policy is that structural vulnerability is being created through the policy changes but then presented as an issue of individual capacity.

Parenting and early intervention

As suggested previously, the notion of 'early intervention' entered policy discourse under New Labour in the context of Every Child Matters, and indeed the particular direction of early intervention policy under the Coalition is set by a report written by the Labour MP, Graham Allen. His view is encapsulated in the introduction to his report (entitled *Early Intervention: The Next Steps*), where he states: 'I use the term Early Intervention to refer to the general approaches, and the specific policies and programmes, which help to give children aged 0–3 the social and emotional bedrock they need to reach their full potential' (Allen 2011, p.xiii). He also states that:

> Early intervention is an approach which offers our country a real opportunity to make lasting improvements in the lives of children, to forestall many persistent social problems and end their transmission from one generation to the next, and to make long-term savings in public spending.
>
> *(Allen 2011, p.vii)*

These opening remarks clearly indicate that for Allen the first three years of a child's life are the key ones for intervention to break the cycle of deprivation, but equally he makes reference to reducing the costs associated with welfare provision. It is also significant that throughout this review report commissioned by the Coalition government, Allen refers to evidence from research and practice to support his recommendations. He states that:

> The economic benefits of early intervention are clear, and consistently demonstrate good returns on investment. One example documented in research is estimated to have provided benefits, in the form of reduced welfare and criminal justice expenditures, higher tax revenues and improved mental health of up to five times greater than its cost.
>
> *(Allen 2011, p.xiv)*

He asserts that, 'A key finding is that babies are born with 25 per cent of their brains developed, and there is then a rapid period of development so that by the age of three their brains are 80 per cent developed' (Allen 2011, p.xiii). He then goes on to claim that, 'In that period, neglect, the wrong type of parenting and other adverse experiences can have a profound effect on how children are emotionally "wired"' (Allen 2011, p.xiii). Finally Allen makes his most significant statement with respect to recommended actions to address social problems when he claims, 'What parents do is more important than who they are. Especially in a child's earliest years, the right kind of parenting is a bigger influence on their future than wealth, class, education or any other common social factor' (Allen 2011, p.xiv). It is in these telling words that Allen clearly indicates that, in his opinion, the locus of social problems or vulnerability lies in the actions of parents and their relationships with their children, whilst at the same time he dismisses the influence of broader social factors.

This review signalled a significant shift in the focus of Coalition social policy in terms of addressing social problems and the intention to place parents in the spotlight. This can be evidenced by the subsequent review of the core purpose of Sure Start Children's Centres in 2011 which, in aiming to improve the outcomes for young children from the most disadvantaged families, moved from providing parenting support to improving parenting skills. This indicated a significant shift from supporting parents in managing their responsibilities (whilst acknowledging that a wide range of approaches and styles can and do exist) to a position where a particular set of skills were seen as preferable and needing to be instilled. This was to be reinforced by the introduction in 2011 of a 'payment by results' trial in 30 local authority areas, where Sure Start Children's Centres were to be measured and financially rewarded directly in terms of their success in relation to the new core purpose. In addition to this, a two-year pilot scheme was launched in the summer of 2012 which offered all parents with a child under five in three local authority areas free vouchers to attend parenting classes. It is significant that the chosen areas had either medium or high levels of deprivation. Clearly, improving the parenting skills of certain parents was to be at the forefront of Coalition early intervention policy. This was further reinforced when the government in October 2011 set up its 'Troubled Families Team' tasked with turning around the lives of the 120,000 'most troubled' families thought to be responsible for a disproportionate use of welfare resources.

It is important, then, to be clear about the rationale and evidence base from which this specific focus on parenting as the genesis for social problems has emerged. In his review report, Graham Allen makes specific reference to research undertaken in 2008/2009 by the organisation Demos – which was led by an advisory board on which he himself sat, alongside Iain Duncan Smith – published as *Building Character* (Lexmond and Reeves 2009). This research was based on the millennium cohort study data and utilised the data sets of approximately 9,000 households. It aimed to measure five-year-olds according to what it termed their 'character', which it considered to be a significant predictor of a child's future success. It defined character in terms of application (the ability to stick with things), self-regulation (an ability to regulate emotions) and empathy (the ability to put yourself in another person's shoes) and looked at which factors had the biggest influence on its development. The research took into consideration three broad areas of potential influence on a child's development of character, namely structural factors (poverty, ethnicity, family structure, disability, and parental background), parenting style (approach to parenting) and psychological vulnerability (genetic, pre-natal and early environmental factors affecting temperament). The report concluded that parenting style had the biggest impact on the development of a child's character and its subsequent outcomes. It went further by classifying four specific parenting styles and identifying 'tough love' (warm and responsive approach with clear boundaries) as the most successful and 'disengaged' (low in warmth and discipline) as the least successful. It also identified that tough love was less prevalent in low-income households and disengaged parenting was most prevalent in these households.

This evidence appears to provide a clear rationale for both promoting a tough-love approach and focusing on the transmission of these 'parenting skills' to disadvantaged parents/those on low-incomes. However, other significant outcomes are hidden in this data. Close examination of the results shows that in fact income is as, if not more, significant than parenting style in terms of the outcomes for children. Of the children from families with the lowest incomes only 11 per cent were in the top 20 per cent for outcomes compared with 36 per cent in the bottom 20 per cent for outcomes, a more significant difference than those of the children from disengaged parents (10 per cent in the top 20 per cent, 30 per cent in the bottom 20 per cent). Furthermore, of children from the richest families, 28 per cent were in the top 20 per cent for outcomes compared with 10 per cent from the bottom 20 per cent, again a more significant difference than those of tough-love parents (26 per cent in the top 20 per cent, 11 per cent in the bottom 20 per cent). The results in respect of income were dismissed in the report, as it was argued there was evidence that confident poor parents could achieve as much as high-income parents. It is clear that the messages from this report were intended to support an ideological shift towards explanations of vulnerability that were exclusively focused on individuals and their need to change, in this case their 'parenting style'. This report was followed up by a further piece of research by Demos published as *Under The Influence* (Bartlett *et al.* 2011) which attempted to reinforce the significance of parenting style with a specific focus on problem drinking. However, again the results of the research fell short of establishing any significant links between the parenting style experienced by children in their early years and the course of their later life. In spite of the frailty of these pieces of evidence they have been used by the Coalition government to justify a return to social policy approaches which identify individual behaviour change as the main cause of disadvantage and the focal point for solutions, as indicated above.

Reflective Activity

- Is it possible to categorise parenting by the use of particular prescribed 'styles'?
- What problems can you envisage arising in the effort to train parents to utilise a 'preferred' parenting style?
- Can you think of alternatives to this model of working with parents?

Before leaving Coalition policy in the context of parenting and early intervention it is important to mention two other specific interventions, social investment bonds (sometimes called Social Impact Bonds) and the Troubled Families Unit. Turning first to social investment bonds, these are a new funding model in which money is raised from private investors to undertake early intervention or family support work. Depending on the 'outcomes' of the work against pre-set criteria, investors will recover some or all of their investment or make a profit. This, it can be argued, takes marketisation of welfare services into a new domain, introducing market relationships directly into frontline services for the most vulnerable families. It can also be argued that it may well stifle imaginative or creative practice, as one of the suggestions made in *Early Intervention: The Next Steps* is that funding should only be available for programmes which can demonstrate an 'evidence base'. Leaving aside the very real debate about what can be said to be evidence and whether certain sorts of evidence – for example, those gained through particular forms of 'scientific' trial – are given priority, there is the important question of whether more innovative methods will be able to secure this sort of funding.

Turning now to the Troubled Families Unit, this was announced in the aftermath of the riots in 2011 and is intended to co-ordinate work with the 120,000 'most troubled' families in England and Wales. Its approach will in many ways mirror the model being developed to support early intervention, though it will at least initially receive a higher level of government spending to distribute to local authority-based schemes.

Changes to health and social care

We now turn to the reform of health and social care. This is another large and complex topic, which in the first place can be characterised as a move to a more marketised model of provision, with an accentuated role for the private sector; it can be argued that it builds on policy following the implementation of the NHS and Community Care Act 1990, which has seen ever-increasing private sector involvement in the NHS. Nonetheless, looking initially just at NHS reform, it is clear that the speed and scale of the proposed reforms mean that this is, in the words of the health policy 'think tank', the King's Fund, 'revolutionary' – despite the fact that on most indicators the NHS provides a good service in terms of the return on spending.

Looking at social care reform, three elements seem to dominate current government thinking, as indicated by the Care and Support bill which forms part of the Coalition's current legislative programme: first, the need to clarify and standardise assessment and funding arrangements – though there is a tension here with the proposal to open up the assessment process to a range of providers; second, an emphasis on further marketisation and choice; and third, a desire to improve the safeguarding of vulnerable adults. It is important to note that the fundamental issues of how to ensure adequate levels of funding for social care services and what the balance should be between individual and state in terms of who pays what have once again not been properly addressed. Adult social care spending is currently around £16 billion a year and in the context of the current spending restrictions is inevitably of considerable policy interest. Some of the proposals have received a cautious welcome – for example, there have been suggestions that the social work practice pilots introduced in 2011, where social workers work in co-operatives or social enterprises rather than for local authorities, may be able to provide more flexible and imaginative ways of working with a range of service users. There is as yet very little evidence on the impact of the adult social care pilots, but a recently published review of the children's social work pilots suggests that the picture is very mixed, with some benefits but also some significant problems; the report sums it up this way:

> The evaluation has yielded mixed findings with stronger evidence in relation to some aspects of the pilots' work than in others. The views of stake-holders ... as to whether the SWPs performed better than their local authority counterparts or whether they represented good value were divided. There were also variations found in perceptions of different pilots with some emerging as stronger performers than others. Despite this variety, there is some evidence of positive change for children, parents, carers and the workforce that can be attributed to the pilots.
>
> *(Stanley* et al. *2012, p.ii)*

Another important angle that should be considered but does not often feature in the analysis is the impact on the workforce of some of the changes. The Low Pay Commission reports have highlighted for several years the very high proportion of care workers on or around the minimum wage, especially in the private sector, and an analysis by Hussein (2012) suggests that around 200,000 care workers are actually being paid less than the minimum wage. This raises some very difficult issues; those who are recruited to work with the most vulnerable groups are themselves in a position where their pay and conditions may make them and their families vulnerable. A central problem of a marketised system of care is that as such a high proportion of the costs of providing care services are staffing costs, any attempt to develop 'flexible' or 'efficient' services is likely to be at the expense of low-paid (and often part-time or casual) workers. As a consequence, the care workforce sees a high turnover and in some cases finds it difficult to recruit properly qualified staff. Whilst it is simplistic to make a link between high profile 'failures' within the social care system and salaries and conditions, the fact remains that providing quality care needs to be seen as an area in which people can develop a constructive and sustainable career, something that is currently difficult for front-line carers. Any book which concerns itself with the issue of vulnerability needs to acknowledge the way in which market forces impact not just on those who use care services but also on those who provide them.

Conclusion – policy and vulnerability

This chapter has sought to look at the way in which the dominant elements of policy reform over the past thirty years or so have moved away from at least the assumption of universal services provided in the spirit of either social democracy or the one-nation tradition within conservative thinking. The so-called post-war consensus which emphasised notions of social solidarity and mutual responsibility has largely disappeared, to be replaced – as successive governments have reacted to wider social and economic change – by the implementation of increasingly harder-edged versions of neo-liberalism, with a focus on market-based services, individualisation and residual services for targeted groups and with an increasingly explicit distinction being made between those perceived as 'deserving' and 'undeserving'. As this conclusion is being written in autumn 2012, the government has announced it is seeking to cut a further £10 billion – beyond the £18 billion previously announced – from the welfare budget. In seeking to do this it will have to shift greater responsibility for their circumstances onto those who are vulnerable. In a recent speech, the Secretay of State for Work and Pensions, Iain Duncan Smith, said:

> This Government will always stand by its promise to protect the most vulnerable and provide support for those whose sickness or disability puts them in difficulty. Nevertheless, my belief is that where they are able, those in the welfare system should be on a journey. It should be taking people somewhere, helping them move from dependence to independence … . To achieve this journey requires an internal and external cultural change – whereby the welfare system supports people in need, but not to remain in need.
>
> *(Duncan Smith 2012)*

Elsewhere in the same speech he talks about the need for much greater conditionality within the system and an emphasis on making claimants responsible. As far as it is possible to predict at this point, the emphasis in policy development is likely to be on ever-greater elements of conditionality and targeting. The choice of the binary expression '*dependence to independence*' is significant, chiming as it does with individualisation rather than with notions of interconnectedness and mutual support which, as argued elsewhere in this book, seem to be key aspects of constructive ways of working with vulnerability.

References

Allen, G. (2011) *Early Intervention: The Next Steps*. Available online at www.dwp.gov.uk/docs/early-intervention-next-steps.pdf (accessed 20 November 2012).

Audit Commission (1994) *Seen but not Heard: Co-ordinating Community Child Health and Social Services for Children in Need*. London: HMSO.

Bartlett, J., Grist, M. and Hahn, B. (2011) *Under The Influence*. London: Demos.

Clarke, J. (2004) 'New Labour's Citizens: activated, empowered, responsibilized, abandoned?' *Critical Social Policy*, November 2005, 25(4): 447-463.

Daniel, B. and Wassell, S. (2002) *Adolescence: Assessing and Promoting Resilience in Vulnerable Children*. London: Jessica Kingsley.

Department of Health (1995) *Child Protection: Messages from Research*. London: HMSO.

——(2001) *The Children Act 1989 Now: Messages from Research*. London: The Stationery Office.

Disability Rights UK (2012) 'Disability and universal credit', Citizens Advice. Available online at www.citizensadvice.org.uk/index/policy/policy_publications/er_benefitsandtaxcredits/disability_and_universal_credit.htm (accessed October 2012).

Duncan Smith, I. (2012) Speech to Cambridge Public Policy Forum (25 October 2012). Available online at www.dwp.gov.uk/newsroom/ministers-speeches/2012/25-10-12.shtml (accessed 27 October 2012).

Fergusson, D.M. and Lynskey, M.T. (1994) 'Adolescent Resilience to Family Adversity', *Journal of Child Psychology and Psychiatry*, 37(3): 281-292.

Fonagy, P., Steele, M., Steele, H., Higgitt, A. and Target, M. (1994) 'The Emanuel Miller Memorial Lecture 1992: The Theory and Practice of Resilience', *Journal of Child Psychology and Psychiatry*, 35(2): 231-257.

Giddens, A. (1998) *The Third Way: the Renewal of Social Democracy*. Oxford: Polity Press.

HM Government (2010) *The Coalition Agreement: A Programme for Government*. Available online at http://programmeforgovernment.hmg.gov.uk/foreword/index.html (accessed September 2012).

Hussein, S. (2012) 'The scale of very low pay for care workers is much larger than previously anticipated and demands immediate attention', British Politics and Policy at LSE online forum – blog entry (17 January 2012). Available at http://eprints.lse.ac.uk/44071/ (accessed February 2013).

Lavalette, M. and Pratt, A. (2006) *Social Policy: Theories, Concepts and Issues*. London: Sage.

Lexmond, J. and Reeves, R. (2009) *Building Character*. London: Demos.

Murray, C. (1984) *Losing Ground: American Social Policy, 1950–1980*. New York: Basic Books.

——(1990) 'The emerging British underclass', in IEA Health and Welfare Unit (1996) *Charles Murray and the Underclass*. Choice in Welfare No. 33. London: IEA/Sunday Times.

——(1994) 'Underclass: the crisis deepens', in IEA Health and Welfare Unit (1996) *Charles Murray and the Underclass*. Choice in Welfare No. 33. London: IEA/Sunday Times.

Rutter, M. (1999) 'Resilience concepts and findings: implications for family therapy', *Journal of Family Therapy*, 21: 119-144.

Sassoon, D. (1996) *One Hundred Years of Socialism: The West European Left in the Twentieth Century*. London: I.B.Tauris.

Stanley, N., Austerberry, H., Bilson, A., Farrelly, K., Hussein, S., Ingold, A., Larkins, C., Manthorpe, J., Ridley, J. and Strange, V. (2012) *Social Work Practices: Report of the National Evaluation*, DfE Research Report DFE-RR233.

The National Evaluation of Sure Start (NESS) Team (2012) *The impact of Sure Start Local Programmes on seven year olds and their families*, DfE Research Report DFE-RR220.

Timmins, N. (2001) *The Five Giants: a Biography of the Welfare State*. 2nd ed. London: Harper Collins.

Wolfe, A. and Klausen, J. (2000) 'Other people', *Prospect*, December.

4

CHILDREN WITH SPECIAL EDUCATIONAL NEEDS AND DISABILITIES

Chris Collett

Introduction

Article 23 of the United Nations Convention on the Rights of the Child (UNCRC (1989)) specifically addresses the rights of children with disabilities to enjoy 'a full and decent life' that promotes dignity, self-reliance and active participation (Lansdowne 2009: 16). The key to the realisation of those rights is seen as education (Smith 2010). This chapter will examine the role of inclusive education in England in ensuring that the rights of children with special educational needs and disabilities (SEND) are upheld and consider what has been achieved.

Children with disabilities are disproportionately more likely to live in poverty, be vulnerable to physical and sexual abuse and have limited access to education (Lansdowne 2009). The disadvantage and social exclusion experienced by many disabled people is not the inevitable result of their impairments or medical conditions but rather stems from attitudinal and environmental barriers (Knowles and Lander 2011: 141). Those barriers persist as an outcome of the historical prejudice, discrimination and cruelty to which disabled people have been subjected for hundreds of years, resulting in a tradition of segregation and ill-treatment across work, education and social life. It is important to understand in the first instance where these attitudes originated and why they remain so deeply embedded in the public consciousness. Whilst in recent decades disability rights movements have made significant progress in tackling the inequalities that exist between disabled and non-disabled people, there is growing evidence of the lasting impact, and even a recent resurgence of those negative attitudes and their repercussive effects, on the experiences of disabled children and young people in everyday life.

Terminology that describes disability in an acceptable way has changed over time. According to the Disability Discrimination Act (1995) and its successor, the Equality Act (2010), a disability is an impairment that has a *substantial and long-term* effect on the individual's ability to carry out tasks of everyday life. The 1981 Education Act states that a child has special educational needs if they require provision over and above what is generally provided in schools (Hodkinson and Vickerman 2009). There is considerable overlap between the two definitions so, for the purposes of this chapter, the term Special Educational Needs and Disabilities (SEND) has been used where appropriate.

Historical context

Disability has long been seen as a threat to non-disabled people (Reiser in Cole 2012). Finkelstein (1980) and later Harris and Roulstone (2011) propose models that describe three distinct phases in the history of disabled people: the pre-industrial or feudal period; the industrial capitalist period and finally the post-industrial phase that brought with it the decline of industrial thinking (Hodkinson and Vickerman 2009; Harris and Roulstone 2011). Certainly, as will be later illustrated, the industrial revolution played a key role in shaping approaches and attitudes towards disability. But the foundations for those attitudes were laid down long before this. Ancient history tells a grim story of the treatment of disabled children. The ancient Greeks and Romans regarded imperfection and deformity as abominations, and any such affliction an indication of the Gods' displeasure (Reiser 2012; Quarmby 2011; Brignall 2008). Disabled people were considered of little worth except for entertainment, and it is recorded that 'dwarves, hunchbacks and fools' were much in demand amongst the wealthy for this purpose (Quarmby 2011: 24). Reiser (in Cole 2012) notes that alongside the spectacle of blind gladiators pitted against one another in the Roman arena was the 'sport' of throwing disabled children beneath the hooves of galloping horses. A requirement to register births some days after a child was born allowed time for a deformed or disabled infant to be discreetly disposed of, and infanticide was positively encouraged by scholars such as Aristotle – this meant that disabled babies were commonly drowned or simply left out in the wild to be devoured by wild animals (ibid.). Those disabled children who did survive into adulthood were often outcasts, perceived as economically inactive and thus a burdensome drain on resources, unable to make a useful contribution to society (Quarmby 2011).

Links between disability and impurity were reinforced by the major organised religions, which established the perception of disability as a 'punishment' for moral weakness or evil, carrying with it a shameful stigma. Dominant figures like Martin Luther denounced disabled people as being 'possessed by the devil' (Quarmby 2011: 33). The importance of so-called 'miracle cures' added to the belief that disability, by definition, was an undesirable and unacceptable aspect of the human condition (Reiser in Cole 2012). Where there was more tolerance shown towards disabled individuals in small rural communities, they were nonetheless consigned to the 'lowest echelons of their society' (Hodkinson and Vickerman 2009: 35), a status that has been evident ever since and a guiding factor in the framing of social policy. Reiser (in Cole 2012) points out that it is no coincidence that one of the most common disability labels historically used is 'cripple', derived from the German word 'kripple', meaning 'without power'. This differential was reinforced by the often paternalistic tolerance of disability and the giving and receiving of alms and charity, a phenomenon that came to the fore in a structured way during the nineteenth and early twentieth centuries.

The suspicion surrounding disability was further strengthened during the Middle Ages by the witch hunts which targeted women with deformities, who were perceived as being either sinners or involved in witchcraft (Quarmby 2011). The theme of disabled people as scapegoats persists through folklore, with the portrayal of witches and goblins in fairytales as grotesques – with afflictions or disfigurements – and purveyors of evil (Reiser in Cole 2012). The exploitation of disabled people as entertainment continued through Victorian freak shows and country fairs (Quarmby 2011) and was later to be extended by the opening up to the public of the 'lunatic asylums', the most famous of which was Bedlam (ibid.). While all of these practices helped to establish negative perceptions of disability, the biggest tangible upheaval in the lives of disabled people was still to come.

The industrial revolution of the nineteenth century triggered a mass migration from rural communities, in which disabled people had to an extent been integrated, to the factories of industrial towns and cities. Local and family-based support for disabled people rapidly and catastrophically declined (Hodkinson and Vickerman 2009). 'Able-bodied' and 'whole' became synonymous with usefulness and the individual tragedy of disability was turned into a burden and a problem for society (ibid.). Disabled people who were unable to function within the rigidly structured and demanding environment of mass production became superfluous; they were rendered economically impotent and consequently consigned to the poor- or workhouse, shut away from the remainder of the population. Unable to fulfil a useful role for which they could be rewarded, large numbers of people with disabilities became dependent on the goodwill of the more advantaged and on meagre handouts from the state. The Poor Law of 1601 had established the notion of the 'deserving' and 'undeserving' poor and aimed to make sure that for those receiving handouts life would be considerably less comfortable than for those who worked for a living. The 1834 Poor Law Amendment Act led to the mass institutionalisation of disabled people, reinforced the stigma of the workhouse and consigned the vast majority of people with disabilities to a miserable existence (Reiser in Cole 2012). This period marked the emergence of the power of medical professionals in determining who was eligible for the work- or poorhouses, giving a licence to those in authority to make decisions about the lives of disabled people (Borsay 2005). This kind of autocratic intervention in the lives of disabled people continues to this day. Diagnosis and categorisation became the key to accessing what few resources were available (Harris and Roulstone 2011), contributing to the domination of a discourse around disability which saw it as an aberration, only to be resolved by a 'cure' (Borsay 2005).

The rise of philanthropy through charitable organisations, while offering practical relief, helped to perpetuate the notion of disabled people as pitiable and inferior and compound the culture of dependency (Harris and Roulstone 2011). All of these developments signalled the beginning of a segregationist approach that has taken many decades to overturn. In 1990, disabled activist Mike Oliver proposed two theoretical frameworks to describe and explain perspectives of disability. The first, which he calls the medical model, has its roots firmly embedded in this historical period. A deficit model, it defines disabled people by what they are unable to do, focusing on stereotypes of the disabled as burdensome, pitiable and passive recipients of support; the emphasis is on curing the condition so that the disabled individual can 'fit in' (Oliver 1990). It describes vividly the prejudice and discrimination faced by disabled people during this period and beyond.

Reflective Activity

Consider the main features of the medical model of disability.

To what extent do these ideas continue to resonate today?

The wholesale removal of disabled people from mainstream society did nothing to alleviate the fear and superstition that surrounded them, and such attitudes were given further weight by the growth, towards the end of the nineteenth century, of social Darwinism and the emergence of the eugenics movement (Hodkinson and Vickerman 2009). Francis Galton's attempts to apply Darwinian theories of 'natural selection' and 'survival of the fittest' to human beings meant that, almost inevitably, disabled people were among those seen as a threat to the future of humankind, potentially weakening the population and, at a time of economic hardship, taking up valuable resources. In Germany, Karl Binding and Alfred Hoche calculated the greater cost to the state of a disabled person compared with that of a non-disabled person (Kevles 1995), and parallels may be drawn today. In China as recently as 1995 the Maternal and Infant Health Care Law took steps to reduce birth numbers of those deemed to be inferior quality, and so strengthen the population (Potts 1999).

Although laws making the sterilisation of disabled people compulsory – passed elsewhere in the world – were rejected in England, the policy of segregation, with the added incentive now of preventing the propagation of people with disabilities, became an active strategy, justified by legislation such as the Mental Deficiency Act of 1913 (Harris and Roulstone 2011). Distinctions between the disabled, the degenerate and the criminal became blurred: as late as 1942 the Beveridge Report identified five 'evils', and these included a disproportionate representation of disabled people (ibid.).

Prior to 1944 educational provision for children with disabilities in England was inconsistent at most. Segregated provision evolved from the institutions created during the eighteenth and nineteenth centuries, when there were a number of specialist schools set up by charitable or church organisations, predominantly for children with specific impairments – especially deafness and blindness (Borsay 2005). Children with less clearly definable disabilities were consigned indiscriminately to the workhouse or asylum, often for life, on the strength of what would today be considered relatively minor disabilities. They were construed as helpless, their denial of rights justified by eugenicist fears (Borsay 2011). Life in such institutions was harsh, with children often subjected to cruel medical 'treatments' and experimentation and at risk of abuse (Borsay 2005; Quarmby 2011). Thus, disabled children and young people were vulnerable due to both the general population viewing disability as threatening and undesirable and – often – the activities of the very people who were meant to be caring for them.

Reflective Activity

Think about the children who were segregated from their families at a very young age.

What effect would this have had on them and their families?
How does this compare with the experiences of children today?

Post-World War Two and the atrocities of the Holocaust, there was the beginning of change in attitudes towards the disabled and other marginalised groups (Quarmby 2011). From the late 1940s, newly formed charitable organisations such as Mencap and Mind began pressing for reform (ibid.), and in 1948 the UN Declaration of Human Rights proclaimed, 'All human beings are born free and equal in dignity and rights', introducing principles of equal opportunities, dignity, self-determination and non-discrimination, crucial for the protection of vulnerable minority groups, including those with disabilities (Smith 2010).

The 1944 Education Act introduced universal education that included provision for children with a wide range of disabilities, based on medical categorisation and 'offering such variety of instruction and training as may be desirable in view of their different ages, abilities, and aptitudes' (Education Act 1944). Disabled children were left at the bottom of the pile, with few allocated resources and a continuing medical model approach consisting of medical interventions, therapies and treatments, the primary aim of which was cure and 'normalisation' (Farrell 2010). Many children, especially those with learning difficulties who were deemed 'ineducable', continued to be cared for in large mental handicap hospitals or were offered occupational therapies in NHS-run junior training centres; all of these fell under the remit of health authority, so any potential the children had tended to go unrecognised.

During the 1950s and early 1960s a number of reports began to disclose the scandal of abuse that was occurring in the large mental handicap institutions – some of it catalogued by Morris (1969) – and it was becoming increasingly difficult to justify the long-term incarceration of people whose only digression was disability (Quarmby 2011). In 1961 Enoch Powell began to call for the closure of the costly large psychiatric hospitals, and community care was favoured (ibid.). In response to a changing human rights landscape, the 1970 Education (Handicapped Children) Act deemed that all children had a legal entitlement to a 'full and broad' education, bringing all children, even those with the most complex needs, into the remit of local education authorities (Hodkinson and Vickerman 2009). For the first time it was acknowledged that such children were capable of benefiting from education, although a segregated system of special education continued to develop, consistent with the medical model of disability (Frederickson *et al.* 2007). According to Armstrong *et al.* (2010) children with disabilities continued to be seen as problematic, and the new arrangements simply reinforced the existing social hierarchy and meant the avoidance of unreasonable public expenditure or disturbance to the smooth running of normal schools. These segregated special schools, usually catering for specific categories of disability, were few and far between and often meant that children travelled long distances or were forced to board. Borsay (2011) highlights the isolating effects and long-term damage of these practices, which were compounded by low expectations, few opportunities for gaining academic qualifications and consequently poor employment opportunities. The rights of children with disabilities, and even of their parents in relation to choice of provision, were not keeping pace with what was happening in the wider world.

The rise of the disability rights movement, which originated in the US amongst injured veterans returning from the war in Vietnam, began to take hold in Britain, and there was an increasing recognition that disabled people were being denied the opportunity to participate in affluent post-war society (Quarmby 2011). While there had been earlier examples of activist groups, this was the beginning of a co-ordinated approach to tackling the injustices which disabled people were subjected to (ibid.).Traditional concepts were being challenged and, increasingly, disability was being viewed as 'a form of social oppression' (Hodkinson and Vickerman 2009: 37).

Instrumental in this movement was Mike Oliver, who, after describing the medical model framework, proposed an alternative approach to disability that acknowledged this shift towards societal responsibility. According to the social model, disability is defined not as an individual 'personal tragedy' (Shakespeare 2008) but as an outcome of the organisational barriers to full participation that exist, such as inaccessible physical environments and discriminatory and prejudicial attitudes. An individual is disabled by the environment in which he or she lives, works or is educated (Oliver 1990). Although this presents a clear challenge to continuing medical model perspectives, Harris and Roulstone (2011: 44–45) highlight tensions between the two, and critics argue that the social model fails to take account of the reality of impairment that contributes to disability.

This changing understanding of disability was reflected in changes in educational provision for disabled children. The move to reverse segregation began in the 1970s and 1980s with the increasing recognition internationally that children with disabilities should have access to the same opportunities as others (Frederickson et al. 2007). The comprehensive system that evolved in England in the 1970s additionally argued the moral case for a fairer inclusive system, and progress for disabled children was formalised by the Warnock Report 1978, which paved the way for their 'integration' into mainstream schools (Hodkinson and Vickerman 2009; Frederickson et al. 2007; Clough and Corbett 2001). The 1974 committee chaired by Mary Warnock conducted the first major review of education for disabled children, and it heralded a move away from medically imposed categories of disability, proposing instead an all-embracing term, 'special educational needs', which also shifted the emphasis away from individual deficits and towards the provision that would be required to effectively support learning. The additional resources required would be accessed through the mechanism of individualised 'statements of need' (Hodkinson and Vickerman 2009; Frederickson et al. 2007; Clough and Corbett 2001). The Warnock committee was ahead of its time, recognising the importance of the early identification of needs and speedy interventions, the creation of effective partnerships with parents, and the need to take a co-ordinated multi-agency approach (Baldock et al. 2009). The key recommendations of the Warnock Report were subsequently enforced through the 1981 Education Act. From that point on, 'integration' into (later 'inclusion' in) mainstream schools became the central plank of education policy for children with SEND. And whilst the concept of inclusion has been an evolving one, its aims remain firmly rooted in human rights imperatives.

Armstrong et al. (2010: 6) point out that 'a society that values social justice and equal participation cannot, at the same time, justify [segregated] special education', going on to describe inclusion as rhetoric that, on principle, few would oppose. But the gap between ideology and practice is wide and the transition from segregated to inclusive provision has not been an easy one. In recent years there has been growing evidence that many children with SEND have been poorly served by the policy of inclusion and have suffered from the inevitable degree of 'experimentation' that has characterised the change.

Shaped by the international human rights conventions of the 1970s and 1980s, the concept of inclusion has been interpreted in the UK as meaning full inclusion in mainstream (Hodkinson and Vickerman 2009). Driven by national disability rights movements such as the British Council for Disabled People (BCDP) and the Centre for Studies on Inclusive Education (CSIE) (Cigman 2007), successive governments have pursued policies to close segregated special schools in favour of an inclusive education system (Hodkinson and Vickerman 2009). Policy has been underpinned by disability legislation, the most influential of which has been the 2001 Special Educational Needs and Disability Act (SENDA) (derived from the 1995 Disability Discrimination Act), which makes it unlawful for schools and settings to exclude children with SEND without legal justification (Frederickson et al. 2007; Hodkinson and Vickerman 2009). Increasingly, at policy level, the approach has followed the social model of disability and 'integration' has given way to 'inclusion', which requires a whole-school approach and ensures that the needs of a wide range of children are met. This is reflected in the 2004 government guidance, 'Removing Barriers to Achievement', introduced as part of the Every Child Matters initiative (DfES 2004) in an attempt to improve educational and social outcomes for all children (Hodkinson and Vickerman 2009).

The current position

Despite these policy drivers, in recent years in the UK there has been a growing recognition that the system is failing to meet the needs of many children with SEND currently included in mainstream, and in 2005 Mary Warnock confirmed this, citing the 'disastrous legacy' of her 1978 report, and the 'limits to what can be achieved in mainstream schools, given the diversity of children's needs and the finite available resources' (Cigman 2007: xii). More recently, the Lamb Inquiry (2009) observed that 'while the aims of the SEN framework remain relevant, implementation has often failed to live up to them', leaving children with SEND educationally vulnerable (Haines and Ruebain 2011: 3).

Reflective Activity

Look at these definitions of inclusion.

- An attitude or a principle, a means of promoting an ethos which redefines 'normality' as accepting and valuing diversity (Jones 2004: 13)
- A system of education which recognises the right of all children and young people to share a common educational environment in which all are valued equally regardless of differences in perceived ability, gender, class, ethnicity or learning styles (Armstrong 1999: 76)
- Inclusion is a process of identifying, understanding and breaking down barriers to participation and belonging (NCB no date)
- Inclusion is a process that maximises the entitlement of all pupils to a broad, relevant and stimulating curriculum, which is delivered in an environment that will have the greatest impact on their learning (NAHT 2005)

What is the author saying?
Do you agree/disagree?
What might be the challenges of translating these into practice?

There are a number of ideological and practical tensions inherent in the system that has evolved, not least a model that links funding directly to the individual child's needs (Meijer 2003). Education settings, both state-maintained and non-maintained, are legally required to identify, assess and provide for children with SEN through procedures set out in the 2001 SEN Code of Practice (Jones 2004). The focus is on the early identification, with a view to placing children and meeting needs appropriately, as early as possible (ibid.). Local authorities both determine those needs and take responsibility for meeting them within a defined budget. This funding arrangement has long been viewed as a conflict of interests and a 2006 House of Commons select committee went as far as making recommendations for change (Audit Commission 2007): however, this is yet to be implemented. Meanwhile it has prompted concerns that children may be placed in mainstream provisions without the required support, leaving them vulnerable to educational failure and bullying. A lack of clear, tight criteria for funding also means that 'schools and LEAs can follow procedures to the letter and yet come to quite different conclusions about how similar types and levels of need can be met' (Dyson and Millward in Farrell and Ainscow 2002: 21). Consequently, the statementing process has become an adversarial one that is open to abuse, whether intentional or not, resulting in the parents who are the most assertive having their children's needs met (Warnock and Norwich 2010), and conversely putting those children who lack strong advocacy at a significant disadvantage. Notably, the children and young people who additionally 'lose out' are children with SEND from black minority ethnic groups or who are looked after by the state. Many parents describe the process of accessing the required resources as 'a constant battle', reporting difficulties in negotiating the educational procedures and in constantly 'fighting the system' (Rogers 2007: 66).

A statutory process based on a requirement to identify deficits undermines the more enlightened social model approach (Hodkinson and Vickerman 2009). Warnock herself (2005) identifies what she considers to be a flaw in the term 'special educational needs', which imposes a false homogeneity on the population of children with SEND, whose differences are, in reality, many and varied. Haines and Ruebain (2011: 2) additionally identify the conflict inherent in trying to 'dismantle the rigid labelling of disabled children in favour of a rights based approach, whilst maintaining a system that allocates resources in accordance with that very labelling'. Florian (2008) too questions whether it is possible to provide effectively for learners' differences without stigmatising them as different, highlighting the continuing tension between medical model approaches and inclusion.

A further tension has arisen from the conflict between the inclusion agenda and the drive to raise standards and create competition between schools that began with the introduction of the National Curriculum in 1988. Rogers found that many children supposedly 'included' in mainstream, were, in practice, excluded in various ways: removed from the group for individual tuition, unable to access material presented to them or unable to form meaningful relationships with their peers and 'engage with others socially' (Rogers 2007: 63). This, she asserts, is made worse by the continuing lack of knowledge and understanding about difference, but also by the stringent 'testing and examination' structure in our schools. In addition, the caveat that has traditionally accompanied inclusion – that it is viable only if it does not compromise the education of non-disabled children – means that many SEND

children, chiefly those with emotional and behavioural difficulties, are subject to short-
or long-term exclusion and left at the mercy of overstretched and inconsistent support
services, with little family support.

The real test of the success of inclusive policy should be whether or not it has
made a difference to the lives of children with SEND. Kalambouka *et al.* (2007)
claim that creating more inclusive schools should lead to better outcomes for children but, despite the fact that policy has been driven in this direction for thirty
years, there is a surprisingly small body of evidence regarding its impact, with most
studies being small scale and based to a large extent on evidence from the US
(Farrell *et al.* 2007). Similarly, Frederickson *et al.* (2007: 105) highlight the failure to
systematically evaluate 'affective and social outcomes' of inclusion in the UK. The
assessment of outcomes can be problematic given the continually changing population of children with SEND (Cigman 2007), and many outcomes are described in
subjective terms that are not easily definable.

Lunt and Norwich (1999) drew a correlation between reduced performance at
GCSE and schools who had higher levels of children with SEN. However, Farrell
et al. (2007) criticise the report as being a crude comparison. The development of
the National Pupil Database (NPD) made more detailed information available and
enabled Farrell *et al.* (2007) to carry out a more sophisticated study, which looks at
the impact of inclusion on achievement at both school and local authority level.
Key findings were that there was no correlation between inclusion and achievement at local authority level (national examination results), and that it would take
large increases in the number of children with SEND to make any significant
impact. It was felt that other factors, such as poverty and social deprivation, may
have a more significant influence over outcomes than disability, though it should
be acknowledged that the relationship between these two is a complex one. Whilst
Farrell *et al.* found nothing to suggest that LEAs should not continue with inclusion
policies, their enthusiasm is muted and they express concern regarding the potential
effects of the complete closure of special schools. And this does not begin to
address what might be the experience of individual children with SEND regarding
their future life opportunities. Russell (2003) found that children with disabilities
are still twice as likely as non-disabled children to leave school with no formal
qualifications.

OfSted (2006) reported that the best outcomes for pupils with learning difficulties and disabilities (LDD) were determined not by the type of provision but by its
quality. Inspectors found effective provision distributed equally across mainstream
and special schools, with 'more good and outstanding provision in resourced
mainstream schools than elsewhere' (OfSted 2006: 2). The most important factors
contributing to good progress were: 'the involvement of a specialist teacher; good
assessment; work tailored to challenge pupils sufficiently; and commitment from
school leaders to ensure good progress for all pupils' (OfSted 2006: 6) – all of
which, it could be said, are more likely to occur in specialist provisions. Additionally,
the report found that children with emotional behavioural difficulties (EBD) were
least likely to receive effective support, and usually received it too late. However,

underlying the report is an acknowledged lack of agreement regarding what 'good progress' for pupils with LDD actually means.

Warnock (2005: 15) argues that 'the concept of inclusion must embrace the feeling of belonging, since such a feeling appears to be necessary both for successful learning and for more general well being.' Throughout the 1990s studies found that there were some positive effects of inclusion for children with SEND in terms of social skills, self-concept and a 'reduced fear of differences' (Kalambouka *et al.* 2007: 367). But research findings are not exclusively positive and unspecified negative attitudes towards SEN children were noted by Petch-Hogan and Haggard 1999 (cited in Kalambouka *et al.* 2007). Using a range of criteria, including socio-metric measures and a 'belonging scale', Frederickson *et al.* (2007: 109) looked at one particular inclusion project in the UK and found that former special school children were positively accepted by their peers, whereas other SEND children were not. But this may simply have been because particular care was taken by staff to assimilate the children from special schools (Frederickson *et al.* 2007). Peer-attitude research, conducted chiefly in the US, would appear to contradict these findings, indicating that children with SEND who are included experience higher levels of social rejection, bullying and victimisation, and are less accepted than their mainstream peers (ibid.).

Concerns have been raised, too, about the common practice of supporting children with SEND through the extensive use of teaching assistants (TAs), whose 'lack of training has been highlighted as has a major concern in the successful undertaking of a pedagogical role' (Lindsay, in Reindal 2008: 136). Farrell and Balshaw (2002: 38) are equally critical, viewing TAs as 'a cheap resource'. At the same time, the SENCO role is undertaken by teachers with varying levels of expertise and experience, and a nationally recognised qualification has only relatively recently been introduced (TDA 2009). All of which would indicate that the status and value of disabled children continues to be seen as less than that of non-disabled children, so that resources cannot be justified.

Special schools have historically been criticised for their low expectations of children with disabilities, and the Lamb Inquiry (2009) found that this was not necessarily different for children included in mainstream provisions. The Achieve-ment for All Strategy (AfA) (2010) has been an effort to raise expectations and achievements in the broadest sense for all children, including those with SEND. It recognises the indirect impact on attainment of the raised self-esteem and con-fidence that arise from success in a range of out-of-school activities, and attempts to address the fact that children with SEND have traditionally had fewer opportu-nities to take part in these activities. AfA takes a rights-based collaborative approach and reports significant improvements in relationships, pupil behaviour and atten-dance, along with a reduction in the number of children identified with SEND within the schools that espouse AfA (Ekins 2012). However, despite the positive outcomes reported, it is interesting to note that, rather than being adopted as a mainstream strategy – which would suggest a level of entitlement – AfA has recently acquired charitable status, which means, one suspects, a less certain future and a return to the reliance on 'goodwill' to meet the needs of disabled children and young people.

Critics of 'full inclusion' would assert that it overlooks the obvious 'practical realities' of disability and the rights of other children to an effective education (Hodkinson and Vickerman 2009: 80). This has led to the growing belief that inclusion should not be about location but about choice – about access to a high-quality education that leads to equal opportunities in later life, placing special schools within the definition of inclusion as part of the spectrum of provision (Tutt 2007). She goes on to assert that the increased co-operation between mainstream and specialist services sectors in the UK creates this 'flexible continuum of provision', in which special schools co-exist with mainstream to create what the DfES (2004: 4) calls 'a unified system where all schools and their pupils are included within the wider community of schools'. This allows for continuing segregation and would seem to be at odds with the United Nations Convention on the Rights of Persons with Disabilities (UNCRPD) which recognises the distinct situation of children with disabilities, stating that 'children with disabilities should have full enjoyment of all human rights and fundamental freedoms on an equal basis with other children' (Gabel and Danforth 2008: 3) and, in Article 24, calls for children with disabilities not to be excluded from the general education system (Lansdowne 2009). It is interesting to note that whilst the UK has ratified the convention, it is with the following caveat:

> The UK reserves the right for disabled children to be educated outside their local community where more appropriate education provision is available elsewhere.
>
> *Article 24, clause 2 (a) & (b)*

In consequence, policy in England has become increasingly vague about what is meant by inclusion (Hodkinson and Vickerman 2009). On the one hand there is the rhetoric of inclusive education as a fundamental human right (Wedell 2005), embraced by organisations such as the Centre for Studies in Inclusive Education (CSIE) and the Alliance for Inclusive Education (AllfIE), which continue to press for the closure of all special schools by the year 2020 (AllfIE 2010). On the other hand, despite ideological commitment, there is a definite ambivalence, both at practitioner level, where lack of resources and continuing negative attitudes are seen as barriers to inclusion (Evans and Lunt 2002), and at the wider policy level. Armstrong *et al.* (2010) claim that in the UK inclusion continues to be about assimilating children into the existing system, rather than attempting to change the system itself, and Farrell (2010) observes that the growing body of specific strategies such as the online 'Inclusion Development Programme' (Ekins 2012), designed to meet the needs of individuals, does not address the need for more radical systemic change. Barton (2005: 5) cites a 'lack of political will on the part of government to unreservedly support inclusion' and, since Warnock's *A New Look* (2005), it has even been argued that segregation could be perceived as being *positive* discrimination for children with SEND (Low 2007). However, this would seem to deny the right to participation of children with SEND and thus limit their opportunities in later life.

Certainly since the turn of the twenty-first century the emphasis has shifted away from a blanket policy of mainstream inclusion, and some influential policy makers are calling for a resurgence of the special school sector (Tutt 2007). The parents' lobby has also been important. Batten *et al.* (2006), in their report, *Make school make sense. Autism and education: the reality for families today*, found that parents were in favour of a range of provision, including mainstream schools, special schools, resource bases in mainstream schools and dual placements. Over 40 per cent of children with autism surveyed had experienced bullying at school, with one in five children being excluded and 67 per cent of those excluded more than once. Over 50 per cent of the children surveyed were not in the type of school their parents believed would best support them. In addition, some groups –such as those with sensory impairments (blind, deaf, and deafblind) – see inclusive education as an opportunity to deny children with disabilities the individualised support they need, and actively campaign to retain the opportunity for segregated learning (Inclusion International 2009).

Cigman (2007) differentiates between the presumption and assertion of inclusion; advocating it as the default position, rather than the other way around. But even this stance has been challenged by recent policy developments. Concerns about flaws in the current system have prompted a number of reviews of SEND provision. The Lamb Inquiry (2009) was followed by the consultative green paper, *Support and aspiration: A new approach to special educational needs and disability*, which proposed a 'removal of the bias towards inclusion' (DfE 2011: 4); however, the newly published SEN and Disability draft provisions (DfE 2012) makes this less explicit, again indicating indecision on the part of policy makers.

The newly formed free schools and academies, while required to meet the same obligations as maintained schools with regard to SEND legislation, will nonetheless encourage over time a more selective and segregationist approach (Ekins 2012). What's more, the creation of 'special academies' serves to reinforce the role of segregated specialist provision for children with SEND, which, as Ekins points out, would again seem to indicate that the rights-based approach to ensuring equality of opportunity for children with disabilities is being lost (ibid.). Whether due to a lack of commitment to equality of opportunity, a lack of investment in appropriate resources, low levels of expectation or simply the unsatisfactory nature of their educational experience, disabled children remain vulnerable to the whims of policy makers.

In recent years there has been a recognition that while education policy has promoted the inclusion and participation of children with SEND, many families of such children remain at a significant social disadvantage and experience lowered status. Russell (2003) notes that children with disabilities have a far greater likelihood of living in poverty than other disadvantaged groups and a greater chance of being socially excluded. The Quality Protects programme (Council for Disabled

Children 2003) highlighted wide variations in the availability of services and support for children and young people with disabilities and there is strong evidence that this situation still exists. The role of voluntary sector organisations in meeting these needs continues to be a prominent one. Research reported in the 2007 Disabled Children and Child Poverty briefing paper showed a powerful relationship between low income and social exclusion among families who have a disabled child. The two particular challenges faced were found to be the considerable and ongoing costs of caring for a disabled child and the barriers parents experienced to entering and sustaining employment. A response to these issues came from four important disability charities, Contact a Family (CAF), Mencap, the Council for Disabled Children (CDC) and the Special Educational Consortium (SEC), acknowledging that disabled children were inadequately provided for in the 2004 Every Child Matters agenda and concluding that a separate drive asserting 'rights and justice for every disabled child' was necessary. This resulted in the influential Every Disabled Child Matters campaign (EDCM). Although EDCM has made a significant impact on policy, reports from Bercow, Lamb and OfSted have all since all flagged up the dearth of services and the difficulty families have in accessing them (Ekins 2012). Added to which, families are subjected to numerous assessments to determine their eligibility for services that simply enable them to lead lives on an equal footing with the rest of the population. While Russell (2011) recognises that better understanding now exists of the need to support families of children with disabilities, she also identifies the ongoing need for more flexible, responsive and personalised services and the eradication of discrimination. However, the cuts to welfare services prompted by the current economic climate are already having an impact and will lead to increased vulnerability for children and families. Under the new Universal Credit system, the Hardest Hit Coalition has identified at least 100,000 families that will lose up to £28 per week (Hardest Hit Coalition 2012).

Scope's 2012 Keep Us Close campaign highlighted a further issue: that even when provisions are available, they are often miles from where a child and her family live and involve lengthy travel or even the need for the child or young person to live away from home and community – not from choice but from necessity (Scope 2012). Services are often fragmented (Russell 2003), and the shift from centralised to localised services can also lead to a lack of equity. The current drive to reduce bureaucracy may, on a positive note, mean that local authorities can be more flexible in delivering services, but it can also lead to the removal of ring-fencing on certain funding streams, leaving some services for disabled children and their families at the mercy of other local government priorities. Ekins (2012) also points to the damaging effects of the current recession and the drive for greater 'efficiency' that is often focused on measurable outcomes – which are unhelpful in considering the needs of disabled children and will serve only to exacerbate vulnerability.

The trend in social policy towards encouraging parents back into work has highlighted the lack of affordable child care available to parents of children with SEND – especially older children and those with more complex needs – which means that employment opportunities for the parents of disabled children are often limited (Russell 2003). The situation is exacerbated by changes in the population of disabled children, with a trend towards more children with complex medical needs and overlapping conditions and a rise in the number of children diagnosed with autism spectrum disorders and ADHD (Russell 2003; Tutt 2008). The educational and social needs of these children and young people are more challenging to meet and their parents are more likely to have to remain at home to care for them. Not surprisingly, in recent years there has also been a marked increase in the need for 52-week residential care (Russell 2003).

The identified need for broader support, a 'joined-up' approach and greater parental autonomy has prompted the proposal of combined Education, Health and Social Care plans, along with personal individual budgets with which parents can buy in services from a 'local offer' presented by the local authority, all of which are central to SEND reforms under consultation (DfE 2011, 2012). These measures are currently being trialled through 20 pathfinders across 31 local authorities, along with a substantial scaling up of the key worker role for family support. There are concerns, however, about the time it has taken to establish the basic pathfinder projects, and fears that the evidence may therefore follow policy rather than inform it; doubts exist too, about the practicalities of translating what takes place in one locality to the national arena. There is a lack of clear guidance regarding definitions of, for example, complex needs, and the refocus on children with more severe disabilities has led to worries that some children may miss out on support altogether. In addition, the pathfinders have identified difficulties around the sustainability of the enhanced key worker role and community sector involvement (SENCO Update 2012). It could also be argued that the parents who have sought increased autonomy are those who have the capacity to manage the necessary processes, and that there will be many for whom the day-to-day commitment of caring for their child will prevent them from opting for this. Without the most stringent of accountability measures there is the potential for this system to fall foul of the same inequities as the current statementing process. Some disability groups are also realistic about the pressure this will place on the agencies involved at a time when services are being radically cut (ibid.).

Conclusions

So what of the wider impact of inclusive education on participation, equal opportunities, dignity and self-determination for children and young people with disabilities? One of the overarching aims of inclusion has been to dispel the negative attitudes and fears that surround disability and promote a culture of acceptance in which there is no place for prejudice or discrimination. According to CSIE, the route to an inclusive society is an inclusive education system that helps create a society in which disabled children, young people and adults can enjoy the same rights freedoms and opportunities as everyone else and have the same chances of experiencing success in later life. After 30 years of inclusive policy, how far can we say that has been achieved?

The EDCM agenda for the new government notes that 17 per cent of disabled young people are not in education, employment or training, compared with only seven per cent of non-disabled young people; that disabled children are over eight times more likely to be excluded from school than their non-disabled peers; and that 80 per cent of disabled children have been bullied compared with fewer than two-thirds of their peers. At a time when harassment and victimisation are a routine part of everyday life for disabled people (EHRC 2011), when disabled adults can be subjected to sustained abuse by professional carers (BBC News 2012), when the highly publicised overhaul of the benefit system for disabled people by Atos encourages public perceptions of the words 'disabled' and 'benefit cheat' as synonymous, and when cruel 'jokes' at the expense of disabled people are considered 'edgy' rather than offensive, it would seem that we, as a society, are far from accepting disability as 'normal and part of the natural variation in the human condition' and that disabled children, young people and adults will continue to be vulnerable (EHRC 2011). Within this context, a return to increased segregation of children with disabilities would seem a retrograde step in terms both of optimising educational achievement – and therefore life opportunities – and promoting social inclusion. But if a policy of inclusive education is to be pursued, then it needs to be firmly grounded in the rights and entitlements of children with SEND, within a system that recognises and values individual difference and, while accepting the need for adequate resources, is flexible enough to support all learners whilst not institutionally disadvantaging others.

References

AllflE (Alliance for Inclusive Education) (2010). Available online at www.allfie.org.uk/pages/articles/vol14.html (accessed 25 February 2013)

Armstrong, A.C., Armstrong, D. and Spandagou, I. (2010) *Inclusive Education: International Policy and Practice*. London: Sage

Armstrong, F. (1999) 'Inclusion, curriculum and the struggle for space in school'. *International Journal of Inclusive Education*, 3(1), 75-87

Audit Commission (2007) *Special Educational Needs: separation of assessment of need from funding of provision*. Education and Skills Committee. Available online at www.publications.parliament.uk/pa/cm200607/cmselect/cmeduski/memo/specialedneeds/ucm2802.pdf (accessed 26 June 2010)

Baldock, P., Fitzgerald, D. and Kay, J. (Eds) (2009) *Understanding Early Years Policy*. 2nd Edn. London: Sage

Barton, L. (2005) *Special Educational Needs: an alternative look*. Available online at www.leeds.ac.uk/disability-studies/archiveuk/barton/Warnock.pdf (accessed 14 March 2010)

Batten, A., Corbett, C., Rosenblatt, M., Withers, L. and Yuille, R. (2006) *Make School Make Sense*. National Autistic Society. Available at http://trialogue.org.uk/msms/msmsengland.pdf (accessed 25 February 2013)

BBC News (2012) *Winterbourne View Abuse Scandal*. Available online at www.bbc.co.uk/news/uk-england-bristol-20078999 (25 February 2013)

Borsay, A. (2005) *Disability and Social Policy in Britain since 1750*. Basingstoke: Palgrave

Borsay, A (2011) 'Disability and education in historical perspective'. In Haines, S. and Ruebain, D. (2011) *Education, Disability and Social Policy*. Bristol: The Policy Press

Brignall, V. (2008) 'Disability in the Ancient World'. *New Statesman*, 7 April

Cigman, R. (2007) (Ed.) *Included or excluded? The challenge of the mainstream for some SEN children*. London: Routledge

Clough, P. and Corbett, J. (2001) *Theories of Inclusive Education*. London: Paul Chapman

Council for Disabled Children (2003) *Analysis of Quality Protects 2002 Management Action Plans: Services for Disabled Children and their Families*. London: Council for Disabled Children/ Joseph Rowntree Foundation

DfE (2011) *Support and Aspiration: A new approach to special educational needs and disability: a consultation*. Norwich: The Stationery Office

DfE (2012) *Draft legislation on the reform of provision for children and young people with Special Educational Needs*. Norwich: The Stationery Office

DfES (2004) *Removing Barriers to Achievement. The Government's Strategy for SEN*. London: DfES

Dyson, A. and Millward, A. (2002) 'Looking them in the eyes: is rational provision for students with "special educational needs" really possible?' In Farrell, P. and Ainscow, M. *Making Special Education Inclusive*. Abingdon: David Fulton.

Education Act (1944). London: HMSO. Available online at www.legislation.gov.uk/ukpga/ Geo6/7-8/31/enacted (accessed 25 February 2013)

EHRC (2011) Hidden in Plain Sight: inquiry into disability-related harassment available online at http://www.equalityhumanrights.com/legal-and-policy/inquiries-and-assessments/ inquiry-into-disability-related-harassment/hidden-in-plain-sight-the-inquiry-final-report/ accessed October 2012

Ekins, A. (2012) *The Changing Face of Special Educational Needs*. Abingdon: Routledge

Evans, J. and Lunt, I. (2002) 'Inclusive Education: are there limits?' *European Journal of Special Education*, 17(1), 1-14

Farrell, M. (2010) *Debating Special Education*. Abingdon: Routledge

Farrell, P. and Balshaw, M. (2002) 'Can teaching assistants make special education inclusive?' In Farrell, P. and Ainscow, M. (2002) *Making Special Education Inclusive*. Abingdon: David Fulton

Farrell, P., Dyson, A., Polat, F., Hutcheson, G. and Gallanaugh, F. (2007) 'Inclusion and achievement in mainstream schools'. *European Journal of Special Needs Education*, 22(2), 131-145

Finkelstein, V. (1980) *Attitudes and Disabled People*. New York: World Rehabilitation Fund. Available online at www.leeds.ac.uk/disability-studies/archiveuk/finkelstein/attitudes.pdf

Florian, L. (2008) 'Special or Inclusive Education: future trends'. *British Journal of Special Education*, 35(4), 202-208

Frederickson, N., Simmonds, E., Evans, L. and Soulsby, C. (2007) 'Assessing the social and affective outcomes of inclusion'. *British Journal of Special Education*, June 2007, 34(2), 105-115

Gabel, L. and Danforth, S. (2008) *Disability and the Politics of Education: an International Reader*. New York: Peter Lang

Haines, S. and Ruebain, D. (Eds) (2011) *Education, Disability and Social Policy*. Bristol: Policy Press

Hardest Hit Coalition (2012) *The Tipping Point*. Available online at http://thehardesthit. wordpress.com/our-message/the-tipping-point/ (accessed 25 February 2012)

Harris, J. and Roulstone, A. (2011) *Disability, Policy and Professional Practice*. London: Sage

Hodkinson, A. and Vickerman, P. (2009) *Key Issues in Special Educational Needs and Inclusion*. London: Sage

Inclusion International (2009) *Better Education for All*. Available online at http://ii.gmalik. com/pdfs/Better_Education_for_All_Global_Report_October_2009.pdf (accessed 27 April 2010)

Jones, C. (2004) *Supporting Inclusion in the Early Years*. Abingdon: Open University Press.

Kalambouka, A., Farrell, P., Dyson, A. and Kaplan, I. (2007) 'The impact of placing pupils with special educational needs in mainstream schools on the achievement of their peers'. *Educational Research*, 49(4), 365-382

Kevles, D. J. (1995) *In the Name of Eugenics: Genetics and the Uses of Human Heredity*. Cambridge, MA: Harvard University Press

Knowles, G. and Lander, V. (2011) *Diversity, Equality and Achievement in Education*. London: Sage

Lansdowne, G. (2009) *See Me, Hear Me: A Guide to Using the UN Convention on the Rights of Persons with Disabilities to Promote the Rights of Children*. Save the Children Publications

Low, C. (2007) 'A defence of moderate inclusion and the end of ideology'. In Cigman, R. *Included or Excluded? The challenge of the mainstream for some SEN children*. London: Routledge.

Lunt, I. and Norwich, B. (1999) *Can Effective Schools be Inclusive Schools?* London: Institute of Education.

Meijer, C.J.W. (2003) (Ed.) *Special education across Europe in 2003: trends in provision in 18 European countries*. Available online at www.european-agency.org/publications/ereports/special-education-across-europe-in-2003/special_education_europe.pdf (accessed 15 March 2010)

Morris, P. (1969) *Put Away: A Sociological Study of the Institutions for the Mentally Retarded*. London: Routledge & Kegan Paul

NAHT (2005) Policy Paper on Special Schools (revised) available at www.naht.org.uk (accessed October 2012)

NCB (no date) Participation and belonging in Early Year Settings. Inclusion: working towards equality available online at http://www.ncb.org.uk/media/216977/ecf_inclusion_leaflet.pdf (accessed October 2012)

OfSted (2006) HMI 2353 *Inclusion: Does it matter where Pupils are Taught?*

Oliver, M. (1990) *The Politics of Disablement*. Basingstoke: Macmillan

Potts, P. (1999) 'Human rights and inclusive education in China: a western perspective'. In Armstrong, F. and Barton, L. (1999) *Disability, Human Rights and Education*. Buckingham: Open University Press

Quarmby, K. (2011) *Scapegoat: Why We Are Failing Disabled People*. London: Portobello Books

Reindal, S. M. (2008) 'A social relational model of disability: a theoretical framework for special needs education?' *European Journal of Special Needs Education*, 23(2), 135-146

Reiser, R. (2012) 'The struggle for disability equality'. In Cole, M. (2012) *Education, Equality and Human Rights*. 3rd Edn. Abingdon: Routledge

Rogers, C. (2007) 'Experiencing an "inclusive" education: parents and their children with "special educational needs"'. *British Journal of Sociology of Education*, 28(1), 55–68

Russell, P. (2003) '*Access and Achievement or Social Exclusion?' Are the Government's Policies Working for Disabled Children and Their Families?* National Children's Bureau

Russell, P. (2011) 'Building brighter futures for all our children: education, disability, social policy and the family'. In Haines, S. and Ruebain, D. *Education, Disability and Social Policy*. Bristol: The Policy Press

Scope (2012) *Keep us Close*. Available online at www.scope.org.uk/sites/default/files/Scope_Keep_Us_Close_policy_report_final.pdf (accessed 25 February 2012)

SENCO Update (2012) *SEND pathfinders: will evidence affect policy?* Issue 139, October 2012

Shakespeare, T. (2008) 'Disability, genetics and eugenics'. In Swain, J. and French, S. *Disability on Equal Terms*. London: Sage

Smith, R. K. (2010) *Textbook on International Human Rights*. Oxford: Oxford University Press

Swain, J. and French, S. (2008) *Disability on Equal Terms*. London: Sage

TDA (2009) *Special Educational Needs Co-ordinators*. Available online at www.tda.gov.uk/teachers/sen/advanced_skills/senco.aspx (accessed 10 June 2010)

Tutt, R. (2007) *Every Child Included*. London: Sage

Tutt, R. (2008) *Educating Children with Complex Conditions*. London: Sage

Warnock, M. (2005) *Special Educational Needs: A New Look*. London: Philosophy of Education Society of Great Britain

Warnock, M. and Norwich, B. (2010) *Special Educational Needs: A New Look*. London: Continuum

Wedell, K. (2005) 'Dilemmas in the quest for inclusion'. *British Journal of Special Education*, 32(1), 3-11

5

THE CONSTRUCTION OF VULNERABILITY IN THE HOMELESS AND YOUNG PEOPLE THROUGH UK HOUSING POLICY

Mike Seal

Introduction

> Since its inception, housing policy in the United Kingdom has been determined by the dominant political philosophy of the time.
>
> *(Balchin 1998, p. 1)*

> Generally 'youth' tends to be seen as a problem: young people are beset by predominantly negative images, are seen as either a source of trouble or in trouble.
>
> *(Roche and Tucker 1997, p. 1)*

This chapter will examine how vulnerability has been socially constructed through housing policy, particularly in relation to people who are homeless and the way young people are expected to leave home. It will argue that, through homeless legislation and provision, homeless people are constructed as being to blame for their predicament and that young people, particularly working-class young people, are made vulnerable through housing policy. Furthermore, I believe, following Balchin (1998), that legislation and related social policy divide homeless people into categories of deserving and undeserving, underpinned by an individualist view of the causes of homelessness which ignores its structural and personal dimensions. Similarly, following Roche and Tucker (1997), I concurrently argue that housing policy for young people has been informed by two contradictory constructions, both with social and economic manifestations. One is to keep young people at home for fear of the immoral potential of being away, combined with the need for them to economically contribute to the home, and a contradictory push that they should be independent, underpinned by a flawed model of transitions into adulthood. I will trace the development and change in these discourses. I will focus mainly on the last 25 years, but it is important first to examine history further back than this as old constructions often inform more modern constructions, making them conflictual and contradictory.

Reflective Activity

Reflect on, or discuss in a group, the reasons why you left home.

What were the push-and-pull factors in you doing this?
Was it seen as a natural thing, and was there a natural way to do it?
If you had lived in the nineteenth century, what would the factors have been for you then?

Early constructions

Balchin (1998) describes how, prior to the First World War and particularly in the first half of the nineteenth century, housing policy was dominated by a laissez-faire economic approach. As a result the majority of working-class people were in rented accommodation, often of a substandard condition, with rents subject to indiscriminate rises that constituted up to 16 per cent of their income (Gauldie 1974). Interestingly, Rogers (2004) felt that this laissez-faire philosophy extended to how youth was constructed as a concept, or rather not constructed. He states that 'boundaries between child, youth and adult either did not exist or were constituted differently' (Rogers 2004, p. 23). At this time the legal age of consent was 12 for young women and fourteen for young men, illiteracy was normal and people started work from as young as eight (Hammond and Hammond 1947). In terms of 'leaving home', Hareven and Adams (2003) note a similar laissez-faire approach, with children being seen even by their families as an economic asset, with a duty to look after parents and often living with them, even after marriage. While this has modern resonances, it challenges the notion that leaving home is, and always has been, a largely cultural/life transition.

Towards the second half of the nineteenth century, such laissez-faire views were challenged, socially at least, by what Young (1960) calls an 'evangelical moral upsurge'. In short, there was concern about the plight and living conditions of the poor. Politically, there was the development of reform movements aimed at alleviating the worst excesses of poverty, but the gaze was also concerned with the 'moral development' of the poor. Pelham *et al.* (1997) note how the policies tended to be harsh, accompanied by social ostracism of the group, and were underpinned by an attitude that blamed poor people for their situation.

> In the giving of relief, the public should impose such conditions as will help the individual and the country at large. Every penny given, that helps to make the position of the pauper more eligible than that of the other workmen, will encourage laziness.
>
> *(The Poor Law Amendment Act, 1934)*

The reasons for such constructions are contested. Some authors (Young 1960; Rogers 2004) would see them in terms of the prevailing laissez-faire ideology that held people responsible for their own predicaments. Other authors (Mannheim 1936; Marx 1964) would say that while this is true of laissez-faire ideologies, any prevailing ideology needs to construct those at the bottom of the economic heap as being responsible for their own poverty, because then the 'responsibility is shifted from structural components of the stratification system to the individual, and the status quo is legitimized' (Pelham *et al.* 1997, p. 324).

These constructions were particularly applied to homeless people, with individual explanations for homelessness placing them on the periphery of society both culturally and physically (Daly 1996). Culturally, homelessness is seen largely as an individual failure, a personal weakness or, at best, an emergency. He notes that we construct homeless people in one of three ways: bad, meritiing minimal provision; mad, needing paternalistic intervention; or sad, needing pity and charity. Consequently, provision that stems from this philosophy has tended to be minimal and punitive, excluding those who are seen as undeserving and paternalistic in nature (Daly 1996). Provision was in the form of resettlement units. These were documented by authors such as George Orwell in the 1930s and Jack London just before the First World War, although they existed until the 1990s. Tellingly, these institutions were nicknamed 'spikes'. The origin of the term is uncertain. One view is that those who were drunk or deemed 'bad' were made to sleep draped over a rope stretched between two spikes in a corridor – and woken up by the rope being cut; another is that it was the name of the crude tool with which residents broke rocks for their keep. These institutions also deloused people on entry, took away any money they had (as they had to be destitute) and sent them out early in the morning and did not allow them back until the evening, so they could 'look for work'.

Homeless people were not only located on the periphery of humanity in a philosophical sense, they were forced to the edges physically. Spikes were placed on the outskirts of towns to keep homeless people away from tourists, shoppers and businesses. Their regime also encouraged homeless people to form a migratory population. The maximum length of stay varied from one to three days and, as spikes were 20 miles apart, a migratory trail of homeless people moved around the country, from Canterbury to Glasgow. Ironically, spikes were called 'resettlement units' but forced people to be unsettled and mobile (Goodall 1999).

Reflective Activity

Read Chapter 17 of the book *Down and Out in Paris and London* by George Orwell (it is available as a free ebook; just google it).

How would you feel about living in such a place?
What do you think was behind the motivations of the workers and the policy makers in creating such provision?

In terms of the social construction of young people, the late-Victorian moral gaze was similarly intense (Rogers 2004; Griffin 1992). Griffin talks about the 'discovery' of adolescence by G. Stanley Hall in 1904, challenging notions that the teenager emerged in the 1950s. Hall (1904) saw adolescence in terms of a biological phase, focusing on the sexual elements, a construction that some authors (Gillis 1974; Kett 1977) think has resonance in more modern constructions. Griffin sees this as the development of a 'white/Anglo Saxon, middle class, male heterosexual norm' against which all young people are measured. As we will see later, such norms continue to inform constructions about how young people 'should' leave home and the housing policy that supports them in this. There were a series of crusades against poverty and the living conditions of the urban poor by a number of MPs and philanthropists.

In terms of housing, Balchin (1998) is sanguine about the success of such crusades in alleviating conditions. The slum clearance and temporary accommodation laws of the time were largely ineffectual because rate payers were reluctant to spend money and slums were often on prime land. While the Public Health acts led to an improvement in conditions, associated costs were often passed from the landlords directly on to rent payers and the supply of rented property reduced because being a landlord became less profitable. It was not until the Housing of the Working Class acts of 1885 and 1900 that local authorities became landlords themselves in any significant numbers, and even then, the outbreak of the First World War saw 90 per cent of housing still in private hands.

Specific provision for young people was negligible as they mainly continued to live with their families. However, Schürer (2003) talks about how, after the turn of the century, the notion that young people largely lived at home began to shift, chiefly in response to changing economic conditions. Increasing numbers of young men were living in private lodgings, having had to follow work, and young women were in 'service'. In both these cases the housing arrangement was seen as temporary, coming to an end when people got married or moved back into the parental home. Nevertheless, it represents a departure from the notion that young people should 'stay at home' and meant they had new opportunities (Rogers 2004).

After the First World War, attitudes towards housing – and public housing in particular – underwent a philosophical sea change. Lloyd George won an election partly on back of the phrase 'Homes for Heroes', promising decent homes for returning soldiers. Addison brought in the Housing and Town Planning Act of 1919, establishing the principle of high-standard public house-building as a duty of local authorities; this was bolstered by the Wheatley Housing Act of 1924. Part of what underpinned this was an acceptance that young people did indeed leave home, upon marriage, to set up new economic units. They would therefore need housing. Schürer (2003) notes that the construction of young people as staying at home cracked further during this period, with greater numbers of young men leaving home for economic reasons after having lived away from home during the war. Rogers (2004) similarly examines how the image of women was changing, mainly as a result of women working in the munitions factories during the war. In terms of housing for young people, these new provisions, as stated, were for families and, interestingly, public housing was seen as prestigious at the time and tended to go to middle- and lower-middle-class households (Balchin 1998).

Rogers (2004) also notes that there were other social changes in the interwar period that necessitated a change in the view of youth, with fashion in the 1920s being seen as for the young and, in the 1930s, the development of cinema and dance halls as places where young people could meet and socialise. However, the Depression saw a contrary social pull back to the parental home to support the family economically, accompanied by a retraction of public house-building programmes promised in the 1919 and 1924 acts.

Post-war housing policy changed dramatically. This was due to a number of factors. There was a practical need to replace bombed and damaged housing and worn-out stock and meet the general needs of the population, which increased by a million over this period. There was also a change in the macro-economic approach, with Keynesian economic policy preferred over something more laissez-faire, and this required government projects like house-building to stimulate the economy. There was also a political imperative, as the broken promises of 'Homes for Heroes' still had bitter resonance. This post-war period was the 'golden' era of public house-building (Balchin 1998): even when the Conservatives returned in 1951, they continued the policy, pledging to build 300,000 homes per annum. The post-war consensus was that local authorities and the government should expand public housing, and this lasted from 1951 until 1979. Differences in political approaches tended to involve the regulation and de-regulation of private housing rather than the consensus itself. However, the emphasis remained on housing for families (Balchin 1998). In his first housing bill in 1947, Bevan stressed that public housing was for families and was not to be targeted at perceived marginalised groups, which included young people.

In terms of homeless people, the 1948 National Assistance Act changed spike provision from being a parish responsibility to being a state responsibility, yet in many ways it consolidated the earlier attitudes and constructions rather than challenging them. Donnison and Ugerson (1982) note how it created 'a weak obligation to provide temporary shelter for small numbers when the problem of homelessness called for stronger obligations to provide permanent housing for large numbers'. They were also housing within the DHSS and social services, again individualising the problem and seeing it as a personal rather than structural matter. Jacobs et al. (2003), reviewing the schemes, noted that their working practices were often 'predicated upon notions of homelessness as a consequence of vagrancy, alcoholism, destitution, pauperism and unwillingness to work'. Workers were civil servants, not social workers, and processed rather than supported people.

Modern constructions and constrictions: 1970–1996

The late 1960s and early 1970s saw a sea change in constructions of homelessness with the formation of organisations such as Shelter, CHAR and Crisis. Their central aim, as the first director of Shelter expressed it, 'was to relate homelessness to housing scarcity, and not to welfare (in its administrative sense), and to get full recognition of the scale of the problem (Wilson 1970, p. 19). This culminated in the passing of the 1977 Housing Act, which acknowledged the link between homelessness and housing and placed a duty on local authority housing departments to provide both temporary and permanent accommodation to *some* people who were homeless. We should not underestimate the importance of this move, because it acknowledged, in law, that homelessness could be caused by structural issues and that the government consequently had a legal duty to house homeless people – we are still the only European country with this acknowledgement and legal precedence.

Reflective Activity

Watch 'Cathy Come Home' on youtube.com. It was one of Ken Loach's first films and its screening caused the public debate that led to the founding of Shelter. It is the tale of a young family that gets moved from pillar to post until their children get taken off them.

Would this happen today?
What, if anything, has changed?

However, many authors (Neale 1997; Pleace 1998; Hutson and Liddiard 1994) note that this act and all subsequent homeless legislation (the 1985 Housing Act, the Housing Act of 1996 and the Homeless Persons Act of 2002) preserve some of the ideas of deserving and undeserving poor and the individualistic perspective that certain homeless people are to blame for their predicament. One of the conditions of the act is that, as well as being homeless, the person must be in 'priority need', i.e. there is a duty to meet the needs of all homeless people. Priority need groups now include people with dependent children; those experiencing domestic or racial violence; those coming out of the army, care or prison; 16- and 17-year-olds and the elderly; and those with a mental, physical or learning disability: these are the deserving homeless. These categories aside, it is if you are 'vulnerable', defined as:

> whether, when homeless, the applicant would be less able to fend for him/herself than an ordinary homeless person so that he or she would suffer injury or detriment, in circumstances where a less vulnerable person would be able to cope without harmful effects.
>
> *(DCLG 2006)*

This is a personal test that neatly preserves notions of individuality and denies structural causes. It is also an explicitly personal test, with a judgement being made about whether you are personally vulnerable for a reason exclusively to do with you and your circumstances. The denial of structural issues is also enshrined in its being a comparative test – you are compared with others in a similar situation. If, for example, you say you cannot move to an area because it is racist and you are from a black and ethnic minority (BME) community, it will not be sufficient. All BME people are in that situation: the racism needs to be directed towards you personally for some reason. This neatly sidesteps structural issues that may, for example, discriminate against all young people or all BME groups. A national inquiry into the prevention of youth homelessness (Evans 1996) found that, with regard to young people, 'the underlying assumption is that young people without dependants are not vulnerable and can fend for themselves'. Furthermore, it found that this view extended into local authority housing policy generally: 'this view is reflected in both the types of housing provided by the public sector and the access rules and priorities that public landlords apply'. Issues such as individual or structural discrimination by landlords due to race or age are not taken account of, only personal direct discrimination. In fact, case law has been established to explicitly say that if the discrimination is of a structural nature and would cover others with that attribute, then the individual is not vulnerable. The inquiry also found that there is a hangover of the deserving and undeserving construction in terms of priority need, with issues like drug use and alcohol rarely being taken into account in relation to vulnerability, even if the impact on housing is acute in an individualised way. Drug use is seen as self-inflicted and therefore a choice – a choice to be vulnerable – and consequently not legitimate. In addition to being a particularly individualised view of drug use, this echoes the 'sad' construction of 'legitimate' homelessness people: they must have no agency, otherwise they are 'bad' homeless people.

This construction is epitomised in another provision within the homelessness acts, which states that a person must be unintentionally homeless, i.e. they did not deliberately make themselves homeless. The echoes of some homeless people being seen as 'bad' and 'cheats' resound, and again structural factors (Mannheim 1936; Marx 1964; Rogers 2004; Young 1960) are minimised. We do not consider why someone would be desperate enough to get pregnant to access housing; we simply condemn them for doing it. Balchin (1998) believes that it is this perception – that homeless people were jumping the queue for public housing – which resulted in the Housing Act of 1996 removing the right to guaranteed public housing and replacing it with a duty to provide two years' temporary accommodation. Although this was subsequently reversed, the perception remains. More recently, in the name of prevention, there have been initiatives to stop young homeless people getting into the homeless system, with an emphasis on family mediation. While this can be applauded – especially as homeless hostels can be hostile environments that exacerbate young people's issues (Smith and Worley 2001) – it can also mean a young person being deemed intentionally homeless because the housing officer has rung their parents, who say they would take them back, or worse, made a judgment that the parents were colluding with the young person in saying they would not have them back.

Returning to housing in general, the post-war consensus on housing came sharply to an end with the Conservative administration of 1979–1997 and its move away from social housing and towards the private sector. The 1980 Housing Act and subsequent acts cut housing subsidies for local authorities by 50 per cent in real terms between 1979 and 1996, and introduced the tenants' right to buy council housing. Local authority house-building plummeted from 107,000 in 1978 to 37,000 in 1996. At the same time, the Housing Act deregulated private housing, introducing short-hold tenancies and breaking the link between fair and regulated rents in favour of market rents. Money invested in the private sector largely consisted of 'freeing up the market' by, for example, offering tax cuts to investors while cutting renovation grants. As a result, rents in the private sector increased threefold in the period 1980–1996, with a reduction in standards of accommodation (Balchin 1998).

With regard to homelessness, the number of the homeless rocketed, but there was also a change in its dynamics (Seal 2005). The aforementioned change in housing and benefits policy under Thatcherism was one factor. This combined with the failure to provide adequate resources under the 1989 Children Act, which was meant to make provision for young people leaving care. Whether this was causal is debated (Seal 2005). Undeniable is the fact that between 1972 and 1991 the proportion of homeless men under the age of 25 grew from 11 per cent to 39 per cent and the proportion of homeless women from 24 per cent to 60 per cent, with over 50 per cent, in both cases, having been in local authority care (Kemp et al. 1994).

Aside from this creation of vulnerability, other aspects of homeless people's vulnerability were exacerbated. The closing of mental health institutions and the failure to adequately resource legislation such as the Community Care Act meant that many people who were supposedly deinstitutionalised ended up in bed and breakfast (B&B) accommodation, isolated and often unmedicated. Daly (1996) notes that, in Portsmouth alone, the number of B&Bs catering for such people increased fivefold in the 1980s. These individuals did not last long in B&Bs but disappeared into the homeless netherworld. The level of diagnosed mental health issues amongst homeless people in B&Bs rose to 28 per cent, 36 per cent amongst day-centre users and 40 per cent amongst soup-run users, compared to 10 per cent in the 1970s (Daly 1996). Authors such as Gill et al. (1996) put the figure for the incidence of mental illness in hostel dwellers as high as 60 per cent.

Drug use also changed. Several authors have noted how drugs, particularly alcohol, have always been an integral part of the lifestyle of the homeless population (Orwell 1933; London 1913). This need not be seen as an individualist explanation about people choosing the 'lifestyle'. Daly (1996) saw drink and drug use as a functional coping mechanism: 'it dulls pain, induces euphoria, fills idle time, and is a means of fostering sociability amongst homeless men and some homeless women' (Daly 1996, p. 117). What changed in the 1980s and 1990s was the drug of choice, the style of use (i.e. poly-drug use) and the prevalence (Seal 2005), heroin moving from being a rich person's drug to being a poor person's drug. The *Big Issue* estimated in 1998 that 70 per cent of their vendors used drugs not prescribed to them. Heroin was used by 53 per cent, 28 per cent were using crack cocaine, 23 per cent were using diazepam and 21 per cent were using temazepam. Comparative figures for young people generally were only 1 per cent for cocaine, 1 per cent for heroin and 1 per cent for crack cocaine and abuse of prescription drugs was minimal.

By the early 1990s, rough sleeping was endemic, particularly in London. In 1991 the government launched the Rough Sleepers Initiative (RSI) in Central London, providing temporary and permanent accommodation for single 'non-priority' homeless people. However, the RSI has been accused of being a displacement activity, a cure for the aesthetic problem of homeless people (Pleace *et al.* 2008). It originated after a Tory MP famously said that he was 'fed up of stepping over homeless people to get to the opera'. The RSI was as much about social exclusion as it was about inclusion (Pleace 1998). In its first phase new units of accommodation were built; significantly, these tended not to be in Central London but in outer London boroughs – reminiscent of the old spikes.

There was also the wholesale destruction of spaces that homeless people had made their own, an example being the closing of the 'Bull Ring' at Waterloo in London. This had been a recognised cardboard city for over 20 years, with a population in the hundreds, yet it was torn down to make way for a new cinema. As agencies provided services for the displaced – it being a planned eviction – it was cited as good practice (Seal 2005). The principle of it being homeless people's space was not countenanced.

In the final phase of the RSI, a target was set to reduce street homelessness by two-thirds. Behind this policy decision is an interesting assumption that that if the existing street homeless population is resettled it will not be replaced. This is a denial of social closure (Weber 1972) to homeless people. The concept that street homelessness may arise because of fundamental structural issues seems to have been lost. In the subtext of the policy document for the final phase of the RSI there was a distinct indication that homeless people in the street who do not accept the resettlement that is offered will have the police deal with them. This represented a return to the individualist model, characterising homeless people as having chosen their lifestyle and those who do not take what they are charitably offered as 'bad' and needing to be dealt with accordingly. Interestingly, the 'street services' teams that have replaced street workers are obliged to work with the police and there has been an increase in the police using their old powers under the 1834 Vagrancy Act. In Edinburgh homeless people are still cleared away using this legislation before the Festival, then allowed back afterwards. I have heard reports of similar ativity in Nottingham and experienced it during Zero Tolerance measures at the end of the 1990s in King's Cross.

New Labour promised some radical changes in housing policy. But it was a mixed picture. Authors such as King (2005) and Stanley (2006) argue that New Labour in fact adopted and extended many of the housing policies of the Conservative regime – the emphasis was on encouraging private sector investment, subsidised through housing benefit, rather than direct investment in public housing. In 2004 the Barker review of housing supply showed that the private sector had singularly failed to 'take up' the house building that was needed and recommended planning reforms, a major increase in overall housing supply and higher investment in social housing. Gordon Brown set a target of 240,000 homes a year by 2016. This included 50,000 social homes a year from 2015 and meant an overall ambition for 3 million new homes by 2020. On the positive front, in 2007 224,680 homes were built in the UK across all sectors. However, the credit collapse meant only 100,000 homes were built during 2008, with a far greater reliance on the public sector than intended.

The Coalition, unsurprisingly, abandoned most of New Labour's policy: I will discuss some of the implications of their policies in my conclusion, but suffice it to say that the housing figures are dire. A recent Shelter report (2006) found that 1.4 million children in England live in bad housing. In 2008/09, 654,000 households in England were overcrowded; in 2009 the number of repossessions rose to 48,000 (from a figure of 25,900 in 2007), and it is predicted that repossessions will remain high in the coming years; furthermore, 7.4 million homes in England fail to meet the government's Decent Homes Standard. More recently still, Shelter (2012) found that the increase in homeless applications for councils was 18 per cent in 2010/11, and rough sleeping is up by 23 per cent. More generally, the UK is now more polarised by housing wealth than at any time since the Victorian era.

At the same time as this severe constriction in housing supply, constructions of young people and the leaving home process have ebbed and flowed. Kemp *et al.* (1994) notes that during the Thatcher and Major governments, policy initiatives aimed at reducing youth homelessness mainly involved the reduction or withdrawal of benefits, seen by policy makers as 'incentives' to leave home. Jones and Bell (2000) note that housing policy for young people has mostly been based on the premise that single young people remain in the parental home until they can afford to leave it and compete as 'newly formed families in the adult housing market', while at the same time changes in the labour market have necessitated single young people moving away for work. In 1984 those under 25 became entitled to lower levels of benefit than those over 25. The government related this change to housing and household responsibility, arguing that young people normally – and rightly – live with their parents, and do not bear the main responsibility for household expenses. In 1985, Board and Lodging Regulations imposed time and rent ceilings, aimed at under-25s living away, typically for seasonal work. By 1989 boarders could claim housing benefit only for accommodation costs; other costs would have to be met from non-housing benefits. Grants for rent deposits and Exceptional Needs Payments (e.g. for furniture and equipment) were removed and replaced, in 1987, by more restrictive discretionary Social Fund provisions. In 1988, student eligibility for housing benefit was restricted, then removed altogether in 1990. In 1996 most under-25s had their eligible housing benefit capped at the average market rent for a room in a shared property, regardless of housing circumstance, the implication being that they should not have their own flat. In 2010 the Coalition government raised the age cap to 35 and proposed cutting housing benefit for under-25s altogether. The consequences of these assumptions are noted by Jones and Bell (2000):

These policies resulted in an extension of dependency among young people able to continue to live in the parental home, and an increase in the vulnerability of those who have left it. The consequence was not to prevent young people from leaving home, only to make the process more difficult. If anything, the risk of homelessness was increased.

Transitional models of leaving home

Reflective Activity

Read the report *Young people's transition to adulthood* at www.jrf.org.uk/ system/files/sp98.pdf.

Does this have resonance with how you left home, and what has changed since the report?
Do you think it is easier or harder for young people to leave home now?

As several authors note (du Bois-Reymond 1995; Duckett and Smith 2009; Jeffs and Smith 1999), there is a 'transitional model' for leaving home that is constructed as the norm. However, as Duckett and Smith note:

> The 'transitions' model however was developed to fit the life experiences of a specific cohort of babies born in one week in 1958; one of the large sweeps of this cohort was undertaken in 1977 and early transition models were based on this data. The transitions of young people who became young adults in the late 1970s were essentially the transitions of the last 'Keynesian' generation: young people left their parental home to move through different, but smooth, pathways into higher education, work and family building.
>
> *(2009, p. 20)*

Yet this model was still being invoked by the Social Exclusion unit in 2005. Jeffs and Smith (1999) note that 'those who postpone "life" decisions typical for adulthood, such as taking a steady job or building a family' (du Bois-Reymond 1995, p. 79) are perceived as less than adult, less than mature. Duckett and Jones (2009) note a plethora of policy terms to account for these transgressions, including 'damaged transitions', 'ordered transitions' v. 'disordered transitions', 'extended transitions' and 'protracted transitions'.

Jones notes significant class differences in patterns of leaving home, with 'an increasing polarisation between young people who stay on in education and gain qualifications, and those who leave school at 16 or 17, risking bad jobs, low pay and unemployment' (Jones 2002, p. 4). She also noted that working-class families tend to start families in their teens and leave home for that new economic unit, while middle-class families live in shared private housing until they become owner-occupiers. Race was another factor, Jones noting that 'increasing educational achievement of some minority ethnic groups does not seem to be resulting in the expected dividends for them in terms of work and pay' (Jones 2002, p. 4), impacting again on people's realistic housing options.

Ford *et al.* (2002) identify four pathways for people leaving home: a chaotic pathway, an unplanned pathway, a constrained pathway, a planned (non-student) pathway and a student pathway. They note three main factors determining which pathway young people follow: the ability of young people to plan for and control their entry to independent living; the extent and form of constraints that characterise their access to housing; and the degree of family support available to them. There are also gradations of vulnerability for all of these, particularly for the first two. Constrained and planned non-student pathways might be when people move out, often with a lot of parental support, into the local private rented sector, with a long-term goal of owner-occupation. Quilgars *et al.* (2011) have built on this research, finding that in the last ten years the situation has become more acute, with people staying at home for longer before the planned move happens and the goal of owner-occupation – particularly in the South East – getting increasingly distant or even disappearing.

Chaotic or unplanned pathways, in contrast, are often related to push factors, meaning that the planning and family support elements are not there. Centrepoint, a major London homeless charity for young people, found in 2006 that 32 per cent of the young people they saw had run away from home aged 16 or 17, over 80 per cent had left home due to 'push factors' (conflicts, family breakdowns, evictions, abuse), 57 per cent of the young people were black or of minority ethnic origin, and 24 per cent had no source of income and could not support themselves when they first approached Centrepoint (Centrepoint 2006).

For 16/17-year-olds such as these the situation is even more acute. Even being accepted for housing under the new legislation is only part of what will make for a successful pathway. Pleace *et al.* (2008) found that those temporarily housed by the local authority under homeless legislation had the common characteristics of traumatic childhoods: family disruption, poor relations with parents, disrupted education, etc. Almost all had left because of relationship breakdown, with 41 per cent having experienced violence at home. Perhaps unsurprisingly 33 per cent had mental health issues, 37 per cent issues with drugs and alcohol, 57 per cent were NEET (Not in Education, Employment or Training) and 39 per cent had criminal records or ASBOs.

The Coalition and beyond

So what of the Coalition's approach? Has it been radically different or has it re-enforced existing perceptions? In October 2011, the National Housing Federation,

Shelter and the Chartered Institute of Housing launched a new report that assessed the Coalition's record on housing since the government was elected in May 2010, using official data. It was done via a series of traffic-light responses – green for going forward, amber for no progress and red where things had got worse. The government received four red lights, for housing supply, homelessness, help with housing costs and affordability within the private rented sector; three amber lights, for planning, evictions and homeownership; and two green lights, for empty homes and mobility within the social sector. The section on overcrowding was left without an indicator, in the absence of recent data.

In terms of welfare reform, the government is severely cutting housing benefit by putting caps on what people can receive for particular properties. Previously using the mid-point of local market rents as its base, it is now set at the rate of the bottom 33 per cent, which, by the government's own admission, forces vulnerable families into the cheapest housing. The Coalition's argument is that this will drive down market rents. However, Chris Norris, policy manager at the National Landlords Association, recently said: 'We are not aware of any evidence that landlords are reducing their rents in return for direct payment of LHA on any significant scale' (*Inside Housing*, 13 January 2012). Instead, the association's research showed that 77 per cent of landlords who have tenants in receipt of LHA (Local Housing Allowance) are being forced to consider reducing their involvement with tenants on housing benefit 'as they cannot absorb the effects of these cuts'. They found that 10 out of 11 councils contacted said they had seen little or no reductions in rent by private landlords as a result of their receiving direct LHA payments. New guidance (DCLG 2011) has been given on housing allocations: 'families who abide by tenancy agreements, work hard, contribute to their communities and are not a nuisance to their neighbours will be prioritised for housing that becomes available'.

In terms of young people, the single-room rent cap on housing benefit is to be extended to those under 35, and limited to £60 a week. It was mooted (*Inside Housing*, May 2012) that young people should have the right to housing benefit withdrawn completely, although this was not subsequently pursued. The discretionary Social Fund is to be abandoned, with local authorities having some discretion to run local funds – which the poorest local authorities will not be able to afford. Disability and sickness benefits are to be severely cut and limited to one or two years, with extended qualifying periods. There is to be an overall cap on the benefits that any one household receives, set at the typical wage: this has real potential to affect those in temporary accommodation, previously caught in a trap which meant they could not afford to work while living in a hostel. There are also proposals to change child support arrangements, with charges for collection.

Grainia Long, Chartered Institute of Housing interim chief executive, said recently:

> Eighteen months into a new government, there is still a lot to do to turn aspirations into reality on the ground. When so many people are struggling

to get the housing they need, we see that the private rented sector is unaffordable, help with housing costs is being reduced and homelessness is rising.

Reflective Activity

Look at the Shelter, Homeless Link and Chartered Institute of Housing websites for the latest news on housing supply, homelessness, housing costs, the private rented sector, planning, evictions, home ownership, empty homes, mobility and overcrowding.

Have the issues changed since the 2011 report?
Has progress been made or are there fewer green lights coming on?

Conclusion

Economically, young people's access to housing has moved from being part of the laissez-faire approach of the nineteenth century to being the object of paternalistic moral concern – though rarely backed up in material terms – in the early twentieth century. From an interwar period of public housing for the privileged to a post-war one of housing for all (that is, all families), then a return to laissez-faire, with public housing becoming social housing for those seen as deserving, which has rarely been young people. At the same time, young people were seen socially as a pension scheme, with a duty to live with and look after their parents. This fragmented, however, with the shake up of the two world wars, increasing social mobility and a need to migrate to the city for work. Post-war, young people were seen as new economic units, but still as people who would live at home until they married and moved either into public housing or their own home. From the 1960s a number of pathways developed over which government policy had influence, i.e. those concerned with public monies have pushed for young people to remain at home without any pathway for leaving. Public housing is no longer an option and a mortgage seems a dream, especially to those in the South East. This leaves young people who want to leave home to the vagaries and insecurities of an increasingly unregulated private sector. At the same time, those who do not leave to work away from home are condemned as scroungers and for not being independent.

However, some young people are forced to follow a chaotic route, often with a multiplicity of issues and little support – waiting for years in temporary accommodation, often deteriorating, hoping to access a dwindling supply of social housing or finding themselves pushed into the least regulated forms of private accommodation and becoming ghettoised. The fifth 'pathway', not noted by Ford et al. (2002), is when the idea of a transition, of leaving home, is abandoned. Young people do not think about it, there being little point. Allen (2006), conducting a survey of housing aspirations in the North East, noted that the main consideration of many working-class people was to get by from 'day to day'. They judged their housing and neighbourhood on that basis and did not see themselves as being on a property ladder, or of having any chance of ever being so.

Homeless people have historically been portrayed as being responsible for their situation. While there is a law that acknowledges structural issues, it is still under-pinned by a model of deserving and undeserving homelessness. Services have wrestled with these constructions and the government has given out mixed mes-sages and had conflicting priorities. Recently we have seen swathes of cuts to Supporting People (the main funder of support services), with 56 per cent of agencies facing cuts (Homeless Link 2012), and 46,000 people (*Inside Housing*, April 2012) being affected. At the same time it is estimated that the recession has increased homelessness by 25 per cent, with homeless applications to local autho-rities up by 44 per cent. The housing minister Grant Shapps has announced grants of £160 million for local authorities, minuscule compared to what has been cut from Supporting People and the welfare budget. What he and the Coalition see as the priorities for funding is telling. The money is to be used for initiatives to keep people in their own homes (interesting for young people), rent deposit schemes to get people into the private rented sector, and night shelters for rough sleepers, with the idea that no one should sleep rough in the capital for more than one night. While he talks about this last initiative in humanitarian terms, it is in one way a return to the Rough Sleepers Initiative, even the spikes, in terms of keeping rough sleepers away from business, tourists and the city centre and making the issue invisible, to do with 'other' people, who should be pitied at best and reviled at worst.

So where does this leave young people and homeless people? The traditional routes to housing are not working. Recent research from De Montford (Yates *et al.* 2011) found that even the student route is faltering. Young people are going back home after university, with massive debt and little hope of employment. In another article (Seal 2008) I set out five challenges for those who work with homeless young people and young people at home, and I think they still have resonance. First, we need to *campaign for change*. There is a fundamental need for affordable housing, particularly for single young people, in both rural and urban areas, and a secure route to permanent accommodation for homeless people. Housing benefit and social security restrictions for young people must be challenged. For the most vulnerable, local authority homelessness strategies need to be examined, particularly where prevention initiatives have elements of 'gatekeeping' about them.

Second, we need to *challenge the assumptions underlying both policy and provision*. First, there is the assumption that people gain responsibility and independence with age, regardless of social class, gender or cultural variation. Young people and homeless people can take responsibility, but it should not be forced upon them. We should also challenge the construction that young people are or can (or should) remain dependent on their parents, as well as the corollary that parents should accept extended responsibility for their children.

We should also *challenge communities' and young peoples' ideas about adulthood, leaving home and transitions*. Educational programmes need to be developed for young people and communities about the realities of the housing market. Parents need to be made aware that the routes that were perhaps open to them may no longer exist. However, particularly for homeless people, these programmes should be separate from decisions involving their priority status under the legislation, lest it becomes about persuading young people to go back into precarious or damaging family situations.

We should also *be a source of support for young people.* All the studies mentioned have shown that family support is crucial for people on their pathway to housing. However, for those for whom this is not available – particularly homeless people – support workers are essential. Indeed, people's social networks are vital for escaping homelessness (Seal 2005; Lemos 2006) and we need to acknowledge this and work with it. It is not enough just to secure housing for people. The process of it becoming home is far more wide-reaching, and we need to be with people in that process. Finally, we should *make greater links with homeless and other support services.* In my own practice I have found youth workers' knowledge of housing and home-lessness to be minimal. However, our liaison may well go beyond knowledge. Many hostels and temporary accommodation do not offer the level of personal support homeless people need (Neal 1996; Seal 2005, 2008) and we can and should endeavour to bridge that gap.

References

Allen, C. (2006) *Understanding Residential Mobility and Immobility*, London: ESRC.

Balchin, P. (1998) *Housing: The Essential Foundations*, London: Routledge.

Centrepoint (2006) *Who uses our services?* Available online at http://www.centrepoint.org.uk/the-issue/why-young-people-become-homeless (accessed 10 March 2012).

Daly, G. (1996) *Homeless: Policies, Strategies and Lives on the Street*, London: Routledge.

DCLG (2006) *Homelessness Prevention: A Guide to Good Practice*, London: HMSO.

DCLG (2011) *Allocation of Accommodation: Guidance for Local Authorities*, London: HMSO.

Donnison, D. and Ugerson, C. (1982) *Housing Policy*, London: Penguin.

du Bois-Reymond, M. (1995) 'Future Orientations of Dutch Youth: the emergence of a choice biography', in A. Cavalli and O. Galland (eds) *Youth in Europe*, London: Cassell.

Duckett, N. and Smith, J. (2009) *National Report on Youth Homelessness and Social Exclusion in the UK*, preliminary study for the European research project Combating Social Exclusion among Young Homeless People (CSEYHP), Cities Institute, London Metroplitan University.

Evans, A. (1996) *We Don't Choose to be Homeless: Report of the National Inquiry into Preventing Youth Homelessness*, London: CHAR.

Ford, J., Rugg, J. and Burrows, R. (2002) 'Conceptualising the contemporary role of housing in the transition to adult life in England', *Urban Studies*, 39 (13), 2455-2467.

Gauldie, E. (1974) *Cruel Habitations*, London: Allen & Unwin.

Gill, B., Meltzer, H., Hinds, K. and Petticrew, M. (1996) *Psychiatric Morbidity Among Home-less People*, London: HMSO.

Gillis, J. (1974) *Youth and History: Tradition and Change in European Age Relations, 1770– present*, New York: Academic Press.

Goodall, J. (1999) *Homeless for a Thousand Years.* Unpublished.

Griffin, C. (1992) *Representations of Youth: The Study of Youth and Adolescence in Britain and America*, Cambridge: Polity Press.

Hall, G. Stanley (1904) *Adolescence: Its Psychology, and its Relation to Physiology, Anthropology, Sociology, Sex, Crime, Religion and Education*, New York: D. Appleton.

Hammond, J. L. and Hammond, B. (1947) *The Bleak Age*, Harmondsworth: Pelican.

Hareven, T. K. and Adams, K. (2003) 'Leaving home: individual or family strategies', in J. Z. Lee, M. Oris and F. Van Poppel (eds) *The Road to Independence: Leaving Home in Western and Eastern Societies*, Bern: Peter Lang.

Homeless Link (2012) *Survey of Needs and Provision 2012: Homelessness services for single people and couples without dependents in England*, London: Homeless Link.

Hutson, S. and Liddiard, M. (1994) *The Social Construction of a Social Issue*, Basingstoke: Macmillan.

Kemp, P., Oldman, C., Rugg, J. and Williams, T. (1994) *The Effects of Benefit on Housing Decisions*, DSS Research Report No. 26, London: HMSO.

Jacobs, K., Kemeny, J. and Manzi, T. (2003) 'Power, discursive space and institutional practices in the construction of housing problems', *Housing Studies*, 2 (3), 344-356.

Jeffs, T. and Smith, M. K. (1999) 'The problem of "youth" for youth work', *Youth and Policy* 62, 45–66.

Jones, G. (2002) *The Youth Divide: Diverging Paths to Adulthood*, London: Joseph Rowntree Foundation.

Jones, G. and Bell, R. (2000) *Balancing Acts: Youth, Parenting and Public Policy*, London: Joseph Rowntree Foundation.

Kett, J. (1977) *Rites of Passage: adolescence in America, 1790 to the present*, New York: Basic Books.

King, A. (2005) *Conservative Consensus: housing policy before 1997 and after*, London: Imprint Academic.

Lemos, G. (2006) *Steadying the Ladder: social and emotional aspirations of homeless and vulnerable people*, London: Lemos and Crane.

London, J. (1913) *People of the Abyss*, New York: Arrow Books.

Mannheim, Karl (1936) *Ideology and Utopia: an introduction to the sociology of knowledge*, translated by Louis Wirth and Edward Shils, New York: Harcourt, Brace and World.

Marx, Karl (1964) *Selected Writings in Sociology and Social Philosophy*, translated by T. B. Bottomore, London: McGraw-Hill.

Neale, J. (1997) 'Theorising homelessness: contemporary sociological and feminist perspectives', in R. Burrows, N. Pleace and D. Quilgars (eds) *Homelessness and Social Policy*, London and New York: Routledge.

Orwell, G. (1933) *Down and Out in Paris and London*, London and New York: Penguin.

Pelham, J., Link, B. G., Moore, R. E. and Stueve, A. (1997) 'The stigma of homelessness: the impact of the label "homeless" on attitudes toward poor persons', *Social Psychology Quarterly*, 60 (4), 323–340.

Pleace, N. (1998) 'Single homelessness as social exclusion: the unique and the extreme', *Social Policy and Administration*, 32 (1), 46-59.

Pleace, N., Fitzpatrick, S., Johnsen, S., Quilgars, D. and Sanderson, D. (2008) *Statutory Homelessness in England: The experience of families and 16–17 year olds*, London: Department for Communities and Local Government.

Quilgars, D., Fitzpatrick, S. and Pleace, N. (2011) *Ending Youth Homelessness: possibilities, challenges and practical solutions*, London: Centrepoint.

Roche, J. and Tucker, S. (eds) (1997) *Youth in Society: contemporary theory, policy and practice*, London and New Delhi: Sage.

Rogers, S. (2004) 'Making and moulding of modern youth', in J. Roche and S. Tucker (eds) *Youth in Society: contemporary theory, policy and practice*, London and New Delhi: Sage.

Schürer, K. (2003) *Work and Leaving Home: the experience of England and Wales 1850–1920*, ESRC Future of Work Working Paper 12, Swindon: ESRC.

Seal, M. (2005) *Resettling Homeless People: Theory and Practice*, Lyme Regis: Russell House Publishing.

——(2008) 'Youth and housing: construction of a problem', *Youth and Policy*, 100, 45-52, NYA.

Shelter (2006) *Against the Odds: an investigation comparing the lives of children on either side of Britain's housing divide*, London: Shelter.

——(2012) *The Housing Report 3*, London: Shelter.

Smith, J. and Worley, C. (2001) *Moving Out, Moving On: from foyer accommodation to independent living*, London: YMCA.

Stanley, K. (2006) 'A new dawn of housing policy', *Inside Housing*, 5 May. Available online at www.ippr.org/articles/56/185/a-new-dawn-of-housing-policy (accessed 10 March 2013)

Weber, M. (1972) *From Max Weber: Essays in Sociology*, edited by H. H. Gerth and C. Wright Mills, London: Routledge

Wilson, D. (1970) *Speech on launch of Shelter campaign about the recognition of the need for statutory housing for homeless people.*

Yates, S., Harris, A., Sabates, R. and Staff, J. (2011) 'Early occupational aspirations and fractured transitions: a study of entry into "NEET" status in the UK', *Journal of Social Policy*, 40 (3), 513-534.

Young, G. M. (1960) *Victorian England: Portrait of an Age*, London: Oxford University Press.

6

CARE LEAVERS

Mark Cronin

Introduction

In recent years there has been unprecedented interest in the experiences of looked-after children, with a particular focus on how this impacts on their ability to make the transition to independence as care leavers. Most recently, the introduction of the green paper *Care Matters: Transforming the Lives of Children and Young People in Care* (DfES 2006), followed by the white paper *Care Matters: Time for Change* (DfES 2007), and finally the Children and Young Persons Act 2008 represented a clear statement of intent from the then New Labour government in terms of provision of services for looked-after children and care leavers. Of course the welfare of children who enter public care had long been a subject of concern, but these children and young people had been largely overlooked by politicians and policy makers.

This recent political interest seems to have been largely focused around the reported poor outcomes that follow on from admission to public care and as such it is not clear whether this momentum has been driven by a moral, a political or an economic imperative. It is equally unclear whether interest in care leavers has been driven by concerns about the risks to their individual welfare or the risks they pose to society as a group in terms of the cost to the taxpayer of these poor outcomes. This chapter will therefore explore both the historical and policy contexts that have come to define care leavers. It will consider the factors which have contributed to the relatively recent focus on the needs of care leavers and examine the provisions available as a consequence of recent policy and legislation, in relation to both the New Labour and the Coalition government. It will consider the complexity of the issues facing children and young people who have experienced the care system and the challenges they face in terms of leaving care. Consideration will be given to the design of related support mechanisms and the available evidence of what works for care leavers. Throughout these discussions consideration will be given to how concepts of vulnerability have been constructed and applied to care leavers and the associated implications.

Brief history of public care

The concept of being 'in care' can be traced back to the provisions of the Poor Laws which provided 'indoor' relief to the destitute in the form of the workhouse. These institutions, as a consequence of the 1834 Poor Law Amendment Act, were designed to act as a deterrent and people feared having to be admitted due to the meagre provision of relief and the harsh conditions under which they were expected to live and work. The nature of this relationship between the state and its citizens is believed to have been significant in relation to public care, as Frost and Parton (2009, p. 96) suggest:

> the long shadow of the Poor Law, which made provision that state welfare should be 'less eligible' or, in everyday words, of a lower standard than life in the community, has been influential in terms of the stigma associated with being 'in care'.

This emerged as a result of debates around the concept of the 'deserving' or 'undeserving' poor and relied on the assumption that poverty was the consequence of moral deficiency – that is, that some happily relied on the support of others in the absence of the necessary moral values related to self-sufficiency.

In the period following the industrial revolution there appeared to be increasing concern about the welfare of children as ideas of childhood 'innocence' became more influential – whether this innocence was seen as the natural state of children ('little angels') or the product of hard-fought battles against their innate sinfulness ('little devils') (Jenks, 1996). 'Boards of guardians' began to remove children from the workhouse to workhouse schools, education being seen as necessary to tackle the cycle of pauperism. Interestingly, as noted by Stanley (2012, p. 246), 'education was compulsory for paupers before it was for other children'. In the mid-twentieth century the courts began to commit offending children to 'industrial schools' on the grounds of morality and law, being parentless, begging or gang membership, and these schools were later used as a punishment for truancy when education became compulsory for all. The re-education of children coming into public care was seen as the key to their salvation.

As the momentum around child welfare gathered pace in the 1860s and 1870s, associated voluntary organisations emerged which became involved in the 'boarding out' (fostering) of children and the establishment of residential homes. At this time significant numbers of children were admitted into care as a consequence of poverty, but the introduction of the Prevention of Cruelty to Children Act in

1889 enabled courts to place children whose parents were found to be abusive with these voluntary organisations. It is important to note at this point that the state did not directly provide homes for these children, as the preferred option was 'boarding out', with voluntary organisations making the practical arrangements. As highlighted by Stanley (2012, p. 247), 'The Poor Law "deterrence" ethic was based on the idea that support was not assumed to be a municipal responsibility'. Therefore, although the state was increasingly regulating the conditions for childhood, it was still, at this point, reluctant to directly replace parents.

The emergence of specific legislation around the provision of public care took a significant step forward in the shape of the Children Act 1948, which was informed by the work of the Curtis Committee (1946) and the inquiry into the death of Dennis O'Neill (Monckton, 1945) at the hands of his foster father on the 9th January 1945. The inquiry raised serious concerns about the nature of this placement as the carers had been selected without adequate inquiry being made to their suitability and there had been a serious lack of supervision by the local authority. It emerged that the foster father had a history of violence and, although Dennis had been placed with this family for over six months, he had been subject to no medical examinations and was visited only once (Monckton, 1945). The focus of the Children Act 1948 was very specifically those who were living in care, and it led to the establishment of local authority children's departments which took over responsibility for children in care, as well as initiating the first national training programme for childcare officers. Most significant was the concern for these children, as outlined in the Curtis Report (1946, p. 5), which concluded that 'measures should be taken to ensure that these children are brought up in conditions best calculated to compensate them for the lack of parental care'. This was carried through into the act, which stated under section 12(1) that 'it shall be the duty of the local authority to exercise their powers with respect to him so as to further his best interests and to afford him opportunity for the proper development of his character and abilities'. This movement towards a consideration of the welfare of the child is highlighted when looking at the provisions in the former Poor Law Act of 1930, which stated under section 15 that it was the duty of the local authority to 'set to work and put out as apprentices all children whose parents are not, in the opinion of the council, able to keep and maintain their children'. Clearly this development did not represent a significant shift away from seeing children, in the words of James, Jenks and Prout (1998), as 'becomings' (the adults they may be in the future) and a utilitarian perspective in terms of their care, but it did represent some consideration of the conditions of their care and them as 'beings' (active participants). However, it is clear that what did endure was a focus on the child's development with a view to their role in adult life.

In the period following the introduction of the Children Act 1948 there was an expansion of the work of these children's departments towards a more preventative approach which aimed to avoid admission into care. There was an increasing belief that more comprehensive services could be delivered under an enlarged family service, which culminated in the establishment of local authority social services departments in 1971, following the Seebohm Report of 1968 and the Local Authority Social Services Act of 1970. These social services departments would take over direct responsibility for children in care, as well as the registration of children's homes and the use of voluntary organisations.

Changing political landscape

If attention had shifted a little towards concern about the welfare of children in public care in the post-war period, then it was the issue of 'drift', as highlighted in the landmark study by Rowe and Lambert (1973) entitled *Children Who Wait*, which would become the main focus. The authors made reference to children who appeared to live in foster or residential care for years, with no clear plan for permanency, and suggested that the issue related to individual planning as well as broader planning for children's services (Kirton, 2009). The philosophy of permanence emphasised the necessity of securing the futures of children in care, either by facilitating a return to birth parents or, where necessary, through substitute care – preferably via adoption and as quickly as possible. The need for permanence and the associated stability would provide the 'continuity of relationships with nurturing parents or caretakers and the opportunity to establish life-time relationships' (Maluccio, Fein and Olmstead, 1986, p. 5). It is however significant that this focus on permanence would also promote the movement of some children out of care.

This period of history also witnessed a series of events which was to bring social policy and the role of the state into the public consciousness. The death of Maria Colwell on the 7th January 1973 and the subsequent public inquiry, published in September 1974 (Secretary of State for Social Services, 1974), provoked a media campaign which labelled these events as a 'national scandal' and generated unprecedented public interest. Maria's return to her mother's care after being fostered by her aunt for over five years, despite Maria's opposition, resulted in her death at the hands of her mother's new partner, William Kepple, and brought into question the actions of the state. This inquiry and those that followed it (Jasmine Beckford 1985, Tyra Henry 1987 and Kimberley Carlile 1987, amongst many others) suggested that childcare professionals had not made use of their legal mandate to protect children and criticised them for failing to focus on the children's interests and being too sentimental in respect of the parents' needs. This case signalled an increasing role for the public inquiry in influencing public opinion and subsequent policy development.

This was further witnessed with the Cleveland Inquiry (Secretary of State for Social Services, 1988) reporting on the events of the summer of 1987, which saw the removal of 121 children from a small community in Middlesbrough. Social workers, on the evidence of two paediatricians, removed these children as they suspected sexual abuse. However, the tests from which the evidence had been gathered were later discredited and all but 27 of the children were returned to the care of their parents. This inquiry mirrored some of the concerns voiced in previous inquiries around the lack of co-ordination/communication between agencies and inadequate professional practice, but significantly it also raised questions about the appropriate balance between family autonomy and state intervention. The sense of injustice felt on behalf of the wrongly accused 'normal families' in combination with the emotive issues around sexual abuse resonated powerfully with the public, and the Conservative government of the time was not unaware of the power of this feeling (Cronin and Smith, 2010).

In the period prior to the Conservative election victory of 1979 there was increasing disillusionment about the ability of the social democratic state to manage the economy and overcome a range of social problems, as detailed in the public inquiries mentioned above, which led to the growth of the New Right (Parton, 2006). This new political ideology concerned itself with what it perceived as increasing state interference to the detriment of family life. It also stressed the importance of individual responsibility, choice and freedom and urged reductions in state interference, taxation and public expenditure. This generated a fresh impetus to redefine the relationship between the state and the family in the care of children, which was realised in the form of the Children Act 1989.

This act made clear provision for the admission of children into care by way of parents providing their consent under section 20 and by application for a care order under section 31, in cases where there were concerns around significant harm. However, there was also a clear message that state intervention should be avoided where possible, as should a child's admission into public care where possible. The 'no order principle' in section 1 (s.1(5)) of the act set the tone, stating that the court, in considering an application 'shall not make the order or any of the orders unless it considers that doing so would be better for the child than making no order at all'. There was also clear reference under section 17 to the duty for every local authority to 'safeguard and promote the welfare of children within their area who are in need; and' (s.17(1a)), 'so far as is consistent with that duty, to promote the upbringing of such children by their families' (s.17(1b)). In principle this represented a shift towards preventative interventions which supported families; however, the avoidance of admissions to care was also a clear objective of this piece of legislation. In addition to this, new threshold criteria were introduced and had to be satisfied before state intervention into family life was legitimised. A child could be admitted into care under a care order if the court was satisfied that 'the child concerned is suffering, or is likely to suffer, significant harm' (s.31(2a)), where harm is defined as 'ill treatment or the impairment of health or development' (s.31 (9)), and significant indicated thus: 'where the question of whether harm suffered by a child is significant turns on the child's health or development, his health or development shall be compared with that which could reasonably be expected of a similar child' (s.31(10)). These threshold criteria clearly set the context for greater reliance on child development frameworks to inform assessment but almost as significantly used subjective terms which were open to interpretation and reliant on policy guidance and resource allocations.

Reflective Activity

- What impact do you think the use of these 'subjective' terms in the Children Act 1989 might have had on identifying significant harm and subsequent decisions about admission to care?
- Do you think this approach to setting the criteria for admission to care would result in a clear and consistent process?
- How do you think the use of political power might have influenced the application of these duties in practice?

In addition to the concerns raised by public inquiries regarding the nature of state interventions in Cleveland and the case of Maria Colwell (and many others), there was growing concern about the state of the residential care sector and the conditions for children in residential care homes. This culminated in a series of reports – the first of which was Sir William Utting's 1991 *Children in the Public Care* (Utting, 1991), followed by his 1997 *People Like Us* (Utting, 1997) – which reported on the widespread abuse of children in residential care settings. These were followed by the landmark report by Ronald Waterhouse entitled *Lost in Care* (Waterhouse, 2000) which reported on the severe and extended abuse of children in residential care homes in North Wales. These reports had a serious and long-term impact not only on the reputation of residential care in England and Wales but also on the care system in more general terms.

The combination of negative messages regarding the nature and impact of state interventions resulting in the admission of children into care and the emergence of a new political ideology which championed a redefinition of the relationship between the state and the family resulted in a significant scaling down of the care population during this period. Shortly after the election of the Conservative government, in 1979, the care population was reported to be 95,300 children and young people, but it had dropped to 49,300 by 1994 (DoH 2001). To this point the matter of provisions for children who were taken into public care was characterised, despite some limited attempts to consider the children's welfare (albeit with a clear utilitarian motive), by political disinterest, apathy and at times abject neglect. The associated costs of care, both in the immediate sense and in relation to longer-term outcomes, had come to be the driving force behind policy development, and in the words of Parker *et al.* (1991, p. 1,617):

> the weakening of confidence in the public care of children following a number of well-documented tragedies, the attention given to consumer views and the emphasis on cost-effectiveness have all served to produce a climate in which the development of reliable means of assessing outcome is increasingly seen as a necessity.

The early use of conditions of care as a deterrent, alongside the enduring influence of right-wing ideology and the reluctant state, had come to signify the nature of care.

Coming into focus

As noted above, what little attention was paid to the welfare of children in public care appeared to be driven by a utilitarian ideology which concerned itself primarily with the impact of care on their long-term outcomes. The impact of the care experience came further into focus during the 1980s as a result of pressure from young people, their organisations and the publication of key texts such as *Leaving Care* (Stein and Carey, 1986). This study involved a group of 45 16–18-year-olds who had been in care for at least one year. These young people left the care of Wakefield Social Services in 1982 and were followed for over two and a half years. The children and young people involved in this research reported that they experienced a 'stigma' about being 'in care', only a third felt care had been helpful to them (although just under a half felt it was better than the alternatives) and most had issues with identity. The authors called for greater continuity, with fewer changes of placement and more sustained relationships, including those with family and siblings. They also questioned the philosophy of training looked-after children (LAC) for independence because at the time only 0.5 per cent of all 16–19-year-olds lived alone and they felt that, given the experiences of care leavers, this might compound their vulnerability (Stein and Carey, 1986). This report drew attention not only to the impact of care on these children but also how the design of leaving-care processes could contribute to the vulnerability experienced by care leavers. These voices attempted to engage in discussions around broader concepts of vulnerability that considered individual welfare instead of narrowly focusing on an individual's ability to contribute to society.

Shortly after this, in 1987, the Department of Health and Social Security initiated what became known as the 'Looked After Children' project, which aimed to introduce a practical scheme for assessing the outcomes of children in public care (Parton, 2006). The working party produced a report which identified seven 'development dimensions' for the measurement of children's long-term well-being into adulthood; these included their health, education, identity, family and peer relationships, emotional and behavioural development, self-care and competence and identity/social presentation (Parker *et al.*, 1991). Alongside these ran a series of six age-related assessment and action records (AARs) which measured their progress towards recognised developmental objectives and also the services they received to support their attainment. These were used to set the agenda for direct work with children and care planning, but their primary purpose was undoubtedly to provide local authorities with information about the outcomes for looked-after children and subsequently the effectiveness of the service. The clear focus on the use of these processes to produce outcome data which would inform discussions around the cost-effectiveness of services indicated an intensification of the New Right scrutiny of public finances.

There is some limited evidence of legislative interest in care leavers in the form of the duty to 'assist, advise and befriend' in the Children Act 1948 and indications of the growing recognition of associated difficulties as documented in the Short Report (House of Commons, 1984), which called for stronger duties to support care leavers. There was also some new impetus given to developing specialist services for care leavers as a consequence of the Children Act 1989. This contained a duty under section 24 to prepare looked-after children for leaving care, as well as detailing provision for some support until aged 21, and saw the emergence of specialist local authority after-care teams. However, research continued to reveal widespread problems for care leavers in terms of their education, employment, housing, health and young parenthood, as detailed in the *Moving On* research by Biehal *et al.* in 1995 and by Broad in *Young People Leaving Care: Life After the Children Act* (1998). Thus, at the time of the election of New Labour in 1997 it was evident that leaving care issues remained problematic and challenging.

New Labour

One of the first actions of the New Labour government was to include care leavers in its social investment agenda, as they were considered to be one of the groups most vulnerable to the effects of social exclusion. For New Labour, 'social exclusion' was about both individuals not being able to actively participate in society and take advantage of the associated life chances and their not contributing to the prosperity of society as a whole. Thus, care leavers were seen as a group for whom social investment might reap rewards in terms of their individual life chances, but which, more importantly, represented an opportunity to ameliorate the contribution of this group to the prosperity of society as a whole.

The positioning of care leavers in this social investment agenda provided a clear indication of the direction of travel for policy reform in this area. The rhetoric made clear reference to social justice for care leavers, but the policy was underpinned by a broader approach to tackling social exclusion informed by New Labour's 'Third Way' political ideology. This ideology was primarily concerned with a modernisation agenda, positioned between 'old Labour' (essentially pro-state) and the pro-market 'New Right'. In their election manifesto of 1997 New Labour outlined its intentions for reform to create a 'modern' welfare state for a 'modern world' which would enhance the country's broader aims for prosperity and economic competitiveness.

In relation to welfare services this modernisation agenda referred to offering welfare 'rights' with 'responsibilities' – for example, in the form of the flagship 'Welfare to Work' policy, which would provide support to the unemployed on the understanding that they accepted their moral responsibility to enter the workforce. It also adopted a 'what works' approach to welfare provision which enabled delivery of services by the state, voluntary and private sector organisations. As part of this political repositioning New Labour made a commitment to keep to Conservative public spending plans and to avoid increased taxation, which resulted in a programme of targeted social investment that included care leavers. Thus, the concept of 'social exclusion' provided both a means by which specific groups could be identified as worthy of social investment and a clear indication of how the issue needed to be addressed in terms of socially including these groups by primarily re-engaging them in the overall aim of increasing the country's prosperity. As such, the social investment agenda became a central feature of policy reform and, shortly after the New Labour election victory in 1997, Tony Blair set up the Social Exclusion Unit to co-ordinate policy in this area.

Initial indications of New Labour policy in this area were signalled by the now famous statement made by Frank Dobson, the Secretary of State for Health, in his letter to all councillors launching the Quality Protects programme, dated 21st September 1998: 'for children who are looked after, your council has a legal and moral duty to try to provide the kind of loyal support that any good parents would give to their children'. Dobson concluded this letter by stating:

> In announcing this new initiative we wish to help some of society's most vulnerable young people. We have it in our power to alter their future pattern of life for the better. We owe it to all our young people to ensure that they get the best possible start in life.

This letter was followed by the Quality Protects document (DoH, 1999) which aimed to ensure that looked-after children gained maximum life-chance benefits from educational opportunities, health and social care (objective number 4) and that young people leaving care, as they entered adulthood, were not isolated and participated socially and economically as citizens (objective number 5). This rhetoric represented a significant shift in the aspirations of policy makers to the welfare and well-being of children in public care and their subsequent transition as care leavers. However, there remained a clear focus on utilitarian objectives in terms of future participation in society.

The introduction of the Children (Leaving Care) Act 2000, following the consultation document *Me, Survive, Out There?* (DoH, 1999), represented a piece of legislation that extended the provision of support services for care leavers. In the first instance, under section 19(A), 'it is the duty of the local authority looking after a child to advise, assist and befriend him with a view to promoting his welfare when they have ceased to look after him'. It goes on to outline other local authority duties to keep in touch with care leavers until they are 21 (s.23B(1)), appoint them personal advisers (s.23D(1)), prepare a pathway plan mapping out their transition as care leavers (s.23E) and providing assistance until at least 21 and sometimes 24, if in education or employment. These provisions represented an attempt to encourage local authorities to improve their planning and support for young people leaving care with the aim of improving transitions for care leavers. It resulted in specialist after-care teams being introduced in almost all local authorities with the specific task of facilitating these new duties and provisions.

Significantly, ongoing support was reliant on state-approved transitions into adulthood, i.e. education or employment.

Shortly after the introduction of this piece of legislation Tony Blair decided to personally lead a review of the adoption process which clearly indicated the government's preferred option for children entering public care. He stated that 'It is hard to overstate the importance of a stable and loving family for children. That is why I want more children to benefit from adoption' (DoH, 2000, p. 3). The subsequent reforms and the introduction of the Adoption and Children Act in 2002 proved to be successful, with adoption rates increasing significantly (Office for National Statistics, 2011). However, this merely served as a reminder of the government's continued preference for the family as the privileged location for children and did nothing to improve confidence in the ability of the state to provide adequate care (Frost and Parton, 2009). It also indicated a desire to reduce the care population.

In 2006 the New Labour government published *Reaching Out: An Action Plan on Social Exclusion* (HM Government, 2006) in which it outlined its intentions and aims for progressing its social exclusion agenda, as well as reaffirming its belief that 'no one should be shut off from the opportunities, choices and options in life' (p. 8), but with the reminder that 'Tackling social exclusion also matters because failing to do so creates a cost for society' (p. 8). This document outlined five key principles that emphasised: the importance of early intervention, identifying what works, promoting multi-agency working, the personalisation of rights and responsibilities, and managing underperformance. It also made reference to the government's intentions to publish a green paper later that year on children in care, which will be considered in the next section.

Care Matters

In October 2006 the green paper *Care Matters: Transforming the Lives of Children and Young People in Care* (DfES, 2006) was published, setting out a clear rationale for reform, as outlined in the foreword by the then Secretary of State for Health, Alan Johnson, who stated that 'goals for children in care should be exactly the same as our goals for our own children' (p. 3). He went on to state: 'we want their childhoods to be secure, healthy and enjoyable – rich and valuable in themselves as well as providing stable foundations for the rest of their lives' (p. 3). There is clear evidence in these words of a commitment to the welfare of children in care, as well as to their transition to adult life. Johnson also goes on to acknowledge that 'our care system fails to enable most children who enter it to achieve these aspirations' (p. 3). The evidence of this failure is set out in Annex C of the green paper, which refers to the significant differences in educational achievements between children in care (11 per cent gaining five or more GCSEs grade A–C) and all children (56 per cent gaining five or more GCSEs grade A–C), their likelihood of being excluded from school (0.9 per cent for looked-after children, versus 0.1 per cent for all children) and the percentage of 19-year-olds who are NEETs (not in education, employment or training) – 60 per cent for care leavers compared with only 15 per cent for all young people.

The focus of the outcomes data contained in Annex C is almost exclusively concerned with educational attainment and potential employability, but there is also reference to offending behaviour, which outlines that 9 per cent of children in care have received a warning, reprimand or conviction compared with 3 per cent of all children. It is also telling that this annex begins by making reference to the significant increase in the care population – approximately 10,000 between 1995 and 2005. This, coupled with the major concern at the time about the spiralling cost of public care – quoted in a parliamentary debate in 2003 as rising from £435 per child per week (£1.3 billion per annum) in 2000 to £585 per child per week (£1.9 billion per annum) – and the debate around potential savings associated with the increased educational attainment of children in care – as outlined in the *Times Education Supplement* of 12th May 2006 – indicated a desire to reduce the costs to wider society of the care population. When considering the 'value' of childhoods and the necessary 'foundations' for the rest of children's lives, the measures of success appeared to be closely associated with the terms of reference of New Labour's social investment agenda. These may have also been supported by the desire to ameliorate the costs of public care.

This focus on education was further reinforced when the subsequent white paper, *Care Matters: Time for Change* (DfES, 2007), was published in June 2007. Although the paper presented seven key priority areas it was clear that its main focus was on improving the educational outcomes for children in care. The key priority 'Delivering a first-class education' was awarded by far the biggest proportion of the associated finance, primarily in the form of a £500 annual personal budget for all children in care not meeting expected educational standards, but also in terms of associated policy, which aimed to prevent the disturbance of school continuity in years 10 and 11. It also saw the role of the designated teacher in all schools put on a statutory footing and the extension of the 'virtual school head' scheme, both of which were intended to support educational performance.

Another of the key priority areas, 'Transition to adulthood', made explicit reference to care leavers and included initiatives to look at ways of preventing the premature discharge of children in care and pilots to explore the extension of foster care to 21. However, other initiatives in this priority area reinforced the educational focus, with a £2,000 bursary for care leavers entering higher education and the extension of a personal adviser for care leavers – if in education – up to 25. There were some other key policy developments of note in this paper, controversially the introduction of social care practices which opened the way for private companies to manage the care of looked-after children. However, it was clear that educational performance was the main priority, a position that was further reinforced when the Children and Young People's Act 2008 received royal assent. The act provided legislative support for the statutory role of designated teacher, higher education bursaries and the extension of the personal adviser role to support care leavers in education/training up to the age of 25.

It appears that this policy reform was driven by a utilitarian approach concerned primarily with improving the ability of care leavers to contribute to the prosperity of wider society. There is clear evidence to support this argument, but almost as significant is the comparative attention paid to other key priority areas identified in the white paper. The first priority, 'Corporate parenting: getting it right', set out to improve the performance of local authorities and their delivery of services to children in care, but there was no associated funding to support these aims. Local authorities were expected to absorb any additional costs and were to be subject to additional inspections to monitor their progress. Most significantly, the key priority area entitled 'Promoting health and well-being' received very little additional funding. Resources associated with this priority were intended to provide young pregnant women with a named health professional, raise awareness of the health needs of children in care and promote their leisure activities.

It is well documented that children who enter care have often endured significant trauma and emotional disturbance in their pre-care experiences (DfES, 2006). It is not surprising then that almost half of all children in care have been diagnosed with a mental health disorder, compared with 10 per cent of all children (Office for National Statistics, 2003). It is astonishing then that there is no reference in the Care Matters initiative to addressing the social/emotional needs of children in care. Even in terms of the focus on improving educational attainment it is surprising that consideration has not been given to the potential for social and emotional problems to create a significant barrier to educational achievement.

Reflective Activity

- What impact might a growing culture of performance management and the accountability of public finances have had on the omission of a commitment to addressing the social/emotional needs of LAC?
- How easy is it to evidence outcomes when providing therapeutic interventions?
- What level of resource commitment would be necessary to adequately address the mental health needs of the LAC population?

This omission may offer some explanation for the lack of significant progress in narrowing the gap in educational performance between children in care and all children. It appears that there has been some improvement in terms of the percentage of children in care gaining five or more GCSEs grade A–C, from 11 per cent in 2005 to 15 per cent in 2009. However, it is significant that this percentage for all children has increased at a much faster rate, from 56 per cent in 2005 to 70 per cent in 2009 (DCSF, 2010), which in effect has resulted in a broadening of this gap.

Reflective Activity

- What factors do you feel might be contributing to the prevalence of mental health disorders in LAC?
- How might these issues impact on LAC and their educational progress?
- What effect might a focus on therapeutic interventions to address mental health issues for LAC have on educational performance?

Impact of care

Having established that the main focus of Care Matters is on improving the educational attainment of children in care, it is important to consider the main reasons for this relative underachievement and begin to explore how well recent policy developments are designed to meet the needs of children in care. In 2006 Barnardos carried out research entitled *Failed By The System: The views of young care leavers on their educational experiences* (Barnados, 2006), which asked young people involved in their leaving care projects to reflect on their educational experiences. The study involved 66 young people between the ages of 16 and 21 who were receiving leaving-care support from Barnardos. Only 14 of these young people reported having left school with any educational qualifications and only seven of them had five or more GCSEs grade A–C, which meant that the vast majority (52) left school with no educational qualifications. Half of the group (33) had been in four or more placements and 27 of these had been in both residential and foster care, with four of the group having had more than 24 placements. Not surprisingly, on average, group members had attended five different schools and 41 of them had been excluded from school, with 22 of these having been excluded for more than 60 days in total. Nearly half the group (29) reported having received no extra help to catch up on work when moving schools and 26 reported that no one had attended their school's parents' evenings. Over half of the group reported being bullied in school and believed this was directly related to them being in care. Thirty-one of these young people reported having never been praised or rewarded when they did well at school and 24 reported that they had never been involved in making decisions about their education.

For this group of young people educational failure was clearly typified by a lack of stability, lack of support and a lack of engagement. When asked what would have helped them at school, they were clear that greater placement stability and fewer changes of social worker and/or school would have made a difference. They also made distinct reference to the impact of negative assumptions about children in care – i.e. that they are not interested in school/that they cause problems – and the importance of teachers' understanding of their situation. They also felt that if they had been offered greater encouragement even for small achievements then this would have helped with their self-confidence and self-esteem. For this group of young people placement stability and continuity of support workers were key themes in their reflections on their educational experiences, as well as the direct contact with schools/pupils and teachers.

Reference to broader social factors and their influence on education was also a theme in the earlier research published by the Joseph Rowntree Foundation entitled *Into the mainstream: Care leavers entering work, education and training* (Allen, 2003), exploring care leavers' reflections on their care experience and subsequent economic engagement. For this study 36 young people were interviewed, the majority of whom were in their first year as care leavers. It concluded that young people who had enjoyed a relatively stable care experience were more likely to be settled post-16. A key factor in educational achievement for this sample was the number and type of placements they had experienced, as every change disrupted the school routine, prevented the establishment of significant relationships, undermined key support networks and impacted on the young person's attitudes and self-esteem. What emerges from these studies is that a young person's placement stability and the associated relationships/support networks are key to both their educational progress and their general well-being.

As mentioned earlier there has also been some interest in the over-representation of children in care in the criminal justice system, as indicated in Annex C of the Care Matters green paper. This issue was explored by a report produced in 2011 by the Prison Reform Trust entitled *Care – a stepping stone to custody? The views of children in care on the links between care, offending and custody* (Blades et al., 2011). For this research 23 in-depth interviews were conducted with children in care between the ages of 13–17 years old, the majority of whom were either in or had been in custody. The report begins by making reference to the high prevalence of children in young offender institutions who are, or have been, in care and asks those involved in the study to identify how being in care impacts on the likelihood of offending. These young people felt that the loss of contact with family/friends was a significant risk factor for offending, as were their poor relationships with their carers/social workers. They also felt that their often difficult relationships with their peers and the frequent change of placements contributed. When asked about factors that could protect them from offending, they made reference to stable placements, ongoing contact with family/friends, more quality contact with their social workers and being more involved in decisions which affect their lives. In this research the role of social relationships appeared to be key and the young people clearly needed support from at least one trusted adult to provide practical and emotional support.

The notion of risk and protective factors and their contribution to an individual's resilience is central to an important contribution to understanding the care experience made by Mike Stein in his report *Resilience and young people leaving care: Overcoming the odds* (2005). This report represents a review of literature that has attempted to capture the experience, views and reflections of young people leaving care over a 20-year period. It begins by making reference to studies which have looked at the issue of placement stability and concludes that between 30 and 40 per cent of care leavers have experienced four or more placements, between 6 and 10 per cent have had a single placement and the same percentage have had 10 or more placements. Stein states that 'overall the picture suggests that those *in loco parentis* are failing to provide the basic stability required by young people to promote their resilience' (p. 8). He goes on to state that another key factor in promoting resilience is a sense of identity, which is about understanding our personal narrative or 'who I am' and contributes to self-esteem and self-confidence. Stein also makes reference to the development of an individual's self-efficacy/ self-control through their engagement in problem-solving and decision-making with respect to their life choices. He also makes reference to the impact of a positive school experience, but adds that the evidence suggest that in many cases these resilience-promoting factors are denied care leavers due to the disruption and instability they experience. Stein (2005, p. 8) does acknowledge that:

> for some young people care has provided them with a turning point, by removing them from a damaging family background and giving them an opportunity to develop their potential in new families, communities and at school.

But he concludes that 'for too many their experience of care, far from helping overcome the damaging emotional legacy of family problems, had rendered them unable to form the very relationships they needed so much' (p. 8). With specific reference to care leavers, he concludes that for the majority who leave care at 16/17 years old, the transition into adulthood is by comparison to the experience of other young people compressed and accelerated. He goes on to classify care leavers into three groups according to their experience of care and subsequent transition into adulthood as: the 'moving on' group whose stable care experience has enabled a planned move to independence with ongoing support from secure relationships; the 'surviving' group, who, despite having experienced placement instability, leaving care early and making an unplanned/rushed move to independence, are – with quality personal/professional support – managing; then the 'being a victim' group whose care experience has not compensated for poor pre-care experience and as a consequence have significant placement instability, no secure attachments, tend to leave care early and their transition to independence is fraught with problems. The work of Stein not only strengthens our understanding of the role played by instability and its subsequent impact on education, it also clearly locates the importance of identity and self-efficacy alongside the development of self-esteem/self-confidence and confirms the central importance of secure relationships. All of this makes clear reference to the emotional health and well-being of care leavers.

These issues were explored by Stanley (2007), who asked looked-after adolescents in two local authorities in England about their ideas and experiences relating to their mental health needs. In addition, carers in the same local authorities were asked to report their views on the mental health of looked-after children. For this study the views of 14 looked-after young people between the ages of 12 and 19 were gathered during four focus groups. The factor they reported as being significant in terms of impacting on their mental health was the availability and continuity of staff, and they stated that a lack of consistency was an issue. They also reported that the stigma attached to being in care affected their willingness to confide in friends and was a barrier to developing important relationships. They also felt that the level of control they were able to have over receiving professional help and the sharing of confidential information was a significant issue. It appears that for this group of young people secure and consistent relationships with key people are a protective factor in terms of their mental health, but again instability and the associated problems are a real concern. The issue of self-efficacy and self-control in terms of decision-making also appears to be key to positive mental health.

The views of 159 carers in this study were obtained using postal questionnaires and they reflected on their experience of caring for young people and on the young people's mental health. They reported young people displaying anxiety, fearfulness and low self-esteem and commented on their poor relationships with both peers and adults. For these carers the key issues associated with the mental health of these young people was the lack of consistency in care associated with placement changes and the subsequent changes in care staff, which inhibited the development of secure relationships. They also commented on problems encountered accessing specialist mental health support services in terms of both availability and the preference for contact with these services being made via social workers, which created unnecessary delays. In his discussion Stanley suggests that 'a lack of trust consequent on repeated losses and breakdowns in caring relationships may make young people particularly challenging and unattractive to carers and contribute to further placement breakdowns' (2007, p. 265). It appears that not addressing the mental health needs of looked-after children may not only impact on their educational progress but also result in a cycle of placement disruption which, as has been detailed above, is a consistent theme in poor outcomes for care leavers. Another important feature coming from this and previously mentioned research is the role of key adults/carers and the specific position of the young person's social worker. In her paper 'Who owns my pain? An aspect of the complexity of working with looked after children', Rocco-Briggs (2008) reflects on working with looked-after children and their care network as part of the Children and Adult Mental Health Service (CAMHS). She explores the difficulties encountered by professionals when attempting to develop relationships with children who have experienced abuse and trauma. In her conclusions she emphasises the importance of a 'network' around the child and for these professionals to have the space to think about the child in order to facilitate relationships which support therapeutic interventions. Clearly for Rocco-Briggs the key to supporting these young people's mental health is the existence of secure and meaningful relationships with key professionals who have the space and time to understand and respond to their needs.

The conditions for such a secure and meaningful relationship between a child in care and their key professional (i.e. social worker) is explored by McLeod (2007) in the paper 'Whose agenda? Issues of power and relationships when listening to looked-after young people'. In this research 11 young people in care aged between 9 and 17 and 11 social workers were interviewed and the focus was on communication and the participation of the young people in decisions that affected their care. For McLeod, 'listening is closely bound up with issues of power' (2007, p. 279) – clearly relevant to this relationship, with social workers in a significant position of power in terms of the care of looked-after young persons and conversely, as argued above, young people feeling they have relatively little power. For the young people in this study a key issue was that they felt social workers who did not act on their wishes had not really listened to them. They also reflected on the resource issues of placement availability and social work time. It seems that trust can only be established when communication leads to significant actions in the areas that matter most, i.e. time spent with young people by social workers, and some control over where they are placed. McLeod (2007, p. 285) suggests that 'reaching an understanding of the viewpoint of a marginalised young person is a time-consuming business requiring the sustained relationship central to the traditional notion of casework'. Unfortunately, the issue of social work time has been of concern for a number of years and the recent work of the Social Work Task Force has attempted to address a number of significant issues which are impeding the profession. However, progress appears to be slow, as the recent Ofsted report *High Expectations, High Support and High Challenge* (2012b) found that 38 per cent of social workers surveyed felt they did not have sufficient time to work effectively with children and young people and 27 per cent of managers did not believe there were sufficient numbers of suitably qualified staff in their team to meet the needs of children and young people. McLeod concludes that 'it could be that the biggest barrier to effective listening is when adults do not really want to hear what children have to say' (2007, p. 285). It seems most likely that the professional constraints placed on social workers in terms of both time and available resources create an environment which significantly undermines the very relationships which are key to the welfare and well-being of children in care.

Reflective Activity

- What do you understand to be the issues facing the social work profession which might be undermining this key relationship?
- What professional dilemmas might social workers face in terms of committing more time to the development of this relationship?

> • What broader factors might undermine the development of the trust required to enable more effective listening?

Current context

It is important at this point to consider the implementation of Care Matters by the New Labour government and the subsequent changes as a result of the election of the Coalition government in May 2010. Early reports of the success of these initiatives pointed to their fragility, even in relation to their main focus, i.e. improving educational attainment. In respect of the personal education allowance, reservations were voiced about the fact that these resources were not ring-fenced and therefore were taken into the whole school budget. Sarah Gentles, education manager at the charity Shaftsbury Young People, reported in *Children & Young People Now* in September 2009 that in her experience this provision was patchy and that not all young people were getting it (Crane, 2009). There were also concerns that generic equipment was being purchased using the personal education allowance finance, with the justification that looked-after children would have access to it. This allowance was later abolished by the Coalition government in April 2011 as part of its review of guidance for looked-after children. The new 'pupil premium' will, according to the Coalition government, address the educational needs of the vulnerable. However, again, early reports indicate that its ability to meet the needs of the vulnerable will be hampered by widespread budget cuts. A survey of 2,100 teachers carried out by the Sutton Trust in November 2010 (Lewis and Pyle, 2010) indicated that their priorities for spending the pupil premium would be reducing class sizes and employing more teachers/support staff; measures which would provide benefit for all pupils but do not relate specifically to the needs of the vulnerable.

There has also been concern raised about the introduction of the free school initiative, which will give headteachers greater autonomy and power in respect of school admissions and exclusions and could undermine attempts to improve educational consistency for looked-after children, who might be viewed as potentially disruptive to overall school performance. In this age of austerity coupled with a government led by a centre-right ideology we have also seen the emergence of more worrying developments. There have been discussions in some local authorities, as noted in *Community Care* (Pemberton 2011), about money-saving plans to charge parents whose children are admitted to care. This is seen as potentially having the dual function of generating income and providing a deterrent.

In their most recent report, *After care: Young people's views on leaving care*, Ofsted (2012a) provides some useful reflections on the experience of leaving care today. This research collected the views of 308 young people, most of whom had left care, with some preparing to leave. Just over 40 per cent of these young people reported that entering care made their lives better, making reference to getting a better education and being involved in positive activities. However, over one-third felt entering care had made their lives worse, due to their losing contact with family/friends, having poor peer relationships, having limited support from social services and being made to grow up too fast. Just over half (51 per cent) felt they had been reasonably well prepared for leaving care, making reference to acquiring financial management and domestic skills. However, 49 per cent felt they had been badly prepared, making reference to a lack of financial skills, practical help and, significantly, having no one to talk to. Only 25 per cent felt they had left care at the right time, with 46 per cent believing they needed more time in care. In terms of educational achievement, 29 per cent felt they did better than they would have done if they had not entered care; however, 35 per cent felt they did worse. When asked what was the best thing about being in care these young people reported a sense of safety and having a family, as well as getting help with their education. The worst things about care were losing contact with family/friends, too many moves/changes in carers and social workers, not being able to contact social workers and not being consulted/listened to. What emerged from this survey was that many of the young people were not aware of their rights, and the suggestions they made for changes included taking action to ensure they are heard, better contact with their social workers and the availability of greater emotional support to help them cope with the changes they were experiencing.

Conclusion

A brief exploration of the history of public care identified the establishment of a relationship between the state and children in care, characterised by both a reluctance to take responsibility and the design of associated services to act as a deterrent. It can be argued that, to a degree, this relationship has persisted and the limited interest in and resources committed to meeting the needs of children in care is indicative of an ongoing view that this population is a drain on public finances and that admissions to care should be avoided. It was also established that the primary focus of care should be the re-education of these young people to ameliorate their impact on the state, which has also been maintained in policy terms via an almost exclusively utilitarian approach to their care.

Regarding vulnerability, apart from some limited references to welfare, this again has been conceptualised as the risk this population poses to the prosperity of broader society. As a result there is little evidence of any substantial effort to address the welfare needs of such children and, consequently, the prognosis for their successful transition into adult life is severely limited. All of this has emerged in the context of compelling evidence which indicates the areas in which improvements could and should be made in order to address the welfare needs of children in care. Time and time again care leavers have made reference to the importance of stability in their care placements, schools and relationships with key professionals. They have clearly indicated their lack of knowledge of their rights and feeling they have no say and are not consulted in decision-making about their care. They have also clearly stated their need for emotional support both during their care experience and after leaving care. Addressing these welfare needs has, of course, significant resource implications, as iterated by a recent report produced by a collection of well-respected charities working with care leavers entitled *Access All Areas* (NCAS, 2012), which highlighted the need for a more strategic, cross-departmental approach to their support. However, until a real commitment is made to meeting these needs, public care will continue to be frequently a damaging experience, one which can both inhibit transitions into adulthood and act as a deterrent to families seeking support.

References

Allen, M. (2003) *Into the mainstream: Care leavers entering work, education and training.* York: Joseph Rowntree Foundation.

Barnardos (2006) *Failed By The System: The views of young care leavers on their educational experiences.* Barnardos Policy and Research Unit.

Biehal, N., Clayden, J., Stein, M. and Wade, J. (1995) *Moving On: Young People and Leaving Care Schemes.* London: HMSO.

Blades, R., Hart, D., Lea, J. and Willmott, N. (2011) *Care – a stepping stone to custody: The views of children in care on the links between care, offending and custody.* London: Prison Reform Trust.

Broad, B. (1998) *Young People Leaving Care: Life After the Children Act.* London: Jessica Kingsley.

Children Act 1989. London: HMSO.

Children (Leaving Care) Act 2000. London: HMSO.

Crane, P. (2009) 'Children in care lose on allowances', *Children & Young People Now*, 17 September.

Cronin, M. and Smith, C. (2010) 'From Safeguarding to Safeguarding' in Brotherton, G., Davies, H. and McGillivray, G. (eds) *Working with Children, Young People and Families.* London: Sage, pp. 97–117.

Curtis Committee (1946) *Report of the Care of Children Committee.* London: HMSO.

DCSF (2010) *Outcome Indicators for Children Looked After: Twelve months to 30 September 2009 – England.* Department for Children, London: Schools and Families.

DfES (2006) *Care Matters: Transforming the Lives of Children and Young People in Care.* London: Department for Education and Skills.

DfES (2007) *Care Matters: Time for Change.* London: Department for Education and Skills.

DoH (1998) *The Quality Protects Programme: Transforming Children's Services* (LAC (98)28). London: Department of Health.

DoH (1999) *Me, Survive, Out There? New Arrangements for Young People Living in and Leaving Care.* London: Department of Health.

DoH (2000) *The Prime Minister's Review of Adoption.* London: Department of Health.

DoH (2001) *Health and Personal Social Services Statistics 2000.* London: Department of Health.

Frost, N. and Parton, N. (2009). *Understanding Children's Social Care: Politics, Policy and Practice.* London: Sage.

HM Government (2006) *Reaching Out: An Action Plan on Social Exclusion.* London: Cabinet Office.

House of Commons (1984) *Children in Care, Volume 1: Second Report of the Social Services Committee, 1983/4.* London: HMSO.

James, A., Jenks, C. and Prout, A. (1998) *Theorising Childhood.* Cambridge: Polity Press.

Jenks, C. (1996) *Childhood.* London: Routledge.

Kirton, D. (2009) *Child Social Work: Policy & Practice.* London: Sage.

Lewis, K. and Pyle, K. (2010) *NFER Teacher Voice Omnibus: November 2010 Survey.* London: NFER.

Maluccio, A., Fein, E. and Olmstead, K. (1986) *Permanency Planning for Children: Concepts and Methods.* London: Tavistock.

McLeod, A. (2007) 'Whose agenda? Issues of power and relationships when listening to looked-after young people', *Child and Family Social Work*, 12, pp. 278–286.

Monckton, Sir W. (1945) *Report on the Circumstances which Led to the Boarding-out of Dennis and Terence O'Neill at Bank Farm, Minsterley, and the Steps Taken to Supervise their Welfare.* London: HMSO.

NCAS (2012) *Access all Areas*, report by Catch22 National Care Advisory Service, The Care Leavers' Foundation, The Prince's Trust and A National Voice. NCAS.

Office for National Statistics (2011) *Statistical Bulletin: Adoptions in England and Wales 2010.* Newport: Office for National Statistics.

Office for National Statistics (2003) *The mental health of young people looked after by local authorities in England.* Norwich: HMSO.

Ofsted (2012a) *After care: Young people's views on leaving care. Reported by the Children's Rights Director for England.* Manchester: Ofsted.

Ofsted (2012b) *High expectations, high support and high challenge: Protecting children more effectively through better support for front-line social work practice.* Manchester: Ofsted.

Parker, R., Ward, H., Jackson, S., Aldgate, J. and Wedge, P. (1991) *Looking After Children: Assessing Outcomes in Child Care: The Report of an Independent Working Party established by the Department of Health.* London: HMSO.

Parton, N. (2006) *Safeguarding childhood: early intervention and surveillance in a late modern society.* Basingstoke: Palgrave Macmillan.

Pemberton, C. (2011) 'Council wants to charge parents who put children into care' in *Community Care*, 4 October. Available online at www.communitycare.co.uk/articles/04/10/2011/117548/council-wants-to-charge-parents-who-put-children-in-care.htm (accessed 27 February 2013).

Rocco-Briggs, M. (2008) 'Who owns my pain? An aspect of the complexity of working with looked after children', *Journal of Child Psychotherapy*, 34(2), pp. 190–206.

Rowe, J. and Lambert, L. (1973) *Children Who Wait.* London: Association of British Adoption Agencies.

Secretary of State for Social Services (1974) *Report of the Inquiry into the Care and Supervision Provided in Relation to Maria Colwell.* London: HMSO.

Secretary of State for Social Services (1988) *Report of the Inquiry into Child Abuse in Cleveland.* London: HMSO.

Stanley, J. (2012) 'Residential child care policy' in Davies, M. (ed.) *Social Work with Children & Families.* Basingstoke: Palgrave Macmillan, pp. 246–271.

Stanley, N. (2007) 'Young people's and carers' perspectives on the mental health needs of looked-after adolescents', *Child and Family Social Work*, 12, pp. 258–267.

Stein, M. (2005) *Resilience and young people leaving care: Overcoming the odds.* York: Joseph Rowntree Foundation.

Stein, M. and Carey, K. (1986) *Leaving Care.* Oxford: Blackwell.

Utting, Sir W. (1991) *Children in the Public Care: A Review of Residential Child Care.* London: HMSO.

Utting, Sir W. (1997) *People Like Us: The Report of the Review of the Safeguards for Children Living Away from Home.* London: HMSO.

Waterhouse, Sir R. (2000) *Lost in Care: Report of the Tribunal of Inquiry into the Abuse of Children in Care in the former County Council Areas of Gwynedd and Clwyd since 1974.* London: HMSO.

7

CHILDREN OF PRISONERS

Karen Argent

Introduction

In a report published by the charities Action for Children, The Children's Society and the NSPCC entitled *In the eye of the storm: Britain's forgotten children and families* (Reed, 2012), these organisations argue that at the policy development level there is a continuing lack of attention paid to the issues faced by the children of prisoners. Their concern is echoed in a longitudinal academic study, *Risk and protective factors in the resettlement of imprisoned fathers and their families* (Losel et al., 2012: 7), which also recognises that 'parental imprisonment can be one of the most critical life events for families (because) it can disrupt marital and family relationships, have negative outcomes for children, and aggravate material and social problems'.

This chapter will further explore these concerns and argue that because this group of children continues to be largely invisible in political and policy discussions, they are not having their needs adequately recognised or met through appropriate service provision. There has also been a relative lack of independent or academic research undertaken on the practical and emotional needs of this group of vulnerable children – an absence that has been noted by Shaw (1992), Boswell and Wedge (2002) and Murray and Farrington (2008). However, despite this seeming consensus that the needs of this vulnerable group are not being adequately recognised, policy-makers continue to address the issues in a piecemeal and unsatisfactory way.

This happens despite the fact that the impact of family-member imprisonment on a child has been well monitored for at least thirty years by voluntary and campaigning organisations such as Action for Prisoners' Families (APF), Ormiston Children and Families Trust (OCFT), Prison Advice and Care Trust (PACT) and The Howard League for Penal Reform. It is largely as a result of persistent campaigning by such groups that some progress, albeit limited, has been made in changing policy. The *Change for Children* (ECM) (DfES, 2004a) policy of the last Labour administration, for example, was the first to explicitly mention this vulnerable group of children and begin to consider an appropriate response in terms of service provision. Consequently, there have been some real improvements to family support within the prison system, although the extent of such support and its prioritisation is still at the discretion of individual prison governors. There have also been some examples of local authorities responding to this agenda by publishing policy guidelines and offering in-service training to the staff of schools, children's centres and other relevant agencies, although this is not universal. The initial undergraduate and postgraduate training of professionals who plan to work in the community with families in a range of roles such as teachers, social workers, health visitor and family support workers includes some relevant training, although this is still largely an *ad hoc* process.

It also needs to be recognised that many children of prisoners will have other circumstances that contribute to their perceived vulnerability, such as a special educational need and/or a disability and may often be living in relative poverty, possibly as a consequence of the imprisonment of a parent. They will almost certainly fall into the Coalition government's definition of living in a 'troubled' family (Department for Communities and Local Government, 2012).

This chapter seeks to explore in more detail the way in which social attitudes towards certain kinds of families viewed as inherently dysfunctional and problematic contribute to a deficit model that further disadvantages the children living in those families (Condry, 2007). It will examine what makes the children of prisoners particularly vulnerable and what the characteristics of that vulnerability are; but, importantly, it also asks why these vulnerabilities persist and what part is played by public perceptions of prisoners and their families.

Due to limitations of space, the chapter focuses on the implications for children attending school. In England, attendance at school is statutory for all children between the age of five and sixteen and this particular service can be used as something of a case study to illustrate how the needs of the children of prisoners are being met (or not) at a practical level. Many of the points discussed could be applied in other settings.

The scale of the problem

The adult prison population now stands at approximately 86,801, a figure that does not include juveniles in secure training centres and local authority secure children's homes (Williams *et al.*, 2012). Within this group of individuals it is estimated that at least 65 per cent of women and 59 per cent of men have dependent children. Statistics indicate that approximately 200,000 children have a parent in prison and that this is predicted to rise (OCFT, 2011). As such they may be described as 'the unseen victims of the prison boom' (Petersilia, 2005: 68). These are conservative estimates since it is difficult to be precise about the numbers outside official statistics and the data gathering of such information is unreliable (OCFT, 2007). Incarceration is well established as the preferred way to punish crime, with a secondary purpose to provide an opportunity to prepare inmates for eventual resettlement into society. The Coalition government has stated a renewed commitment to making prison more effective as a deterrent, with no specific reference to the needs of prisoners' children either during the period of imprisonment or when the sentence is completed. Prison continues to be regarded by many influential politicians and policy-makers as the best solution for a range of crimes. The imprisonment of a large number of first-time offenders for relatively minor offences as a result of the riots of 2011 indicates a public appetite for and endorsement of prison as an effective response. The UK now has the largest prison population in Europe and, given current attitudes towards crime and deviance, it is likely that it will remain high or even grow further in the coming years. One result of this will be that more and more children will be affected by the incarceration of a parent and by the issues that arise from this.

It is, of course, necessary to recognise that there are times when a child may benefit in some ways from separation from the imprisoned parent; if, for example, a crime relates to child abuse or domestic violence. However, even in these cases the dynamics of the family will be disrupted and the experience traumatic and this will still need to be acknowledged and the right support provided for the children (Mazza, 2002).

Why are these children vulnerable?

Professional guidelines published by OCFT (2007) emphasise that the children of prisoners have the same rights as any other child. This reflects rights as laid down in the United Nations Convention on the Rights of the Child (UNCRC) (United Nations, 1989), which is ratified by the UK and endorsed in the Children Act (1989, 2004).

The emotional impact of loss and separation on a child through, for example, the separation and/or divorce of a parent or the death of a close family member has long been recognised as significant and many schools have strategies in place to provide both immediate and extended support for children in these circumstances (OCFT, 2007). Interviews with twenty-four children under the age of eleven who were the children of prisoners highlighted the negative effects on their schooling, which included experiences of bullying, learning difficulties and trouble resulting from behavioural difficulties and poor relationships with teachers. This research describes 'a sense of fragility about the well-being of most of the children and young people interviewed' and in looking forward to the eventual release of the imprisoned parent resulting in improved relationships, even though in 'these pipe dreams too lay evidence of their deeply rooted vulnerabilities' (Losel et al., 2012: 101).

Reflective Activity

The UNCRC includes the following articles:

- All actions should be in the best interests of the child (Article 3)
- The importance of listening to children and taking their views into consideration (Article 12)
- The need to maintain personal relations and direct contact with both parents on a regular basis (Article 9)
- Protection from abuse, violence and neglect (Article 19)
- The right to education including the development of children's personalities, talents and mental and physical abilities (Article 28 and Article 29)

Think about some ways in which the above rights of a six-year-old child may be affected by having a parent in prison.

Despite these problems, children can develop coping strategies that help them to be relatively unaffected, particularly in terms of their ability to continue and do well in education. The work of researchers such as Daniel and Wassell (2002), Losel *et al.* (2012) and Convery and Moore (2011) shows that children cope with varying degrees of resilience to such circumstances depending on multiple factors, and that they benefit from sympathetic and sensitive intervention and support from relevant adults – including those beyond the immediate family. There is however a danger that the children of prisoners do not always get a desirable level of support in care or, particularly, education settings, partly due to lack of knowledge and awareness on the part of the staff and possibly because the remaining parent chooses not to disclose the information about the imprisonment of their partner to the school or because the child chooses not to disclose.

Key points of stress

The extent to which the experience of parental imprisonment disrupts a child's life will of course be influenced by a number of variables, including the age and stage of development of the child, the nature of the prior relationship with the imprisoned parent, the wider family circumstances, the nature of the crime and the length of the imprisonment. What are described by OCFT (2007) and others as 'key points of stress' for families need to be briefly considered when judging the possible impact on the education of children.

The arrest

This will often occur early in the morning for pragmatic reasons and involve a dramatic and disturbing physical invasion of the family home by the police, often armed and accompanied by dogs. It is likely that the family, including any children, will be asleep when this occurs and that the consequent disruption to the normal early morning routine will be considerable. The invasion of a secure family environment and subsequent searching of the premises (including children's bedrooms and possessions) and probable removal of a parent for further questioning would be a traumatic experience for any child. Lagoette (2011: 39) explains that 'an arrest undertaken with a degree of force can amount to an interference with the child's right to respect for private and family life'. Although the police are now required to consider the needs of any children involved in such an arrest, the priority is to take a suspect into custody with efficiency. An international study designed to contribute to the development of uniform legal rights, policy and administrative practices in the European Union in relation to the interests of the children of imprisoned parents demonstrates that further training about children's rights and detailed practice guidelines for police officers are required to highlight the possible impact on children (Gampell et al., 2011: 224). The study goes on to warn that a lack of attention to improving practice could 'leave children emotionally scarred and contribute to children's hostile views of the criminal justice system'.

It may be that the remaining parent chooses to keep any children away from school on the day of the arrest, but if they do attend it is likely that they will be concerned and distracted. Younger children in particular are likely to be anxious about the sudden removal of the parent and whether they will return. It is not difficult to imagine how the return home after school and consequent bedtime routine would also be affected, as the remaining parent would be preoccupied with a number of urgent practical problems and dealing with the emotional impact.

Witnessing an arrest is clearly a damaging experience, although the sudden arrest and disappearance of a parent whilst a child is at school is equally difficult to come to terms with. If the remaining parent has to convey this to a child, a lack of information about the circumstances may add to the difficulties:

> She [children's mother] knew I had been arrested but she never knew where I was or what was the case. So after two days I was allowed to phone her so the wife and children hadn't seen me for two days or heard from me for two days. (Prisoner, Northern Ireland)
>
> *(Scharff-Smith and Gampell, 2011)*

Research demonstrates that parents have widely differing views about the extent to which the children themselves should be informed about the arrest and subsequent imprisonment. Whilst a degree of honesty about the situation is recommended by the relevant support organisations, this is sometimes a difficult decision and may depend on the age and maturity of the child in question. What the child is told may also relate to the severity and nature of the crime (OCFT, 2007).

Remand

The period between arrest and sentencing presents other challenges for a family. Until a case is heard in court, the remaining parent may choose not to disclose any information to their children. A remand prisoner, whether guilty or not, is separated from the family, usually at a relatively local prison, but the consequent impact of loss of income, probable negative media coverage, and the dominance of legal procedures contribute to considerably changed circumstances for the remaining family. Even if the accused person is released on bail this is a difficult and stressful period that may contribute to changes in routines and relationships that disrupt sleep patterns, appetite, school attendance, concentration and academic progress (OCFT, 2007).

The sentence

It may be that a defendant is found 'not guilty' and returns home. However, there can still be long-term damage to family relationships as a result of the stressful experience. A custodial sentence presents a different range of new experiences and challenges for a child to cope with. There are differing views as to whether it is appropriate to take children on visits to the prison. Many parents feel that it is important to maintain regular physical contact during the period of separation despite the difficulties of travel and consequent absences for school-age children. Some feel strongly that it is a damaging experience for their children:

> 'I would consider letting my children visit if improvements were made to make the visits less intimidating for children. The way the officers speak to the visitors and children is not acceptable. I would not want my children to be spoken to like that.'
>
> '[Child aged 12] gets upset and browned off, because he hates the long journeys there and so doesn't always want to visit although he does want to see his dad.'
>
> '[O]rdinary visits are not long enough. They're too official. He can't be our dad during them' [sisters aged 11 and 15].
>
> *(interview extracts in Boswell and Wedge, 2002: 38, 67 and 71)*

In England and Wales, a convicted prisoner is entitled to receive two visits every four weeks (rules for remand prisoners are far more flexible). Despite the guidelines on prison visits, which seem to recognise the importance of maintaining family links, this entitlement is not always easy to put into practice. For instance, Mills (2004: 14) cites Murray (2003) who gives the example of HMP Camphill on the Isle of Wight, where 55 per cent of prisoners had received no visits since their arrival. This may be because prisoners are often placed at considerable distance from their families, causing logistical difficulties with visiting despite some assistance with travelling costs. Whilst this is clearly distressing for the prisoners, the negative effects on family life are not difficult to imagine and have been docu-mented by a range of evidence-based reports (e.g. OCFT, 2007; Scharff-Smith and Gampell, 2011).

It is important to emphasise that prison visits can only take place at the request of the prisoner and that children under the age of eighteen usually rely on an adult to accompany them. It is clear to see that these constraints mean that a child may not be offered a visit even if he/she wants it (OCFT, 2007). The visit may be a difficult experience, even when it becomes a familiar routine for some children over a period of time.

Reflective Activity

The visiting process is usually constrained by the following rules (depending on the nature of the offence and the category of prison):

- All visitors are searched by a scanner and 'rub down' search – sometimes dogs are used to detect drugs
- No personal possessions can be taken into a visit – this will exclude favourite toys and comforter and any drawing/collage/model that has not been made under supervision in the visitor's centre
- If drawings have been sent in advance by post they will need to be care-fully screened and are not always passed on to the prisoner
- The visit usually takes place at a table – sometimes an embrace is allowed, but not always
- Prisoners must remain seated throughout the visit, which usually lasts between thirty minutes and two hours

Consider how an initial prison visit might affect a five-year-old child. After the experience, how might he perceive a future visit?

The prime function of a prison is to safely incarcerate the inmates and this necessity can often run counter to the more family-friendly regime. Boswell and Wedge (2002: 33) point out this tension as 'relationship continuity versus prison security, the ideal versus the possible'. For instance, if there is a lockdown due to a violent incident on one wing of a prison, planned visits may be cancelled throughout the institution because of overriding security concerns. Similarly, if a prisoner is involved in a breach of good behaviour, he/she may forgo what are regarded as privileges – for instance, participating in planned 'Children's Visits' or 'Family Visits'. These are designed to be more relaxed, child-centred experiences, increas-ingly provided by prisons to meet the needs of children and prisoners in response to the concerns of campaigning organisations. The consequent distress and dis-appointment to a child and the potential damage to the relationship is not considered. It may be difficult to rearrange these visits, particularly since they have waiting lists because they require increased supervision and support from prison staff and trained volunteers.

Visiting a parent in prison is clearly a challenging experience for many children. On the other hand, a child who does not visit their parent may base their ideas of prison on limited information garnered from unreliable sources and may feel very anxious as a result:

> 'He was having nightmares about his dad. When we got to the bottom of it, we discovered that just before he was sent to prison, his dad had taken him to see a film about Robin Hood. The poor little lad thought his dad was chained to a green slimy wall with rats biting his feet, and a jailer throwing in chunks of mouldy bread!'
>
> *(Headteacher of primary school in OCFT, 2007: 16)*

Release and resettlement

It is evident that this represents another time of readjustment for all concerned. In some cases a family situation becomes more fraught when the sentence is completed, particularly if there are associated difficulties with mental health or substance dependency. Whatever the length of a sentence, there will be a need to redefine and reforge often fragile relationships post-release and this places considerable stress on all children. With respect to fathers and their children, the research by Losel *et al.* (2012: 111) indicates that the experience will be more positive if there has been attention to 'good communication' and 'high frequency of contact' during the period of imprisonment.

Changes in circumstances

Children who are affected by the consequences of parental imprisonment may very quickly have to deal with changes in lifestyle that may include the relocation of home and school alongside the emotional trauma of separation and loss. For instance, the total family income could be halved or totally removed. The consequences of such a dramatic change in family income could mean moving into much poorer quality housing in a different area of a town. This could involve a change of school and loss of extended family and friendship networks. Bringing up children is recognised as an increasingly expensive enterprise and parents are expected to make responsible individual choices. The scrutiny of what needs to be 'capable' parenting has increased and there are both official and unofficial sanctions for those that fail to conform (Brotherton, 2010). In order to make these appropriate choices, a certain level of income is assumed. What is now regarded as a decent standard of living and 'normal' for family life is clearly articulated in the latest Minimum Income Standards Report (Davis *et al.*, 2012).This illustrates that adapting to a life on a severely reduced income is difficult and has many consequences for the further social exclusion for children. For instance, the ability to participate in social and cultural events such as school trips and outings can be seriously limited.

Reflective Activity

Other examples that are cited in the Minimum Income Standards Report include:

- Computers and access to the internet are necessary for working-age families
- The importance of eating out for a couple with two children that requires £30 to spend three times a year to celebrate special occasions
- The importance of exchanging Christmas and birthday gifts, with a recommended amount of £15 per present
- Children should be able to have access to a couple of leisure activities outside school on a regular basis
- A second-hand car is necessary because of the unreliability of public transport
- It is essential for families to have a break away from home once a year

How might the above standards be particularly difficult to achieve for families of prisoners?

What could be the impact on the life of a ten-year-old child if they are not achieved?

How might the impact be different for a child of fifteen?

Which parent is imprisoned is also an important factor and there may be differing impact depending on whether it is the mother or the father. Some view the separation of a mother from her child as being particularly traumatic at any age and this is compounded by the relative lack of prison facilities for women that are likely to be within easy reach of families (Myers *et al.*, 1999; Corston, 2007). Separation from fathers can also have severe consequences for future relationships and there are particular difficulties for young fathers who have been imprisoned before their child's birth or during their early years (Boswell and Wedge, 2002). The recognition of the significant role of fathers in parenting was emphasised by the Labour government in the publications *Engaging with Fathers* (DfES, 2004b) and *Every Parent Matters* (DfES, 2007) and continues to be cited as important by the Coalition government. The Family Strategic Partnership programme (DfE, 2012) restates the importance of a father's involvement with their children.

As previously stated, the ECM policy was intended to provide a framework for ensuring that all children's needs are met by services. The five ECM outcomes for children underpin the Children Act (2004) and therefore can provide a useful lens for looking at the barriers faced by the children of prisoners. A guide for teachers and other practitioners by OCFT (2007) clearly points out the ways in which children may be prevented from achieving the outcomes because of their circumstances.

Reflective Activity

ECM suggests that five key outcomes are important to the well-being of children and indicates that there are barriers to achieving these outcomes for the children of prisoners.

- Being healthy

    The child's carer may experience isolation, stress or health difficulties, and as a result the child's needs may not be fully met.

- Staying safe

    Being bullied and becoming a bully are significant issues for children of school age.

- Enjoying and achieving

    Worry and anxiety may interfere with children's relaxation/recreation.

- Making a positive contribution

    Stigma by association – children may be excluded from group activities/hobbies or friendship groups because of their parent's/carer's crime.

- Achieving economic well-being

    The cost of transport for families visiting prison and/or getting access to local services

    (based on OCFT, 2007: 6–7)

    Can you think of some other examples?

    How might these barriers differently impact on children aged five and children aged twelve?

Why is this an 'invisible' group in policy terms?

Evidence that the children of prisoners are a significantly vulnerable group has been established both through (the limited) academic studies and by the recording of first-hand experience by campaigning groups. Given this, the question that needs to be addressed is why social policy still fails to adequately recognise and reflect their needs and why the issue remains 'below the radar' of public perception. This section suggests that there are several possible reasons for this lack of attention and that these are based on societal attitudes.

The 'undeserving' poor

As already discussed, a family may be pitched into very serious financial circumstances as a consequence of arrest and conviction. Even if the family is relatively well off the changed circumstances will have a dramatic impact, but in the case of many families the imprisonment of a parent will have serious effects in terms of income and opportunities. As a consequence, many children are likely to join the 3.6 million deemed to be living in poverty (Child Poverty Action Group, 2012).

Social attitudes to poverty are shaped by a number of powerful influences – personal experience, education, government policy, media attitudes – and Lister (2008) suggests that our sympathy in relation to notions of absolute and relative poverty may have an influence on whether individuals feel empathy for people living in difficult situations. Even more important, perhaps, is the controversial matter of whether poverty is caused largely by unfair social structures or by individual characteristics and personal failings. This debate is particularly important in respect of the children of prisoners, where a parent's behaviour is often seen as directly responsible for the circumstances the children have to live in.

The cuts to welfare benefits implemented by the Coalition government following the election in 2010 have been predicated on the notion that help should only go to those who can be shown to be demonstrably in need. Those who appear to be avoiding work or having large families to qualify for higher benefits or gain social housing advantage have been cast as the 'undeserving' poor, ultimately to be blamed for their circumstances. Others, for instance the elderly or the severely disabled who have no control over their situation, may be viewed more kindly as the 'deserving' poor.

Undeniably, the public discourse casts prisoners – and by association their families – as members of the undeserving poor. Their poverty is cast as a consequence of bad or immoral decisions for which they are reaping their just deserts.

Public attitudes towards crime and punishment

The public discourse in relation to crime, justice and punishment is that society has a responsibility to adequately protect its citizens from those who break the law. It also needs to find the most effective way to punish criminal behaviour while at the same time rehabilitating those spending time in prison so that they can become more productive members of society on release. This has been clearly stated by the current Secretary of State for Justice who, in his speech, 'Prison with a purpose', said: 'our feral underclass is too big, has been growing, and needs to be diminished' (Clarke, 2011). The use of the word 'feral' here is also perhaps indicative of a certain moral panic which chooses to view particular groups of citizens as wild, uncontrollable and dangerous – barely human. Boswell and Wedge (2002: 156) see this process as undermining ideas of social cohesion and challenge the trend towards demonising those who end up as prisoners, suggesting that the criminal justice system needs to find better ways of emphasising common interests and goals and that 'people should be encouraged to treat prisoners' families as human beings in need of compassion and understanding'.

It has long been recognised by all political parties that an acceptable balance between prison as punishment and prison as an opportunity for reform is difficult to achieve. Prisoners are still seen by many people as having put themselves outside the bounds of civilised society and therefore not to be viewed as having rights. The generally negative response to a proposal to allow prisoners to vote in general elections, for instance, proves how prevalent this attitude is. There also continues to be opposition to the suggestion that prisoners be allowed to earn a more reasonable income whilst completing a custodial sentence, despite the obvious benefit in terms of prisoners with families contributing more to expenses and preparing for employment on release.

In consequence, the short- and long-term effects on children with family members in prison is rarely discussed, either at policy level or in the media. Indeed, the lack of attention to these children, and their consequent invisibility, may indicate some unspoken belief that the children of criminals are also to be punished as a consequence of their association with behaviour deemed worthy of incarceration. It is interesting to consider the extent to which society thinks that a prisoner's punishment includes visiting retribution on those most emotionally close to them – for instance, that not only the prisoners themselves but also their close family members – including children – should forfeit 'the right to family life'. An extreme interpretation might be that such attitudes are shaped by an underlying discourse of eugenics that considers there are 'bad genes' – inherited factors making for a criminal 'disposition'.

Recent political discourse has been heavily shaped by the assumption that any parent engaged in criminal behaviour has poor parenting skills and therefore needs to be viewed as in need of 'positive' intervention and support from the state. Condry (2007) suggests that there is a view that only particular kinds of families become involved with crime and that there is some inherent complicity with the criminal behaviour. In exploring this idea, Condry (2007: 1–2) makes reference to the fictional account in *We Need to Talk About Kevin* (Shriver, 2003: 69), where the mother of an underage murderer who has killed nine people in a high school shooting feels 'her own sense of complicity' and, as a result of the blame and prejudice of her community, reflects on being 'infected, contagious, quarantined' (Shriver, 2003: 394). She goes on to explain that blaming and prosecuting the parents of a perpetrator for negligence in real life cases such as these is not unusual in the US.

It becomes easy to see how a deficit view of parents associated with criminal behavior prevails and 'filters through and informs the everyday understanding of lay people', and this view in turn contributes to a dominant cultural script that is regarded as common sense (Condry, 2007: 70). There is often a view taken by state agencies that the parent who has not been imprisoned may need professional help with parenting skills to achieve the 'normal' development for children in the family in order to prevent their veering towards criminal behaviour.

It is worth considering whether public perceptions about the primacy of behaving in a socially responsible and law-abiding way are so deeply entrenched that anyone who transgresses this dominant discourse, and anyone associated with them, is deemed to forgo the rights and considerations of civilised society: criminals spoil other people's lives, so why should we take care of their families? Surely, the argument goes, those who need to be taken care of as a priority are the victims of crime and, in a time of increasingly limited resources, there are more deserving groups of people than prisoners and their families on whom time and means should be lavished?

Condry (2007: 70) discusses the way in which families, including children, are viewed as partly responsible for the criminal behaviour of any of their members – guilt by association, in other words, and an attitude towards crime which, she argues, is deeply embedded. She cites Goffman's (1963: 43) description of what he terms 'courtesy stigma' which means that: 'the individual who is related through the social structure to a stigmatised individual – a relationship that leads the wider society to treat both individuals in some respects as one'. Her research, based on in-depth interviews with the close relatives of thirty-two serious offenders, describes a feeling of either perceived complicity or the lack of ability to be viewed as a normal family. This relative worthlessness is amplified by feelings of guilt, shock and disbelief which contribute to a 'twofold sense of failure' (Condry, 2007: 63). She goes on to propose that families may even be viewed as further complicit in a crime if they choose to maintain contact and provide support for those in prison and that they garner more sympathy if they disown them. Whilst her research focuses on the consequences of crime for the families of serious offenders, it may be that similar views about the consequences of 'bad blood' retain some influence and thereby contribute to a lack of empathy for these families, whatever the nature of the crime. As Nussbaum (2004: 262) suggests, judging the shortcomings of others is a way to make one feel better about one's own family: 'People are typically aware of deficiency in their own family roles, and thus they need all the more to shore up their purity.'

'Troubled families' or a factor in rehabilitation?

Contemporary political discourse also has a major impact on the way prisoners and the families of prisoners are seen. Current Coalition government policy puts

considerable emphasis on the idea that the practice of crime and anti-social behaviour is concentrated amongst a relatively small number of individuals and families
and that they can be relatively easily identified. This has led to them speaking of
the need to fix 'troubled families', which are defined as having 'no adult in the
family working, children not being in school and family members being involved
in crime and anti-social behaviour' (DfCLG, 2012). A government-funded report
based on interviews with sixteen such families reinforces the part played by the
'intergenerational transmission of problems such as being in care, poor parenting,
violence, abuse, low aspirations, non-attendance in school and few or no qualifications … ' (Casey, 2012: 49). The report concludes that 'the problems of these
families are linked and reinforcing. They accumulate across the life course passed
on by parents to their children across generations of the same family' (Casey,
2012: 67). In the majority of cases the children of prisoners would certainly fit this
definition.

However, there is a danger that the rationale behind any interventions with, or
support offered these families, is weighted towards reducing overall costs to society
rather than recognising the fragility of the children involved and the complex
nature of the difficulties they experience. A report commissioned by the Prison
Advice and Care Trust (Pact) to assess the potential economic impact on work
carried out by the Integrated Family Support Programme, which provides sustained
support throughout the period of custody in ten UK prisons, seems to confirm this
economic emphasis. The findings of the report suggest that the programme 'deli-
vers potential benefits to the State of between £515,465 and £3,479,294 over a
one-year period' and that this 'provides good value for money for the taxpayer'
(Estep and Nicholles, 2012: 4–5). The authors conclude that 'the future potential
positive impacts on the children of prisoners should be explored', since this is not
given specific attention (Estep and Nicholles, 2012: 28).

The importance of maintaining and encouraging stable family ties whilst incarcerated is recognised as beneficial for all family members and there are also implications for successful resettlement. However, Codd (2004: 3) cited by Mills (2004: 8)
suggests that the support given to such families may be only encouraged because of
'their instrumental value, not because of any commitment to maintaining families
for their own sake'. In this way the social policies associated with the families of
prisoners are largely linked to future crime prevention and this is how they are
reckoned cost effective. Mills goes on to suggest that this utilitarian bias neglects to
consider how maintaining family ties can also improve the psychological well-
being of all family members by reducing the damaging effects of isolation and
separation.

Implications for policy

Recognition of the damaging effect of parental imprisonment on children and
family life has led to suggestions that reduced or suspended sentences and alternative punishments such as community service and electronic tagging should be

encouraged. In terms of supporting continued family cohesion the alternative punishments may be preferable to a custodial sentence, but they present other problems for children, which need to be acknowledged. For instance, having a parent with a curfew (associated with wearing an electronic tag) may create practical difficulties with, for instance, being driven to out-of-school activities such as football matches or attendance at parents' evenings. However, it also needs to be recognised that the impact of all of these issues is not as well understood as it should be and further funded research is clearly needed:

> The time is ripe for funding agencies and researchers to collaborate in implementing an ambitious research agenda to advance knowledge about the effects of parental imprisonment on children.
>
> *(Murray and Farrington, 2008: 191).*

Implications for practice in schools

Staff in schools may not always be informed when a child has a parent in prison and this lack of disclosure may be for a number of reasons and should be respected (Ramsden, 1998). However, if the home circumstances are known, the child's needs may be highlighted through the Common Assessment Framework (CAF) process, which was instigated as part of ECM and remains in place despite the changes in government priorities and shifts in policy. This process was designed to be part of a proactive response to concern about children's progress and development resulting from home circumstances and the need for multi-agency support in addressing these concerns. The CAF process is designed to highlight problems in terms of how they present themselves in the setting – poor concentration and tiredness, for example – and enable them to be discussed further with relevant professionals and the family. This process would identify possible causes – lack of sleep and consequent exhaustion resulting from disrupted routines and feelings of anxiety after witnessing the arrest – and indicate that the child and his/her siblings might benefit from counselling or other therapeutic support. It might also indicate the need for similar support for the remaining parent. In practice, however, the identified child would have no guarantee of services as a result of the process, and in any case the recommendations would need to have the full consent of both parents (unless there is an associated safeguarding issue) and this may be problematic since, for a number of reasons, parents affected by imprisonment often choose not to disclose their circumstances to services. This lack of disclosure by affected parents contributes to the invisibility of the group.

Beyond the formal CAF process there are several key points of stress – already discussed – at which a school, if aware of the circumstances, may be able to offer sensitive support, in partnership with other agencies (including the prison service).

It is possible to make education professionals more aware of the issues facing the children of prisoners through appropriate in-service training delivered by specialist organisations. There are also implications for the way these issues can be highlighted through revisions to school policies and through the curriculum and the learning materials made available to children (Ramsden, 1998). Boswell and Wedge (2002: 153) suggest that parents often underestimate the problems experienced by their children in the school setting as a result of imprisonment and conclude that there is a need for 'clear strategies for the provision of teacher confidants to children in this situation'. Brown (2001: 73) also stresses the importance of recognising the impact on children and the need to highlight this in initial training for those intending to work with children: 'Issues for children and young people with an imprisoned family member should be incorporated into existing training programmes for teachers, social workers, police and probation workers, health workers and voluntary agencies.'

Conclusion

This chapter has considered some of the ways in which the children of imprisoned parents may be considered vulnerable. It has highlighted some of the points at which the experience may seriously impact on their participating fully in society, particularly as regards younger children in school settings. It has suggested some reasons for the continuing invisibility of this group in social policy and proposed that this is largely due to negative social attitudes towards the criminal backgrounds of these children. It has provided some examples of good practice that have come about as a result of campaigning voluntary organisations such as APF working in partnership with schools, prisons, other agencies and local authorities.

Research indicates that the rapid change in family circumstances as a result of an arrest and subsequent imprisonment places a number of demands on the remaining parent and their children (Lewis *et al.*, 2008). Networks of family and friends, even if available, may be insufficient in terms of ensuring that the children are adequately supported at this difficult time; thus, raising awareness of the issues faced by the children of prisoners is important for all practitioners in agencies working with these children, as is their ability to help in the building of networks of support in partnership with families and prisoners. For all those working with children there needs to be a recognition of and response to the needs of this group as part of a wider commitment to effective inclusive provision.

The extent to which the needs of the children from these families will be considered or prioritised by the current Coalition government remains uncertain, particularly in the climate of cuts to prison services and increasing privatisation. The campaigning voluntary sector organisations are also under considerable threat in terms of funding – especially given the decline in state support and the increasing expectation that financial shortfalls will be filled by private philanthropy (APF, 2010). A funding environment of this kind inevitably disadvantages projects related to prisoners and their families because they are not seen as glamorous or aggrandising.

Because of these challenges it is likely that many practitioners working in schools and other settings will need to consider how to be more responsive to the needs of the children of prisoners. An awareness of some of the negative consequences of imprisonment may help with this, alongside a better understanding of why social policy has failed to prioritise their needs and a recognition of the long-term benefits associated with a different approach.

References

APF (2010) *Demonstrating the impact of work with prisoners' families*, Action for Prisoners' Families AGM and conference, SOAS, London, 18th November.

Boswell, G. and Wedge, P. (2002) *Imprisoned Fathers and their Children*. London: Jessica Kingsley.

Brotherton, G. (2010) 'Working with parents' in Brotherton, G., Davies, H. and McGillivray, G. *Working with Children, Young People and Families*. London: Sage.

Brown, K. (2001) *No-one's Ever Asked Me: young people with a prisoner in the family*, summary report. Federation of Prisoners' Families Support Groups.

Casey, L. (2012) *Listening to Troubled Families*. London: Department for Communities and Local Government.

Child Poverty Action Group (2012) *Child poverty facts and figures*. Available online at www.cpag.org.uk/child-poverty-facts-and-figures (accessed 16 November 2012)

Clarke, K. (2011) 'Prison with a purpose'. Available online at www.conservatives.com/News/Speeches/2011/10/Clarke_Prison_with_a_purpose.aspx (accessed 14 November 2012).

Codd, H. (2004) 'Prisoners' families: issues in law and policy', guest lecture. Institute of Advanced Legal Studies, London, 7th June.

Condry, R. (2007) *Families Shamed: The consequences of crime for serious offenders*. Cullompton: Willan Publishing.

Convery, U. and Moore, L. (2011) 'Children of imprisoned parents and their problems' in Scharff-Smith, P. and Gampell, L. (eds) (2011) *Children of Imprisoned Parents*. Denmark: Jes Ellehauge Hansen, pp. 12–30.

Corston, J. (2007) *The Corston Report*. London: The Home Office.

Daniel, B. and Wassell, S. (2002) *The Early Years: Assessing and Promoting Resilience in Vulnerable Children*. London: Jessica Kingsley.

Davis, A., Hirsch, D., Smith, N., Beckhelling, J. and Pindley, M. (2012) *Minimum Income Standards Report*. York: Joseph Rowntree Foundation.

DfCLG (2012) *Helping troubled families turn their lives around*, Department for Communities and Local Government. Available online at www.gov.uk/government/policies/helping-troubled-families-turn-their-lives-around (accessed 16 November 2012).

DfE (2012) *Family Strategic Partenership*, Department for Education. London: HMSO.

DfES (2004a) *Every Child Matters: Change for Children*, Department for Education and Skills. London: HMSO.

DfES (2004b) *Engaging with Fathers*, Department for Education and Skills. London: HMSO.

DfES (2007) *Every Parent Matters*, Department for Education and Skills. London: HMSO.

Estep, B. and Nicholles, N. (2012) *Economic Study of Integrated Family Support Programmes*. London: New Economics Foundation.

Gampell, L., Martynowicz, A. and Scharff-Smith, P. (2011) 'Conclusions' in Scharff-Smith, P. and Gampell, L. (eds) *Children of Imprisoned Parents*. Denmark: Jes Ellehauge Hansen, pp. 219–234.

Goffman, E. (1963) *Stigma: notes on the management of a spoiled identity*. Harmondsworth: Penguin.

Lagoette, S. (2011) 'The human rights framework' in Scharff-Smith, P. and Gampell, L. (eds) *Children of Imprisoned Parents*. Denmark: Jes Ellehauge Hansen, pp. 31–56.

Lewis, S., Bates, S. and Murray, J. (2008) *Children of prisoners – maintaining family ties*. London: Children and Families Services.

Lister, Ruth (2008) *Poverty*. Cambridge: Polity Press.

Losel, F., Pugh, G., Makson, L., Souza, K. and Lanskey, C. (2012) *Risk and protective factors in the resettlement of imprisoned fathers with their families. Final report*. University of Cambridge and Ormiston. Available online at www.prisonersfamilies.org.uk (accessed 1 July 2012).

Mazza, C. (2002) 'And then the world fell apart: the children of incarcerated fathers', *Families in Society*, September/December, 83(5/6), pp. 521–529.

Mills, Alice (2004) *'Great Expectations?': a review of the role of prisoners' families in England and Wales*. Southampton: University of Southampton.

Murray, J. (2003) *Visits and Family ties Amongst Men at HMP Camphill*. London: Action for Prisoners' Families.

Murray, J. and Farrington, D. (2008) 'The effects of parental imprisonment on children' in Tonry, M. (ed.) *Crime and justice: a review of research*, 37, pp. 133–206. Chicago, IL: University of Chicago Press.

Myers, B., Smarsh, T., Amlund-Hagen, K. and Kennon, S. (1999) 'Children of Incarcerated Mothers', *Journal of Child and Family Studies*, 8(1), pp. 11–25.

Nussbaum, M. (2004) *Hiding from Humanity: Disgust, Shame and the Law*. Princeton and Oxford: Princeton University Press.

OCFT (2007) *Working with Children and Families of Prisoners: A guide for teachers and education professionals*. Ipswich: Ormiston Children and Families Trust.

OCFT (2011) *The role of invisible victims: how working with families of offenders can help with rehabilitation*. Ipswich: Ormiston Children and Families Trust.

Pact (2012) *Troubled families affected by imprisonment*, Prison Advice and Care Trust briefing paper, June.

Petersilia, J. (2005) 'Hard Time: Ex offenders Returning Home after Prison', *Corrections Today*, 64(2), pp. 66–71.

Ramsden, Sally (1998) *Working with children of prisoners*. London: Save the Children Publications.

Reed, H. (2012) *In the eye of the storm: Britain's forgotten children and families*. London: Action for Children, The Children's Society and NSPCC.

Scharff-Smith, P. and Gampell, L. (eds) (2011) *Children of Imprisoned Parents*. Denmark: Jes Ellehauge Hansen.

Shaw, R. (ed.) (1992) *Prisoners' Children: What are the Issues?* London: Routledge.

Shriver, L. (2003) *We Need to Talk about Kevin*. London: Serpents Tail.

The Children Act (1989). London: HMSO.

The Children Act (2004). London: HMSO.

United Nations (1989) *Convention on the Rights of the Child*. Available online at www.unicef.org/crc/crc (accessed 10 September 2012).

Williams, Kim, Papadopoulou, Vea and Booth, Natalie (2012) *Prisoners' childhood and family backgrounds: results from the surveying prisoner crime reduction (SPCR) longitudinal cohort study of prisoners*. London: Ministry of Justice Research Series 4/12 March 2012.

8

YOUNG PEOPLE WHO HAVE SEXUALLY HARMED OTHERS

Sharon Hall

Introduction

Young people who have sexually harmed other children, young people or adults may be dismissed or demonised by society. Professionals who work with these young people may prioritise issues regarding the risks they pose to others and ensuring that other children are kept safe. This chapter will focus on vulnerability in relation to work with this group of young people, who have frequently experienced trauma and abuse themselves before harming other people. The challenge of balancing risks, needs, concerns and vulnerabilities will be shown to have wider applicability for other groups of young people.

Calder (2008: xx) writes that 'the field of sexual abuse ... is the birthplace of many of the recent significant conceptual and practice developments in risk assessment'. A wide range of assessment tools have been developed to facilitate an understanding of risk from these young people, and many of these incorporate issues of the young person's own vulnerabilities and needs. These tools, which initially drew from the field of adult sex offending, are now having a reciprocal influence on work with adults and beyond. It is hoped that notions of vulnerability and a more holistic approach have a similarly wide application beyond this specific field.

Turnbull and Spence (2011: 941) helpfully separate out different notions of risk regarding young people who are seen as being:

> vulnerable to external risks (including abuse and accidents),
> a risk to themselves (from their behaviour or bad decisions) and
> a risk to society, either now or in the future (through unemployment, criminality and antisocial behaviour)

It will be seen that some professionals (particularly from the justice field) are expected to focus on the third of these, the risk young people pose to society.

In contrast, other professionals and family members will have a greater concern for the young people themselves and their own vulnerabilities.

Historical context for responses to youth crime

Sociologists have disagreed about the social construction of childhood, with Ariès (1962) asserting that there was not a separate concept of childhood or youth prior to the seventeenth century. Muncie (2009) summarises how authors such as Pollock (1983) and deMause (1976) have countered Ariès' claims but recognises the value of his notion that childhood has certainly not always been seen in the same way. Children used to mix far more freely with adults and join in much more with adult activities (Empey, 1982). Nevertheless, Omaji (2003) has identified how reduced penalties for juveniles can be traced back to the tenth century and even early Roman law.

Hendrick (1997) sets out two contrasting views of childhood which grew out of Renaissance humanism and the Protestant Reformation, identified as the 'Romantic child', who was innocent and in need of protection, and the 'Evangelical child', in need of discipline and regulation. Related tensions between welfare and justice have characterised youth justice provision over the last century (Smith, 2005). An increase in petty crime by children in the nineteenth century was linked to industrialisation and the passing of legislation which restricted the hours children were permitted to work in factories (Muncie, 2009). The need to rescue and reform these children led to the start of legislation to protect children and institutions such as Parkhurst Prison for boys (established 1838) and reformatory and industrial schools (set up by legislation in 1854/1857). These can be seen as the roots of the welfare model which reached its peak in the late 1960s.

Children under the age of eight (Children Act, 1933) were conclusively presumed to be unable to be guilty of any offence; this was raised to age ten by the Children and Young Person's Act (1963). The proposal to raise the age of criminal responsibility to fourteen was not implemented by the new Conservative government in 1970. Instead, a renewed emphasis on 'justice' included a review of restrictions on liberty, the use of minimum intervention and alternatives to custody which focused on measured responses to offending behaviour. Rather than focusing on the vulnerability of young people and their need for protection, the justice model promoted individual responsibility for behaviour and a freedom from lengthy intervention by the state. This can be seen as part of the wider influence of neo-liberalism in the UK.

Changes under New Labour led to an overhaul of the youth justice system, including the setting up of multi-agency Youth Offending Teams (YOT) in 2000. The principal function of these teams is the prevention of offending and reduction of reoffending by young people (Home Office, 2003) and this led some organisations to raise serious concerns about the lower priority being given to welfare issues (Nacro, 2003; Family Rights Group et al., 2003). Managerial approaches to assessment of risks and a lesser emphasis on the vulnerabilities of young people will be seen to characterise the current youth justice system in England, in contrast to the somewhat stronger 'children first ... offenders second' (Welsh Assembly Government, 2004: 3) approach in Wales following devolution.

Reflective Activity

Think about what has influenced your own ideas of young people who commit crime. Do you see these young people as risky or vulnerable or both?

Young people who have sexually harmed others

A young child who has inappropriately touched another child's bottom clearly requires a very different response to an older teenager who has committed a violent rape. These extremes demonstrate how wide a range of individuals and behaviours can be included in this topic of young people who have sexually harmed others. Recent literature (e.g. Hackett, 2007; Calder, 2008) describes the group as 'heterogeneous', meaning varied, diverse and requiring very different service responses. One size definitely does not fit all. While more of these young people are male (Erooga and Masson, 2006), it is important not to overlook harm by girls and from more particular groups of young people, such as those with learning difficulties.

UK law stipulates that children under the age of ten cannot be charged with a criminal offence, but younger children do engage in sexual behaviour which can be very harmful to others. Younger children might more typically be considered to be acting out something they have experienced themselves and may be treated more as victims with diminished responsibility for their own actions. Behaviour which is more exhibitionist and less coercive (perhaps particularly from girls) may be seen to put the young person at more risk than they pose to others.

Once over the age of eighteen, young adults will be dealt with through the adult court system, although there are young adults serving custodial or community supervised orders relating to sexual crimes committed when a juvenile. Young people aged 10–17 under the youth justice system may be labelled 'young offenders' or 'juvenile sex offenders', but this terminology will not be used in this chapter. As well as defining these young people by one aspect of their past behaviour which they may never repeat, this terminology excludes a group of young people who have been involved in sexual behaviour but for a range of reasons have not been made subject of a court order. In some cases the police may decide it is not in the public interest to prosecute a young person or a victim may choose not to make a formal complaint. It may be considered preferable for a young person to receive some form of support or 'intervention' on a voluntary basis. For these reasons, the term 'young people who have sexually harmed' will be used in this chapter.

Policy and practice responses

While the diversity of these young people and their needs argues against a simplistic, standardised approach, recommendations for some kind of framework or national strategy have been widespread. Back in 1992, NCH recommended that: 'An overall, systemic approach should be developed for dealing with cases (alleged or otherwise) where a child or young person has abused another child' (National Children's Home, 1992: 47). Conferences, working parties and committees have committed numerous hours working on this issue, and government responses have varied from promising a national strategy or framework at changing timescales between 2001 and 2010.

Relevant policy includes mention of young people who have sexually harmed in 'Working Together to Safeguard Children' (HM Government, 2010), but the promised national framework or strategy referred to here and in other key documents, including Department of Health and Home Office (2006), has still not materialised. There is a 'Key elements' title in Youth Justice Board literature regarding young people who have sexually abused (Youth Justice Board, 2008) but, as has been mentioned, some of these young people will not receive a youth justice response. Simon Hackett (cited by Long, 2010) has described a 'postcode lottery' whereby some young people receive an expensive, even excessive, private intervention while others receive a low-key social work-led response or no response at all.

As has been stated, some of the more serious incidents will result in criminal charges, with young people being overseen by Youth Offending Teams (in England and Wales). A minority will lead to custodial sentences, while more are supervised in the community. Some young people may receive a voluntary intervention following concerns raised by a social worker, school staff member or other professional or by a parent or the young person themselves. Services may be offered by statutory teams such as youth offending services and children's services. Some projects are led by third sector organisations such as Barnardo's and the NSPCC. Other teams and residential projects are privately run. Some services may follow a particular workbook approach or base their interventions around particular training from organisations such as AIM and G-MAP. Other services will deliver a more individualised intervention based on the young person or staff/organisational preferences.

Reflective Activity

Why do you think some professionals find it difficult to work with young people who have sexually harmed others? What influences attitudes relating to children and sex in our society?

Priorities and risk assessment

Whether entering the youth justice system or being seen by other social work professionals, an early priority will be assessment, more specifically risk assessment. When a young person has been charged or suspected of sexual harm of another person there is a need to consider what risks they may present in their home environment and other social circles. Immediate concerns of social workers may be whether a young person shares a bedroom or can continue to live at home with other siblings. In some cases a young person may be removed to temporary foster care, residential care or a secure setting. Other measures may be agreed with parents and carers regarding supervision or changed sleeping arrangements. If an incident has occurred in an educational or social setting there may be more specific risk assessments required in these settings.

Such assessments are typically required straight away, while referrals to specialist teams, whether local or further afield, will take longer. Specialist teams may use assessment tools such as AIM or AIM2 (described in more detail later in the chapter) which consider concerns and strengths of these young people. Other tools such as JSOAP, JSORRAT or ERASOR focus more explicitly on risk assessment (see Calder, 2008). Most of these tools are described as empirically guided since, until recently, no validated actuarial instruments for assessing risk of sexual harm by juveniles have existed (Parks, 2007; Viljoen et al., 2009). A new instrument, JSORRAT-II (Epperson et al., 2006), has been described by Rich as 'presently the only actuarial assessment instrument for adolescent sexual offenders' (Rich, 2009: 227). However, Epperson (2009) indicates that the tool is only currently validated for youth in Utah and Iowa, with further studies underway in Georgia and California. The limitations of these tools, however, are not restricted to the lack of geographical evidence for the population. Even if a tool could predict an exact percentage risk of reoffending, the questions would remain about subsequent action and necessary help.

YOT assessment processes include the Asset paperwork (Youth Justice Board, 2006) which has a particular focus on risk of reoffending, although there are also forms which consider the risk of serious harm (ROSH) posed by the young person and the young person's own vulnerability. These can be seen to reflect some of the different types of risk identified above by Turnbull and Spence (2011). The level of YOT intervention proposed according to the more recent Scaled Approach (Youth Justice Board, 2010) is expressly not affected by any concerns for the young person's own vulnerability, although there is a requirement that the young person's vulnerability is assessed and if necessary a 'vulnerability plan' is put in place.

How soon the young person's own vulnerability is assessed will depend on whether the young person reaches a Youth Offending Team or other specialist team which considers this. Otherwise vulnerability may be assessed by social work professionals within the context of a Common Assessment Framework (CAF) assessment or other less formal processes. Both Corby (2006) and 'Working Together to Safeguard Children' (HM Government, 2010) have identified the importance of a more holistic approach to child abuse and the welfare of children and young people in general. A comprehensive assessment should consider all areas of a young person's life, not just behaviour which has been identified as problematic. There is a growing recognition that young people who have sexually harmed have many needs and vulnerabilities in common with other young people with considerable emotional and behavioural disorders (Calder, 2008).

Vulnerabilities of these young people

It should follow from this line of argument that young people who have sexually harmed may experience the wide range of vulnerabilities found across the population as a whole. Careful individual assessment is needed to identify areas of concern and what support will be helpful. However, there are certain areas of vulnerability which may occur more frequently within this group and these will be addressed here. I will discuss how many of these young people are themselves victims of abuse or trauma, including domestic violence. Another key area of vulnerability which was raised within my own research is the fact that some of these young people have been victims of sexual exploitation. Additionally I will consider some of the potential consequences following harmful behaviour which may add areas of vulnerability.

Research findings vary, but some studies suggest that around 75 per cent of young people who commit sexual offences have been victims of sexual abuse (Hunter et al., 2003). Loh and Gidycz (2006: 744) found that young 'men who experienced a childhood sexual victimization were six times more likely to also have a history of sexually aggressive behaviour'. Other research suggests that a greater number have experienced physical abuse or neglect (Way, 2002). Within my own research and clinical experience I frequently found that a young person acknowledging the wrongness of the abuse they suffered themselves was a significant step in taking responsibility for their own harmful behaviour. Helping a young person to resolve past traumatic experiences is recognised as a desirable goal within work with young people who have later harmed others (Hackett et al., 2006).

Many young people who sexually harm have also witnessed domestic violence, and it has been argued that this 'dysfunctional model of behaviour based on an abuse of power' (Scott and Telford, 2006: 182) affects what young people understand about acceptable behaviour. Bentovim (1998) also discussed how maternal history of sexual abuse was a significant risk factor, particularly with young people who had not themselves been victimised. He argued that a general environment of violence in the family has an important influence, along with other trauma during childhood.

The impact of sexual exploitation was another factor mentioned frequently in my own research. Less evidence is available of any link between being a victim of sexual exploitation and harming others and this is perhaps not emphasised by those working with young people who have been sexually exploited as it could decrease sympathy for this group whose members have complex needs. Brayley and

Cockbain (2011) found that while 40 per cent of sexually exploited youth were involved in some kind offending behaviour, only 1 per cent of the offences were of a sexual nature. They did report some additional inappropriate sexualised behaviour and recruiting of friends into exploitation but noted that these behaviours were rarely criminalised as police found a lack of malicious intent.

In the same way that comparatively few victims of abuse go on to harm others, comparatively few victims of sexual exploitation are likely to harm others. The complexities of cause and effect in these cases are difficult to grasp, but it is very different to say that certain factors predispose anyone to certain behaviour, even if this is seen to be a frequent element in the history of those found to display that behaviour.

A helpful analogy may be how most professional footballers will at some time have played for their school football team. However, it would be ludicrous to suggest that just because someone has played for a school team they are likely to become a professional footballer. Statistically they may be *slightly* more likely to do so, but acting on that assumption would be foolish. Far more people are victims of abuse who never go on to harm others, and it would be discriminatory and damaging to suggest that all victims are likely future perpetrators.

Reflective Activity

Does this analogy make sense to you? Can you think of other aspects that might be present in someone's background but which should not be considered to *cause* their behaviour?

Subsequent vulnerabilities

The vulnerabilities to abuse and sexual exploitation may be seen as likely preceding factors to harmful sexual behaviour, but they may continue or develop after incidents of harmful behaviour. One young person in my own research (Hall, 2010) became involved in sexual exploitation as he spent more time on the streets trying to avoid further harm of his own younger siblings. Another young person within my research was a victim of abuse within residential care after he had been removed from his own home environment. Vulnerabilities linked to being a looked-after child are explored elsewhere in this volume. There are clearly complex issues involved, but removal from a family home will likely have some negative consequences for young people even if it is considered the best course of action by all concerned. Placements at a considerable distance from the young person's home environment can be seen to isolate them further, with further challenges arising as they leave the care system (Gilderthorp et al., 2011).

More general issues of exclusion of young people following harmful sexual behaviour may be seen in well-meant attempts by schools and other settings to protect other young people. Young people may be excluded from school trips or certain activities or made subject to particularly strict supervision. On occasion young people may be permanently excluded from school or other social settings (Carson, 2006). Court-ordered sanctions may involve restricted liberty either in custody or within the community. Having a criminal record and in some cases being formally considered a 'risk to children' will have further effects on a young person's employment prospects and own family life in the future.

Other potential vulnerabilities following sexual harm by a young person might be expected in their interpersonal relationships with family members as well as with any victims outside the family (Bentovim, 1998). Young people who have sexually harmed others may have difficulties forming appropriate intimate relationships in the future, affected by their own emotional issues as well as possible interference from professionals keen to avoid any further abuse. Some young people may experience health problems, from mental distress following feelings of guilt and shame to sexually transmitted infections, sometimes from both their harm of others and their own victim experiences (Wilson, 2010).

Victims of abuse and harm

In emphasising the vulnerabilities and needs of young people who have sexually harmed others it is not my aim in any way to denigrate or minimise the needs and vulnerabilities of victims of abuse and sexual harm. It is a sad fact that victims of sexual harm do not always receive the support and justice that would be wished. I would argue strongly for improved and extended services to be offered to victims of any kind of harm and abuse. However, I do want to argue against a simple division of victims and perpetrators of harm, since many young people who have sexually harmed others can also be seen as victims of harm themselves. Some more holistic approaches to sexual harm (e.g. Bentovim, 1998; Hackett et al., 1998) do stress the need to address the needs of victims alongside any work with young people who have sexually harmed, as will be discussed below.

Approaches which balance risks and needs

This section will consider approaches such as AIM and the Good Lives Model which seek to balance risks and needs, using terminology including 'concerns' and 'primary goods'. Recent research touching on issues of resilience and desistance will also be included.

Two particular approaches to work with young people who have sexually harmed will now be discussed to gain some insight into their more balanced views of risks and vulnerabilities. The AIM framework (Morrison and Henniker, 2006), adapted as AIM2, deliberately uses the term 'concerns' rather than risks, and considers these alongside the strengths that are also identified for the young person being assessed. This immediately alters the tone of the assessment, showing the importance of recognising positive factors and resilience rather than only problems, concerns and risks. The type of intervention recommended is determined by consideration of both concerns and strengths. The indicators of concern are drawn carefully from evidence and clinical expertise, although the creators do not claim that this is a validated, actuarial assessment tool.

The Good Lives Model has even more of a positive focus, considering how any harmful sexual behaviour is related to seeking after positive attributes or 'primary goods'. Identifying ten main areas of human need, the Good Lives Model involves helping those who have sexually harmed to understand the acceptable needs they have been trying to meet through unacceptable means. Finding alternative, healthy routes to gain 'goods' like relatedness, friendship, happiness and mastery is seen as a key goal in helping people who have sexually harmed others. In the Good Lives Model, 'criminogenic needs or dynamic risk factors are internal or external obstacles that frustrate or block the acquisition of primary human goods' (Ward and Gannon, 2006: 80).

Both of these models can be seen in the wider context of a focus on resilience and protective factors within social work approaches to helping young people. Strengths-based approaches to young people (see Saleebey, 1996; Powell *et al.*, 1997) have also had some impact within youth justice fields, particularly within solution-oriented interventions (Clark, 1996; Corcoran, 1997). Focusing on how some young people cope with difficulties and move on positively also links into studies regarding desistance from crime (Farrall and Calverley, 2006; Kruttschnitt *et al.*, 2000). More recent research by Hackett *et al.* (2011) has also considered life trajectories of 'young sexual abusers' and identified some factors linked to more positive life outcomes, including having ambitions and optimism, stable partner relationships and educational achievement.

Value of working holistically

My own research has focused on the meaning and importance of working holistically with young people who have sexually harmed. Some movement towards recognising the importance of a holistic approach within social work and general youth justice has been noted by authors (e.g. Smith, 2007: 227) and the 'Working Together to Safeguard Children' document (HM Government, 2010: 134). Part of my initial hypothesis was that many professionals using the term 'holistic' meant different things or were uncertain quite what they meant. This was supported by my findings from the literature and original research. The 'whole' involved in a holistic approach might mean seeing the whole young person, the whole family situation or the whole wider issue of sexual harm. Wider literature demonstrated varied levels of holistic influence, from an overarching holistic ideology seen in wellness models (e.g. Myers and Sweeney, 2008; Weaver, 2002), the influence of holistic attitudes on professional practice (e.g. Ruch, 2005; Allen, 2003) and, most specifically, the use of methods described as holistic, including but not limited to creative and alternative therapies (Ernst, 2004).

Authors who discuss working holistically with young people who have sexually harmed others can be placed on a spectrum (see Hall, 2010) ranging from those who emphasise the need to see the whole young person and focus on all aspects of their needs (e.g. Longo, 2002) to those who look at a much wider holistic picture, taking in the whole family and community and address societal issues of sexual harm (e.g. Durham, 2006). A few authors (Rich, 2003; Bentovim, 1998; Morrison, 2006) present a wider view of working holistically, incorporating both ends of the spectrum. Rich writes:

> Treating the whole child means treating different aspects of the pathology presented by the juvenile in treatment, but it also means recognizing the array of forces at play in the lives of each individual child or adolescent.
>
> *(Rich, 2003: 449).*

The work of these pioneering authors was reinforced by my original research exploring meanings of working holistically, which was mainly conducted through interviews and questionnaires with professionals working with young people who had sexually harmed others.

Four main themes within holistic work were identified through the research study. The themes were: seeing the whole young person; working with wider family and peers; working in a multi-agency way; and using a range of creative methods. In seeing the whole young person, a range of strengths, needs and vulnerabilities will be revealed. While there may be additional needs and vulnerabilities within the wider family and peer group, and within the varied professionals involved with the young person and their family, the theme of seeing the whole young person will be explored in more detail here since it touches most explicitly on issues of assessing and understanding vulnerability.

Seeing the whole young person

In drawing together my findings regarding what it means to see the whole young person who has sexually harmed others, it will not be surprising that I drew on a wide range of literature and models regarding the whole young person and holistic approaches to well-being for children and adults. There were considerable overlaps and similarities within the Good Lives Model (Ward and Gannon, 2006); Griffin and Tyrrell (1997) *Human Givens*, the Lakota Circle of Courage (Brendtro *et al.*, 1990); Hettler's six-dimensional model of wellness (Hettler, undated); Sweeney and Myers (2003) *Indivisible Self*; and Witmer *et al.* (1998) *Wheel of Wellness*. Many of the assessment areas within the Youth Justice Board's (2006) Asset tool also fitted within a similar framework which I chose to base around the seven CAF areas for child development, developed from research by Ward (2001). Rather than completely reinventing the 'wellness wheel' I chose to present a model (see Figure 8.1) which relates clearly to an assessment framework already familiar to practitioners working with children and young people in the UK.

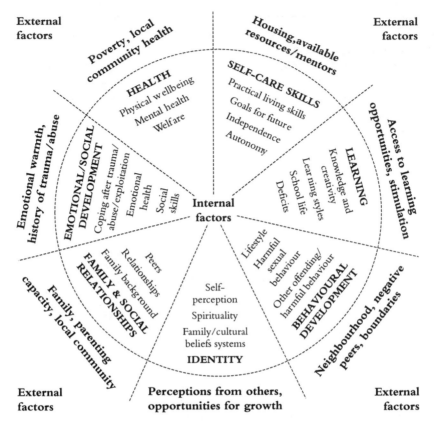

FIGURE 8.1 Connected segments to see the whole young person who has sexually harmed (previously published in Hall, 2011:22)

The diagram combines a thorough review of internal or personal areas of potential strength and vulnerability within a wider recognition of external or structural issues which may represent more contextual assets or vulnerabilities affecting a whole family or community. The boundaries are deliberately dotted to indicate permeability and the interconnectedness of many of the areas. One pitfall of such diagrams would be if they are seen to present a more segmented, atomistic representation of a young person which counteracts any aims for a holistic and integrated approach. Separating out any areas for consideration may be a useful step but awareness of the wider context and connections remains essential.

One YOT staff member explained the range of needs and family context in this way:

> holistically might describe Every Child Matters outcomes, ... health ... education and ... all the other needs that they've got, and obviously, within that would be a need for them not to offend, and then you've got the circle

round the outside, the family's medical and financial needs etcetera, and all of those needs are being met, so that eventually, that whole family, it's 360 degrees around them as well.

This presentation of a wide range of needs relates to the whole-person diagram above, but also to more systemic presentations of the young person embedded in other systems from family to community, as used by multi-systemic therapy (see Bronfenbrenner, 1977; Letourneau and Swenson, 2005). Community approaches to sexual harm and safeguarding have been described by Yokley *et al.* (2007) and Jack and Gill (2010), while Allan (2006) critiqued the complex relationship between poverty and harmful sexual behaviour.

> ### Reflective Activity
>
> Think about a young person you know who you would consider vulnerable. What needs or strengths can you identify in different segments of the diagram above?

Discussion within the research raised a number of benefits of seeing the whole young person who has sexually harmed others. Practitioners stated how important it is to see the young person as 'an okay human being', respecting their autonomy and individuality even while necessarily challenging their harmful past behaviour. They stressed the necessity of understanding the range of needs, vulnerabilities, problems and influences within the young person's life and experiences to be able to see what should be addressed within supportive/therapeutic work. Awareness of elements which could be considered roots of harmful behaviour was seen to be helpful in understanding how to address future risks for that young person and others. Alongside these, the importance of seeing and drawing on strengths and positives was also emphasised, as a way of finding things to build on and use for the future.

A number of challenges and barriers were also identified regarding seeing the whole young person who has sexually harmed others. It was recognised that young people may be reluctant to share, disclose or reveal their whole person, since this can bring further vulnerability. The need for sufficient time and trust with a worker should not be underestimated if a young person is to be enabled to discuss issues of their own victimisation or exploitation. Other challenges were seen to be located in professionals who may have negative attitudes and prejudices, including labelling the young people or wanting to avoid the issues (see Banks, 2006). Overarching system priorities of offence reduction, public protection and compliance were also found to limit how far workers could take the time to see and work with the whole young person. Further challenges were identified within restrictions to time, resources, funding and access to specialists.

Implications of seeing the whole young person

A further section of the research considered the implications of seeing the whole young person who had sexually harmed others. These are mainly linked to the responsibilities of having gained a wider understanding of the young person's needs and vulnerabilities. As particular needs are seen and identified, some action or response may be required, sometimes from the assessing professional but frequently involving other professionals with particular areas of responsibility or expertise. In some more complex families the needs uncovered may be wide-ranging and daunting. One interviewed professional explained:

> The challenge is to work out how we can actually meet those families' needs, because ... they're used to being assessed but not being provided for, I think.

This clearly links in with policy responses to 'troubled families', although the presence of significant safeguarding concerns or sexual harm have not been central to government representations of this group of families who 'cost an extraordinary amount of money' (Cameron, 2011).

The justification of early intervention on a basis of reducing costs (see Allen, 2011) is rather different to recommending early intervention for the sake of harm reduction, tackling inequalities and addressing wider societal failings. Sensitive intervention with young people who have been involved in more minor incidents of sexual harm seems a sensible approach which may prevent further offending. Using classroom-level interventions to emphasise touching which is okay or not okay and good and bad secrets can be seen as a preventative approach protecting all young people. One worker dreamed:

> in an ideal world, my job for example could encompass going into schools, talking to young people, making sure they're aware ... , often kids don't even know what the rules are, and what the boundaries are, and what the legal rules are, and I think particularly nowadays, more and more they are bombarded with messages about sex through the media.

The reason this needed to be in an ideal world was again linked to time and resource pressures.

Supporting and justifying any type of intervention with individual young people or wider groups of peers needs to be seen within a context of an increasing demand for 'evidence-based practice'. The undeniable influence of evidence-based practice has been seen in the 'What Works' agenda in criminal and youth justice (e.g. McGuire and Priestley, 1995; Sherman, 1997; Furniss and Nutley, 2000; Wilcox, 2003); however, the movement has been critically considered by academics, including those from the probation and social work arena (Mair, 2006; Webb, 2001). With ethical objections to any study involving an 'untreated' control group and low base rates of reoffending it is difficult to demonstrate a significant effect for any treatment approach. Goldson (2010) provides an incisive review of New Labour and youth justice, pointing out how policy and evidence have grown further apart, even as the government stressed evidence-based practice. He summarises the evidence for the normality of youth offending, the stable rates of youth crime and the need for diversion, minimum necessary responses and universal, holistic interventions.

Conclusion

Young people who have sexually harmed others can be seen within a complex configuration of risks and vulnerabilities, including risks of harm to others and themselves. Assumptions behind some of these potential risks and vulnerabilities need to be scrutinised since every young person – demonstrating varying behaviours and needs – should be seen as an individual. At the same time as identifying concerns or difficulties it is vital to recognise the young person's strengths and protective factors, which can be used and developed.

Considerable focus within the field has been placed on developing risk assessment tools to predict reoffending. While these may help to identify young people in most need of intervention or assistance, they do not go far towards identifying the areas in a young person's life which may be in most need of attention. Taking time to talk and build a relationship with the young person, their family and other involved professionals will still be the primary sources of information about vulnerabilities and needs. Some of these can be linked to the young person themselves and aspects of their past experiences, while other vulnerabilities can be seen as located within external circumstances and structural issues.

A holistic approach to harm and vulnerability in young people may have an obvious appeal, but the term holistic is used in a wide range of ways to indicate different approaches and focuses on different 'wholes'. In addition to attempting to see the whole young person, professionals also stressed the importance of working with the wider family and with peers, as well as with staff from other agencies. The challenges of balancing the views of this wide range of people mirrors the way concerns about sexual harm are located not just in the individual but also in their surrounding family, their community, wider society and the media.

References

Allan, J. (2006) 'Whose job is poverty? The problems of therapeutic intervention with children who are sexually violent'. *Child Abuse Review*, 15, 55–70.

Allen, C. (2003) 'Desperately seeking fusion: on "joined-up" thinking, "holistic practice" and the new economy of welfare professional power'. *British Journal of Sociology*, 54 (2), 287–306.

Allen, G. (2011) *Early Intervention: Smart Investment, Massive Savings*. London: Cabinet Office.

Ariès, P. (1962) *Centuries of Childhood*. London: Cape.

Banks, S. (2006) *Ethics and Values in Social Work*. 3rd edition. Basingstoke: Palgrave Macmillan.

Bentovim, A. (1998) 'Family systemic approach to work with young sex offenders'. *The Irish Journal of Psychology*, 19 (1), 119–135.

Brayley, H. and Cockbain, E. (2011) *Briefing Document: CSE and Youth Offending*. University College London. Available online at: www.safeandsoundderby.co.uk/blog/wp-content/uploads/2011/06/Child-Sexual-Exploitation-and-Youth-Offending-UCL.pdf (accessed 15 November 2012).

Brendtro, L., Brokenleg, M. and Van Bockern, S. (1990) *Reclaiming Youth at Risk: Our Hope for the Future*. Bloomington: National Education Service.

Bronfenbrenner, U. (1977) 'Toward an experimental ecology of human development'. *American Psychologist*, 32 (7), 513–531.

Calder, M. (ed.) (2008) *Contemporary Risk Assessment in Safeguarding Children*. Lyme Regis: Russell House.

Cameron, D. (2011) Troubled families speech. 15th December 2011. Available online at: www.number10.gov.uk/news/troubled-families-speech/ (accessed 15 November 2012).

Carson, C. (2006) 'Understanding and managing sexual behaviour problems in school settings', in Erooga, M. and Masson, H. (eds) [below].

Clark, M. (1996) 'Brief solution-focused work: A strength-based method for juvenile justice practice'. *Juvenile and Family Court Journal*, 47 (1), 57–65.

Corby, B. (2006) *Child Abuse: Towards a Knowledge Base*. 3rd edition. Maidenhead: Open University Press.

Corcoran, J. (1997) 'A solution-oriented approach to working with juvenile offenders'. *Child and Adolescent Social Work Journal*, 14 (4), 277–288.

deMause, L. (1976) *The History of Childhood: The Evolution of Parent–Child Relationships as a Factor in History*. London: Souvenir Press.

Department of Health and Home Office (2006) *The needs and effective treatment of young people who sexually abuse: current evidence*. London: Department of Health.

Durham, A. (2006) *Young Men Who Have Sexually Abused: A Case Study Guide*. Chichester: Wiley.

Empey, L. (1982) *American Delinquency: Its Meaning and Construction*. Chicago: Dorsey.

Epperson, D. (2009) 'Training the Trainers: Juvenile Sexual Offender Risk Assessment with the JSORRAT-II'. Training given in Sacramento, 8 April 2009. Available online at: www.cdcr.ca.gov/parole/SARATSO_Committee/DOCS/Juvenile%20Sexual%20Offender%20Risk%20Assessment%20with%20the%20JSORRAT-II.ppt (accessed 15 November 2012).

Epperson, D., Ralston, C., Fowers, D., DeWitt, J. and Gore, K. (2006) 'Actuarial Risk Assessment with Juveniles Who Offend Sexually: Development of the Juvenile Sexual Offense Recidivism Risk Assessment Tool – II', in Prescott, D. *Risk Assessment of Youth who have Sexually Abused: Theory, Controversy and Emerging Strategies*. Oklahoma City: Wood & Barnes.

Ernst, E. (2004) 'Disentangling Integrative Medicine'. *Mayo Clinic Proceedings*, 79, 565–566.

Erooga, M. and Masson, H. (eds) (2006) *Children and Young People who Sexually Abuse Others: Current developments and practice responses*, 2nd edition. London: Routledge.

Family Rights Group, Family Welfare Association and Parentline Plus (2003) *Every Child Matters: A Joint Response*. London: FRG, FWA and Parentline Plus.

Farrall, S. and Calverley, A. (2006) *Understanding Desistance from Crime: Theoretical directions in resettlement and rehabilitation*. Maidenhead: Open University Press.

Furniss, J. and Nutley, S. (2000) 'Implementing What Works with Offenders – The Effective Practice Initiative'. *Public Money and Management*, 20 (4), 23–28.

Gilderthorp, N., Whittaker, M. and Dunn, J. (2011) 'Past caring? Issues of after care, attachment and mental health for young people who have displayed harmful sexual behaviour', in Calder, M. (ed.) *Contemporary Practice with Young People who Sexually Abuse: evidence-based developments*. Lyme Regis: Russell House.

Goldson, B. (2010) 'The sleep of (criminological) reason: Knowledge-policy rupture and New Labour's youth justice legacy'. *Criminology and Criminal Justice*, 10 (2), 155–178.

Griffin, J. and Tyrrell, I. (1997) *Psychotherapy, Counselling and the Human Givens*. Chalvington: European Therapy Studies Institute.

Hackett, S. (2007) 'Just how different are they? Diversity and the treatment of young people with harmful sexual behaviours', in Calder, M. (ed.) *Working with Children and Young People who Sexually Abuse: taking the field forward*. Lyme Regis: Russell House.

Hackett, S., Masson, H. and Phillips, S. (2006) 'Exploring consensus in practice with youth who are sexually abusive: Findings from a Delphi study of practitioner views in the United Kingdom and the Republic of Ireland'. *Child Maltreatment*, 11 (2), 146–156.

Hackett, S., Phillips, J., Masson, H. and Balfe, M. (2011) *Recidivism, Desistance and Life Course Trajectories of Young Sexual Abusers. An in-depth follow-up study, 10 years on*. Durham University. Available online at: www.dur.ac.uk/resources/sass/research/briefings/Resear chBriefing7-Recidivismdistanceandlifecoursetrajectoriesofyoungsexualabusersanin-depthfo llow-upsstudy10yearson.pdf (accessed 15 November 2012).

Hackett, S., Print, B. and Dey, C. (1998) 'Brother Nature? Therapeutic intervention with young men who sexually abuse their siblings', in Bannister, A. (ed.) *From Hearing to Healing: Working with the Aftermath of Child Sexual Abuse*. 2nd edition. Chichester: Wiley.

Hall, S. (2010) *Exploring Implications and Benefits of Holistic Working with Young People who have Sexually Harmed Others*. PhD Thesis. Available online at: www.dora.dmu.ac.uk/handle/ 2086/4977 (accessed 15 November 2012).

——(2011) 'Evidence for working holistically with young people who have sexually harmed'. In: Calder, M. (ed.) *Contemporary Practice with Young People who Sexually Abuse: evidence-based developments*. Lyme Regis: Russell House.

Hendrick, H. (1997) 'Constructions and reconstructions of British childhood: an interpretative survey, 1800 to the present', in James, A. and Proat, A. (eds) *Constructing and Reconstructing Childhood*, 2nd edition. Basingstoke: Falmer.

Hettler, W. (undated) *Origins of the Hettler 6 Dimensional Model*. Available online at www. hettler.com/OriginsoftheHettler6DimensionalModel.mht (accessed 15 November 2012).

HM Government (2010) *Working Together to Safeguard Children*. Nottingham: DCSF Publications.

Home Office (2003) *Youth Justice – The Next Steps*. Available online at: www.education.gov. uk/publications/eOrderingDownload/Youth%20Justice%20-%20Next%20Steps.pdf (accessed 15 November 2012).

Hunter, J., Figueredo, A., Malamuth, N. and Becker, J. (2003) 'Juvenile sex offenders: towards the development of a typology'. *Sexual Abuse: A Journal of Research and Treatment*, 15 (1), 27–48.

Jack, G. and Gill, O. (2010) 'The role of communities in safeguarding children and young people'. *Child Abuse Review*, 19 (2), 82–96.

Kruttschnitt, C., Uggen, C. and Shelton, K. (2000) 'Predictors of desistance among sex offenders: The interaction of formal and informal social controls'. *Justice Quarterly*, 17 (1), 61–87.

Letourneau, E. and Swenson, C. (2005) 'Sexual offending and sexual behaviour problems: Treatment with multi-systemic therapy', in Calder, M. (ed.) *Children and Young People who Sexually Abuse: new theory, research and practice developments*. Lyme Regis: Russell House.

Loh, C. and Gidycz, C. (2006) 'A prospective analysis of the relationship between childhood sexual victimization and perpetration of dating violence and sexual assault in adulthood'. *Journal of Interpersonal Violence*, 21 (6), 732–749.

Long, J. (2010) 'Hidden problem of children sexually abusing children'. *File on 4*, BBC, 16 March. Available online at: http://news.bbc.co.uk/1/hi/programmes/file_on_4/8570303. stm (accessed 15 November 2012).

Longo, R. (2002) 'A holistic approach to treating young people who sexually abuse', in Calder, M. (ed.) *Young People who Sexually Abuse: building the evidence base for your practice*. Lyme Regis: Russell House.

Mair, G. (ed.) (2006) *What Matters in Probation*. Cullompton: Willan.

McGuire, J. and Priestley, P. (1995) 'Reviewing "What Works": past, present and future', in McGuire, J. (ed.) *What Works: Reducing Reoffending – Guidelines from Research and Practice.* Chichester: Wiley.

Morrison, T. (2006) 'Building a holistic approach in the treatment of young people who sexually abuse', in Longo, R. and Prescott, D. (eds) *Current Perspectives: Working with Sexually Aggressive Youth and Youth with Sexual Behavior Problems.* Holyoke: Neari Press.

Morrison, T. and Henniker, J. (2006) 'Building a comprehensive inter-agency assessment and intervention system for young people who sexually harm', in Erooga, M. and Masson, H. (eds) [above].

Muncie, J. (2009) *Youth and Crime.* 3rd edition. London: Sage.

Myers, J. and Sweeney, T. (2008) 'Wellness Counselling: The Evidence Base for Practice'. *Journal of Counseling & Development,* 86 (Fall), 482–493.

Nacro (2003) *Youth Crime Briefing.* London: Nacro.

National Children's Home (1992) *The Report of the Committee of Enquiry into Children and Young People who Sexually Abuse Other Children.* London: NCH.

Omaji, P. (2003) *Responding to Youth Crime.* Sydney: Hawkins Press.

Parks, G. (2007) 'Emerging data for risk prediction and identification of offender sub-groups', in Calder, M. (ed.) *Working with Children and Young People who Sexually Abuse: taking the field forward.* Lyme Regis: Russell House.

Pollock, L. (1983) *Forgotten Children: Parent–Child Relations from 1500 to 1900.* Cambridge: Cambridge University Press.

Powell, D., Batsche, C., Ferro, J., Fox, L. and Dunlap, G. (1997) 'A strength-based approach in support of multi-risk families: Principles and issues'. *Topics in Early Childhood Special Education,* 17 (1), 1–26.

Rich, P. (2003) *Understanding, Assessing and Rehabilitating Juvenile Sexual Offenders.* Chichester: Wiley.

——(2009) *Juvenile Sexual Offenders: A Comprehensive Guide to Risk Evaluation.* Hoboken: Wiley.

Ruch, G. (2005) 'Relationship-based practice and reflective practice: holistic approaches to contemporary child care social work'. *Child and Family Social Work,* 10 (2), 111–123.

Saleebey, D. (1996) 'The Strengths Perspective in Social Work Practice: Extensions and Cautions'. *Social Work,* 41 (3), 296–305.

Scott, J. and Telford, P. (2006) 'Similarities and differences in working with girls and boys who display sexually harmful behaviour: the journey continues', in Erooga, M. and Masson, H. (eds) [above].

Sherman, L. (1997) *Preventing Crime: What Works, What Doesn't, What's Promising.* A report to the United States Congress. Available online at: www.ncjrs.gov/works/ (accessed 15 November 2012).

Smith, R. (2005) 'Welfare versus justice – again!' *Youth Justice,* 5 (1), 3–16.

——(2007) *Youth Justice: Ideas, policy, practice.* 2nd edition. Cullompton: Willan.

Sweeney, T. and Myers, J. (2003) *The Indivisible Self: An Evidence-Based Model of Wellness.* Greensboro: Authors.

Turnbull, G. and Spence, J. (2011) 'What's at risk? The proliferation of risk across child and youth policy in England'. *Journal of Youth Studies,* 14 (8), 939–959.

Viljoen, J., Elkovitch, N., Scalora, M. and Ullman, D. (2009) 'Assessment of reoffense risk in adolescents who have committed sexual offenses: Predictive validity of the ERASOR, PCL:YV, YLS/CMI, and Static-99'. *Criminal Justice and Behaviour,* 36 (10), 981–1000.

Ward, H. (2001) 'The developmental needs of children: implications for assessment', in Horwath, J. (ed.) *The Child's World.* London: Jessica Kingsley.

Ward, T. and Gannon, T. (2006) 'Rehabilitation, etiology, and self-regulation: The comprehensive good lives model of treatment for sexual offenders'. *Aggression and Violent Behavior,* 11, 77–94.

Way, I. (2002) 'Childhood Maltreatment Histories of Male Adolescents with Sexual Offending Behaviours: A Review of the Literature', in Calder, M. (ed.) (2002) *Young*

People who Sexually Abuse: building the evidence base for your practice. Lyme Regis: Russell House.

Weaver, H. (2002) 'Perspectives on Wellness: Journeys on the Red Road'. *Journal of Sociology and Social Welfare*, 29 (1), 5–15.

Webb, S. (2001) 'Some considerations on the validity of evidence-based practice in social work'. *British Journal of Social Work*, 31 (1), 57–79.

Welsh Assembly Government (2004) *All-Wales Youth Offending Strategy*. Cardiff: Welsh Assembly Government.

Wilcox, A. (2003) 'Evidence-based youth justice? Some valuable lessons from an evaluation for the Youth Justice Board'. *Youth Justice*, 3 (1), 21–35.

Wilson, H. (2010) 'Health Consequences of Childhood Sexual Abuse'. *Perspectives in Psychiatric Care*, 46 (1), 56–64.

Witmer, J., Sweeney, T. and Myers, J. (1998) *The Wheel of Wellness*. Greensboro: Authors.

Yokley, J., LaCortiglia, J. and Bulanda, B. (2007) 'An overview of social responsibility therapy for preteen children with sexual behaviour problems', in Calder, M. (ed.) *Working with Children and Young People who Sexually Abuse: taking the field forward*. Lyme Regis: Russell House.

Youth Justice Board (2006) *Asset*. Available online at: www.justice.gov.uk/youth-justice/assessment/asset-young-offender-assessment-profile (accessed 15 November 2012).

——(2008) *Key Elements of Effective Practice for Young People who have Sexually Abused*. Available online at: http://yjbpublications.justice.gov.uk/en-gb/Resources/Downloads/KEEP_YPSA.pdf (accessed 15/11/12).

——(2010) *The Scaled Approach*. Available online at: www.justice.gov.uk/guidance/youth-justice/the-scaled-approach/index.htm (accessed 15 November 2012).

9

VIOLENCE IN THE CONTEXT OF PERSONAL RELATIONSHIPS

Graham Brotherton

Introduction – seeking a definition

The issue of violence in the context of personal relationships is a complex and contested one. In trying to analyse and explore the issue this chapter will first seek to give a brief historical overview of the way in which our understanding and analysis has developed and then look at current understandings and policy approaches from a variety of perspectives, including those of both practitioners and those who have used domestic violence services. In doing so, the chapter draws upon the findings of a collaborative European research project and will seek to explore violence in the context of personal relationships in relation to both intimate partner violence and broader violence involving other family, peer or friendship relationships; it will inevitably focus, though, on 'domestic' violence, as this has been the primary focus of most of the research in this area. It will seek to explore factors which influence violence but also strategies for providing effective support based on the experiences of those who have experienced violence. It is of course difficult to cover the full range of issues around vulnerability in a short chapter such as this and as a result the discussion which can be given to any particular issue is inevitably brief.

Reflective Activity

What do you think is the range of actions that could be thought about as violence in the context of personal relationships?

We need first to provide a working definition of violence and a useful starting point is provided by the Women's Aid Federation of England, which suggests:

> Domestic violence is physical, sexual, psychological or financial violence that takes place within an intimate or family-type relationship and that forms a pattern of coercive and controlling behaviour. This can include forced marriage and so-called 'honour crimes'. Domestic violence may include a range of abusive behaviours, not all of which are in themselves inherently 'violent'.
>
> *(Women's Aid Federation 2007)*

This notion of domestic violence as encompassing a range of behaviours rather than just physical violence is an important one, as is the recognition that violence can take place in a range of intimate relationships. There has been pressure for this to be recognised in official policy discourses and in September 2012 the Home Office introduced a definition of domestic violence and abuse as a result of a consultation process. It is important to note that this is a policy definition intended to provide a framework for services rather than a legal definition. However, it is worth noting that the new definition does represent substantial change in some respects. The definition says that domestic violence/abuse is:

> Any incident or pattern of incidents of controlling, coercive or threatening behaviour, violence or abuse between those aged 16 or over who are or have been intimate partners or family members regardless of gender or sexuality. This can encompass but is not limited to the following types of abuse:
>
> - psychological
> - physical
> - sexual
> - financial
> - emotional.
>
> Controlling behaviour is: a range of acts designed to make a person subordinate and/or dependent by isolating them from sources of support, exploiting their resources and capacities for personal gain, depriving them of the means needed for independence, resistance and escape and regulating their everyday behaviour.
> Coercive behaviour is: an act or a pattern of acts of assault, threats, humiliation and intimidation or other abuse that is used to harm, punish, or frighten their victim.
>
> *(Home Office 2012)*

A very significant change here is the explicit recognition that domestic violence can and does occur in relationships between young people. Indeed, the British Crime survey (Home Office 2010) suggests that domestic violence is experienced more by people between the ages of 16 and 19 than other age groups, which contrasts sharply with the traditional view of domestic violence – though, as discussed later in the chapter, issues of definition disclosure and reporting mean these statistics need to be treated with some caution as there may be under-reporting within other groups.

Whilst this definition is specific to domestic violence it can also be said to provide a way of thinking about violence in the context of a range of personal relationships. And this is the way in which we will proceed in this chapter. However, having taken a broad view of what constitutes violence we now need to make explicit the link to the idea of vulnerability which is the theme of this book. In order to do this we need to consider the historical development of attitudes towards violence and how these have reflected broader social attitudes. There is not space here to explore this in depth but there is little doubt that, historically, violence in the context of personal relationships has not generally been seen as a significant issue in policy terms but rather as an issue best left in the private realm of family. Two factors are often used to explain this: first, historic attitudes to women and women's rights, and second, the perceived hidden nature of domestic violence. Each will shortly be considered in turn. Before leaving the issue of definitions, though, it is important to highlight a further key issue: there is a tendency in monitoring or reporting violent events to see them as a series of discrete events rather than as an ongoing process, and this can have important consequences in terms of under what circumstances a decision to intervene is taken. A number of high-profile reviews of the actions of police or social workers have highlighted the failure to build up a picture based on repeated reporting of individual 'events', with significant tragic consequences in some cases.

Reflective Activity

Why do you think violence against women has been accepted in many societies over a long period of time?
  Have attitudes changed or is it still a significant problem?

Returning to the issue of the historical development of attitudes to women, it is well established that violence against women has been accepted – sometimes tacitly, sometimes more explicitly – within many societies across a long time span. Examples would include the way in which women in relationships have been seen in legal terms as a possession in the same way as other 'goods' or the fact that rape within marriage only became an offence in 1981. It is important to also recognise that these only become seen as social issues as a direct result of the so-called 'second wave' of feminism in the 1970s and 1980s which succeeded in problematising a number of key aspects in the context of personal relationships. However, some commentators (see, for example, Farmer and Callan 2012) have suggested that in locating domestic violence within the analytical framework of patriarchy (the assertion that in most societies, most of the time, social structures give men authority over women and which feminist authors argue can be traced back through the history of almost all societies) there has been a tendency to fail to acknowledge the variety of relationships in which violence can occur – for example, in the context of same-sex relationships, or violence by women against male partners. However, it is also argued that explanations which seek to locate violence differently – for example, in the context of particular economic relationships – fail to account for the pervasive nature of men's violence against women across time and in a range of cultural and economic contexts. Many commentators have highlighted the way in which discourses around gender prescribe particular roles for men and woman and the way in which this reinforces patriarchal attitudes, though it has to be acknowledged that this happens in differentiated ways because of other influential discourses around, for example, class and culture. In this sense gender roles can be seen to be performed in particular ways in particular contexts.

In seeking to link this back to the notion of who is vulnerable and in what context, the complex question of incidence reporting and recording arises. Estimates of incidence relate to the extent to which incidents of violence are reported, either formally (usually through the criminal justice system) or informally through research. This in turn relates to definitions used by those undertaking research and legal and policy definitions in force at the time, which is in turn linked to confidence in the process of reporting/recording and the 'ability' to disclose. This in turn might relate to gender, power and status. To give an example, I was involved in a research project which looked at community responses to domestic violence (discussed more fully later in the chapter) (Tucker *et al.* 2011). Part of this research was undertaken in Romania where there was no clear statutory definition in place and services were provided predominately by voluntary groups. The area involved included rural areas with a very poor transport infrastructure and villages built around extended family networks. In this situation it was very apparent that issues around reporting, recording and the ability to disclose were very different to the issues in the large, complex and culturally diverse city where I am normally based. However, even allowing for all of this complexity and uncertainty around the statistics, it is important to highlight that it remains the case that the majority of victims of both repeat violence and fatal or life-threatening attacks are women, though men are also victims and violence does occur in the context of same-sex relationships.

Children and domestic violence

A further key factor which needs to be considered when taking a family perspective is the role of children as actors, as witnesses and as victims. The Home Office consultation referred to previously included an option that the definition might be amended to specifically highlight that children can be victims of domestic violence, but this has not been included in the definition which has emerged; this seems to be because, it is argued, there is already a framework for addressing violence against children through child protection legislation. This is a complex area in terms of the impact on children of either witnessing violence or being themselves subject to violence. Furthermore, they may themselves become willing or unwilling actors in the process as mediators, confidantes or as part of strategies used by the violent person or their partner. A survey by 4Children in 2012 suggested that around one million children are affected by issues of domestic violence; this equates to about one child in 11 so it is a significant policy issue. Holt *et al.* (2008), in systematically reviewing the existing research, suggest that there is an association between childhood exposure to violence and subsequent involvement in violent adult relationships, though as they also highlight this is a complex area and there is no evidence of a causal relationship. The question of which factors might make some children and young people more resilient in this context and how this relates to longer-term outcomes is one where there is a clear and urgent need for further research.

In looking at the relationship between services, children and those who have been violent, Featherstone and Peckover (2007) highlight the ambivalent response of services to violent fathers, for example through the pro-contact approach often adopted in proceedings through the family law aspects of the 1989 Children Act, which can cause difficulties in the context of relationships where domestic violence (in the broadest sense) has occurred. A recent report for the legal rights charity Rights of Women, undertaken by Coy *et al.* (2012), argues that there is already evidence that family court decisions, which tend to place a priority on shared parenting, can exacerbate the problem and that proposed changes to the law make the problem worse. Featherstone and Peckover (2007) conclude by arguing that providing more effective support for women and children in the context of domestic violence must involve more pro-active work with fathers based on challenging dominant discourses of masculinity. They make explicit reference to the work of Giddens and his notion of identity work, as discussed in the first chapter, suggesting that such work needs to support fathers by engaging with the complexities of individual life stories and provide space for them to 're-author' their lives in non-violent ways.

What do we mean by vulnerability in the context of violence in personal relationships?

The term vulnerability is itself particularly complex in the context of personal relationships, as it relates to both personal resources, specific situational resources, the relationship between these and a range of broader socio-economic factors which would include material, cultural and legal dimensions. In seeking to explore this issue of the complex nature of vulnerability we need to consider the way in which this has been theorised or modelled.

One approach was developed by Heise (1998), drawing on the ecological model originally developed by Bronfenbrenner. This seeks to take an integrated ecological perspective in understanding the causes of domestic violence. The model suggests there are 'levels' at which we need to seek to understand violence and a range of factors which operate at each level. Tucker *et al.* (2011) summarise the literature as suggesting that some key factors are:

- at the individual level – being abused as a child or witnessing marital violence in the home, having an absent or rejecting father, use of alcohol;
- at the relational level – male control of wealth and decision-making within the family, marital conflict;
- at the community level – women's isolation and lack of social support, male peer groups that condone and legitimise men's violence;
- at the societal level – the rigid definition and enforcement of gender roles, the concept of masculinity linked to toughness, male honour or dominance, tolerance of physical punishment of women and children, acceptance of violence as a means to settle interpersonal disputes, the perception that men have 'ownership' of women.

It is of course important to highlight that these are not simple 'causal' links and they may have widely differing impacts in different situations. Each individual and relationship is subject to a specific set of influences and whilst some, such as cultural perspectives or the legal context, may be apparently pervasive in a particular society at a particular point, they will still be influenced by 'class', economic status and even the particular dynamics of interpersonal relationships. Vulnerability may have significant shared characteristics but the experience of vulnerability is unique and differentiated. This highlights the need for approaches which both seek to identify common features and experiences and recognise the uniqueness of individual circumstances.

Who is vulnerable?

This is another highly complex and contested area, there being a tendency to see domestic violence in particular as something associated with working-class culture and poverty. However, a number of authors have highlighted that violence is no respecter of class or cultural boundaries and that this is especially true if a broader conception of violence is used. Nonetheless, Phipps (2010) highlights that, looking specifically at sexual violence, women with low incomes are more likely to experience sexual violence than women with higher incomes and argues that there has been a failure in both policy and research to acknowledge that violence is a 'classed' experience. This is reinforced by the way in which the media choose to portray sexual violence, with some victims constructed as 'good' victims, assaulted despite the way they choose to dress and present themselves, and others as 'bad' victims, whose behaviour, dress, etc., is deemed to make them complicit in their own assault. Phipps argues that these distinctions draw on class discourses about both femininity and masculinity which see working-class women as deviant and in some case predatory. Furthermore, working-class masculinity is itself constructed as deviant, especially in terms of a propensity for violence. Their vulnerability of working-class people is therefore located in their own behaviour and attitudes. Whilst Phipps locates this discussion purely in the context of sexual violence, it can be argued that it also applies in the context of other forms of violence where particular actions are constructed in particular ways dependent upon context. There are also links to broader discourses about the 'underclass' and to the current debate about a group of so-called 'troubled' families who are alleged to be disproportionally responsible for a range of anti-social and criminal activity (Department of Communities and Local Government 2012).

A further complicating factor is the role of culture; there are clearly differing attitudes around women's roles and the notion of rights which link to both culture and faith across a range of faith and cultural traditions. The evidence about how much this has an impact on attitudes to violence is very limited. The study by Anitha (2010) which looks at the issue of women with 'no recourse to public funds' – that is, women in the UK but without citizenship status (usually as a result of either marriage or being trafficked) and therefore without access to either welfare provision or legal support – is one of the few to highlight the complex role played by culture and the behavioural expectations associated with it.

A further point is that there is some evidence that, as Sokoloff and Dupont (2005, cited by Tucker *et al.* 2011) highlight, a failure to acknowledge class, culture, etc., leads to problems in providing services that meet the needs of particular individuals and groups. This is particularly true for groups that can be said be 'hidden' and/or 'undeserving', such as those with no recourse to public funds or viewed in the context of the debate around social class. We now turn to considering some of the factors identified in the literature as being significant in exploring vulnerability.

The specific role of drugs and alcohol

There is clearly a relationship between drugs, alcohol and violence but again it is not a simple or straightforward one. There is some evidence that men may be more likely to commit acts of violence after drinking – for example, the Faculty of Public Health (2005) suggest around one-third of domestic violence is linked to alcohol consumption – but the amount of research undertaken in the UK is limited, especially the context of drug use or violence within same-sex relationships. Galvani (2006) explored the views of women who had experienced violence on the role of drinking by both perpetrators and their partners. A number of themes emerge: for example, a number of women highlighted the role of alcohol in opening up the possibility of discussing issues which could not be talked about when the perpetrator was sober but said that in itself was a possible trigger for violence; the impact of the victim also drinking was raised, and was felt by the women in this study to be an indirect influence. Furthermore, whilst all the women interviewed saw alcohol as playing a key role, they did not see it as more significant than other factors. Whilst Galvani's study is a fairly small-scale one, it is almost the only study which looks at the issues from a survivor's perspective.

Community

Wilcox (2006) argues that community has been a missing element in the debate around domestic violence, in the UK at least, and this dimension is particularly significant in the context of the debate about vulnerability and resilience. She suggests that whilst there has been positive change in terms of both policy frameworks and professional attitudes, it is less clear that this is reflected in communities at large. Furthermore, she argues that the construction of domestic violence as a private issue reinforces the notion that it is the responsibility of statutory agencies rather than community networks. The absence of women from leadership roles in many community groups also contributes to domestic violence not being seen as an issue at community level. She also highlights the way in which, for many women and children facing violence, informal support through community networks plays a highly significant role, often much more important than the role of formal services. However, it needs to be acknowledged that the term community is constructed in a variety of ways and that there are class, cultural and ethnic dimensions which have an impact on the way in which community is both understood and experienced. Communities can be a mechanism for reproducing dominant discourses around the 'causes' and nature of violence which may have an impact on who seeks support and under what circumstances and indeed on what conceptions of support are considered acceptable. Wilcox cites the example of a working-class woman leaving a support group because, despite having experienced persistent and long-term domestic violence, she was unable to feel comfortable with the feminist analytical approach used within the support group.

This raises the issue of ambivalence or even hostility from the wider community to groups perceived as operating with an anti-men or anti-family agenda. Understanding the complex mediating role of community is important for a number of reasons: firstly, and perhaps tautologically, because it is where those experiencing violence live, but also because it is the context in which informal advice is sought and where decisions to seek more formal support are made. There is evidence that decisions to seek support are often made over a longish time period and that many people never reach the point of making a formal decision to seek formal support. Thus, understanding the factors which influence this process is vital to our understanding of both vulnerability and our responses to it.

Listening and vulnerability

Wilcox concludes her article referred to in the previous section by highlighting the need for research which actively involves the perspective of those who have experienced violence. The issue of who is listened to and under what circumstances was a key part of the research undertaken by Tucker *et al.* (2011) and is a crucial area of practice. For an evaluation, though, we need to separate the process of listening into different stages, ranging from listening in the context of initial allegation/disclosure, through the process of listening whilst in contact with services, to being involved in the evaluation of services. We will consider each of these stages in turn. Looking first at initial allegation or disclosure, there are still for many people seeking to disclose significant difficulties, ranging from identifying appropriate services (especially outside the criminal justice system) to finding a way of accessing these services despite physical or other barriers – language, psychological readiness, etc. One of the findings of Tucker *et al.* (2011) is that better information is needed to help people access services and that survivors need to feel that they are likely to be believed when they do access services.

As Hague and Mullender (2006) suggested, the voice of the service user has been increasingly heard in the evaluation of services in recent years; however, this voice is still patchy and uneven. Services have had to change to become more 'professional' in a context where funding is often dependent on being able to demonstrate particular outcomes, especially in the current financial situation, and this has the potential at least to lead to a diminution of the voice of the service user. A study in New Zealand by Fanslow and Robinson (2004) which sought to look at wider issues of awareness of services suggests that community outreach services have a key role in both raising awareness and providing ongoing support. Unfortunately, examples of such services are very limited, a key issue for the most marginalised and vulnerable individuals and groups.

Same-sex relationships

Donovan and Hester (2010) argue that the focus on violence within heterosexual relationships has led to the issue of violence in same-sex relationships being overlooked because it doesn't fit with dominant policy discourses. They also highlight that there are patterns in violent relationships regardless of gender which include, for example, what they describe as 'practices of love', strategic declarations of love by the violent partner, especially at points where the non-violent partner suggests that they may leave. They also highlight that the violent partner tends to see the relationship in terms of their own needs, whereas the non-violent partner sees the relationship as a mutual project. This can have important implications in terms of the dynamics of a relationship so that when a violent partner makes an intimate disclosure this can lead to the other partner seeking to provide care and support, but when the reverse happens this is used to further enhance the control of the violent partner. They also highlight the fact that as the violence in same-sex relationships is often emotional violence, which doesn't fit neatly with discourses around what domestic violence is, then it can be very difficult for victims of violence in same-sex relationships to recognise themselves as such, making them vulnerable to ongoing abuse. A further key point is the rejection by many of those spoken to in this study of the word victim on the grounds that, first, they were not passive or accepting of the violence against them and second, the complex nature of violence in 'loving' relationships makes the term inappropriate and unhelpful. Once again the fact that this is a single study needs to be taken into account; however, some of the insights into the nature of interpersonal dynamics highlighted here may have wider usefulness in seeking to understand how vulnerability is 'played out' in the context of interpersonal relationships.

The impact of disability

Hague *et al.* (2011) examined the particular issues facing women with disabilities, highlighting the limited nature of previous research in this area. They identified a range of issues, including the fact that women with disabilities appear to experience a higher incidence of violence of all types – physical, sexual, emotional, financial and neglect. This can include both partner violence and violence from carers, who of course in some cases are the same person. They highlight that this can be particularly difficult and traumatic and may be associated with a sense of both rejection and vulnerability and therefore have a significant impact on a survivor's sense of self. They argue that this needs to be seen in the context of multiple systems of disadvantage which make disabled women in particular potentially vulnerable, linking issues around gender, disability and poverty. Hague *et al.* go on to make the important point that often, rather than recognising the complex intersecting nature of these various dimensions of disadvantage, disability is often treated as an 'add-on' factor. They further highlight the particular issues for women who have particular care needs in gaining access to supportive services which can cater for those needs, especially where children are also involved.

No recourse to public funds

Anitha (2010) highlights the specific issue of 'no recourse to public funds' for women who are not UK citizens but are in the UK as a result of either marriage or trafficking. If they find themselves in the position of seeking leave to remain as a result of being the victim of violence, then they find themselves ineligible for services such as benefits, housing or publicly funded refuges. This leaves them with the impossible choice of either remaining in a dangerous situation or becoming destitute and possibly facing deportation, which places them in a uniquely vulnerable situation. She highlights the fact that the women and in many cases their children find themselves facing not only major financial difficulties but also issues of isolation, exacerbated in many cases by language difficulties. This has an impact in terms of physical and emotional wellbeing. Whilst Anitha does identify a number of examples of good practice in some local authority areas and through the provision of a limited range of specialist services, she also identifies the need for significant legal changes giving this particular group of women equal access to the full range of supportive services. These issues may be at their most acute for those women with 'no recourse' but they may also apply for a wider range of people when there are problems of language or geographical isolation.

'Race' and culture

Developing the points made in the previous section, the role played by cultural factors is a complex one and evidence, especially in the context of the UK, is rather thin on the ground. Kellock (2010) sought to explore some of the issues in a small-scale study in Manchester which highlighted a number of specific issues: the impact of arranged marriage, the fact that living with in-laws is a feature of married life within some cultural communities – notably south Asian communities – and the impact this can have on a woman's status. In particular respondents highlighted: the abuse by mothers-in-law that can follow from this, the role played by perceptions of gossip or being gossiped about in some linguistic communities, especially where someone hired as a translator is perceived by the victim to be part of the community they feel marginalised within. The issue of differing perceptions when one partner in a marriage is from outside the UK and may have a slightly different cultural understanding is also highlighted as significant. However, whilst this can be said to be a useful indication of the urgent need for further research, there is not enough here to allow even tentative conclusions to be drawn. It does, though, highlight the fact that there is a range of key policy and practice issues which are often marginalised in the debate about vulnerability and which remain relatively poorly understood.

Trafficking

One area which has received slightly greater, though still not significant, emphasis in policy terms in recent years is trafficking. Whilst trafficking occurs for a number of reasons, including to supply people for low-paid work in a number of sectors (for example, through the so-called 'gangmaster' system) and often children or young people to work as domestic servants, both of which may involve those who are trafficked being subjected to considerable and often routine violence, we will use here the issue of those trafficked as forced sex workers, because here the boundary with interpersonal relationships is particularly blurred. In the research by Tucker *et al.* (2011) which interviewed a number of survivors of trafficking, a recurring theme was the way in which they had been recruited by 'boyfriends' who offered them lucrative work abroad. The links here between geographical isolation and predatory personal relationships make this group of survivors particularly vulnerable. Women who had been trafficked talked about the difficulty in knowing how to access supportive services and their fears about the consequences for themselves and their families of seeking escape. They also talked about the way in which their circumstances potentially criminalised them and the way in which they perceived that there was often a trade-off between their willingness to give evidence against perpetrators and their future access to assistance.

Reflective Activity

From what you have read so far, what do you think might be the characteristics of effective services to support those who have experienced violence?

Understanding vulnerability from a service user perspective

Between 2009 and 2011, I along with colleagues from the UK, Romania and Germany were involved in a project funded by the European Union's DAPHNE 3 programme which sought to look at violence in the context of personal relationships and how this was defined and responded to at local, national and international levels. As part of the research a series of interviews were carried out in the three countries with women who had experienced violence in the context of interpersonal relationships. Despite the fact that the interviews were carried out in very different contexts, a number of common themes emerged and provide some useful insights. This section attempts to summarise the findings and is adapted from Tucker *et al.* (2011).

Looking first at the decision to seek support, the interview data established the existence of a number of triggers that can lead to a victim of domestic violence leaving their partner. These included:

- the act of rape within marriage;
- prolonged and systematically repeated acts of violent aggression;
- exposure of children to violence or other forms of physical or sexual abuse, and neglect;
- other family members condoning the actions of the perpetrator (including becoming involved in violence and abuse themselves);
- victims starting to self-harm, over-reliance on medication (often anti-depressants), excessive use of drugs and alcohol;
- where strong cultural and/or religious ties exist and the intervention of external agencies is unwelcome;
- situations where individuals are geographically and socially isolated.

What is less clear is the relationship between the factors described here and the actual decision to leave, i.e. what causes someone to actually act often after a considerable period of abuse. Furthermore it is of course important to note that those involved in this research had already taken the decision to leave their partner and therefore it was not possible in this study to look at the perspective of those who chose to seek at least initial support whilst staying with their partner which may have been easier where some of the factors above were not present.

Within the interviews were a number of women who 'married into a family' only to find them in a relationship based on domestic servitude and who experienced violence as a direct result of this. Through these interviews it proved possible to identify a range of common characteristics that contribute towards providing high-quality community-based provision. These included:

- respect for the rights of the individuals involved;
- acceptance of the veracity of the circumstances described by victims of domestic violence;

- availability and access to information that is accurate, relevant and simply written;
- staff who are supportive, sympathetic and appropriately trained;
- speedy access (through referral mechanisms as appropriate) to health, social care, education and legal services;
- support to provide a degree of continuity in lives of dependent children, e.g. continuation of their education;
- advice, counselling and a 'listening ear' as necessary;
- provision of emergency food, clothing, etc;
- provision that is appropriately situated geographically and offers a high level of personal security.

Whilst these issues were particularly pertinent in the context of the circumstances described above, it is important to note that they also apply in the context of work with survivors more generally.

To return to the specifics of trying to develop services which can be said to minimise vulnerability, in developing community-based support for victims of violence a number of challenges appear to impact on service organisation and delivery. These include:

- the challenging and breaking down of cultural and social barriers/stereotypes that 'conceal' perpetrators, accept violence as a 'normal' part of family life and/ or childhood and foster discrimination and disrespect;
- engaging with service, and potential service, users in ways that encourage them to explore their experiences and define their needs and expectations of community-based services;
- the creation of a network of formal and informal services that will build 'resilience', offer access that is non-threatening and can be used as a mechanism for immediate support and protection, and preventative work;
- the managing of a reduced financial resource that will not add to the risks, uncertainties and challenges that many women, children and young people already face.

At the time of writing this chapter, UK services operating in the area of domestic violence are facing very substantial cuts. Walby and Towers (2012) suggest that around 30 per cent cuts were imposed on domestic violence services between 2010/11 and 2011/12 and that around 9 per cent of those seeking places in women's refuges were turned away because of a lack of places. With further cuts likely over the next three years the gaps in services are likely to increase. Some specialist services have already experienced even higher levels of cuts. There is a real danger here that some very vulnerable groups of people who have experienced violence will find it more difficult or even impossible to access services.

Conclusion

A central argument of this book as a whole is that vulnerability is complex and multi-faceted and nowhere is this more true than in the context of violence. Violence occurs in a range of personal relationships and in a variety of contexts and there are a significant number of factors which have an impact on the extent to which a person can be said to be vulnerable to violence. How then can we make sense of this complexity? First, there can be no simple causal model which entirely captures the nuanced interplay between the range of factors which may play a role. At one level relationships are individual and unique – especially from the perspective of those involved – but they take place within the context of a range of normalising discourses at the local, national and global level, stemming from a range of sources of power and influence. In seeking to respond to vulnerability in the context of violent personal relationships, then, we need to develop a more subtle understanding, which has to start from getting a much fuller picture of what the issues look like from the perspective of those who have experienced violence and which recognises that this experience is itself profoundly influenced by issues of class, gender, ethnicity, culture, etc. Furthermore, it needs to be acknowledged that existing legal and policy discourses may play a significant role in actually creating vulnerability for some groups experiencing violence.

References

Anitha, S. (2010) 'No recourse, no support: state policy and practice towards South Asian women facing domestic violence in the UK', *British Journal of Social Work*, 40(2): 462–479

Coy, M., Perks, K., Scott, E. and Tweedale, R. (2012) *Picking up the pieces: domestic violence and child contact*, research report, Rights of Women and CWASU. Available online at www.rightsofwomen.org.uk/pdfs/Policy/Picking_Up_the_Pieces_Report_final.pdf (accessed November 2012)

Department of Communities and Local Government (2012) *Helping troubled families turn their lives around*, policy document, DoCLC. Available online at www.gov.uk/government/policies/helping-troubled-families-turn-their-lives-around (accessed November 2012)

Donovan, C. and Hester, M. (2010) 'I hate the word "victim": an exploration of recognition of domestic violence in same sex relationships', *Social Policy and Society*, 9(2): 279–289

Faculty of Public Health (2005) *Alcohol and Violence*, briefing statement, RCP Faculty of Public Health. Available online at www.fph.org.uk/uploads/bs_alcohol_violence.pdf (accessed October 2012)

Fanslow, J. and Robinson, E. (2004) 'Violence against women in New Zealand: prevalence and health consequences', *The New Zealand Medical Journal*, 117(1206). Available online at https://researchspace.auckland.ac.nz/bitstream/handle/2292/4673/15570342.pdf?sequence=1 (accessed September 2012)

Farmer, E. and Callan, S. (2012) *Beyond Violence: breaking cycles of domestic abuse*, policy report, Centre for Social Justice. Available online at www.centreforsocialjustice.org.uk/client/media/DA%20Full%20report.pdf (accessed October 2012)

Featherstone, B. and Peckover, S. (2007) 'Letting them get away with it: fathers, children and domestic violence', *Critical Social Policy*, 27(2): 181–202

4Children (2012) *The Enemy : 4 million reasons to tackle family conflict and family violence*, 4Children report. Available online at www.4children.org.uk/Files/.fa81./TheEnemyWithin_Report.pdf (accessed June 2012)

Galvani, S. (2006) 'Alcohol and domestic violence: women's views', *Violence against Women*, 12(7): 641–662

Hague, G. and Mullender, A. (2006) 'Who listens? The voices of domestic violence survivors in service provision in the United Kingdom', *Violence Against Women*, 12(6): 568–587

Hague, G., Thiara, R. and Mullender, A. (2011) 'Disabled women and domestic violence: making the links, a national UK study', *Psychiatry, Psychology and Law*, 18(1), 117–136

Heise, L. (1998) 'Violence against women: an integrated ecological approach', *Violence Against Women*, 4(3): 262–90.

Holt, S., Buckley, H. and Whelan, S. (2008) 'The impact of exposure to domestic violence on children and young people: a review of the literature', *Child Abuse & Neglect*, 32(8): 797–810. Available online at http://dx.doi.org/10.1080/13218719.2010.509040 (accessed October 2012)

Home Office (2010) *Crime in England and Wales 2009/10: Findings from the British Crime Survey and police recorded crime*, Home Office statistical bulletin. Available online at http://webarchive.nationalarchives.gov.uk/20110218135832/rds.homeoffice.gov.uk/rds/pdfs10/hosb1210.pdf)

Home Office (2012) New definition of domestic violence and abuse to include 16 and 17-year-olds, Home Office statement. Available online at www.homeoffice.gov.uk/media-centre/press-releases/new-def-of-domestic-violence (accessed November 2012)

Kellock, V. (2010) 'Domestic abuse: Black and minority-ethnic women's perspectives', *Midwifery*, 26(2): 181–188

Phipps, A. (2010) 'Violent and victimized bodies: sexual violence policy in England and Wales', *Critical Social Policy*, 30(3): 359–383

Tucker, S., Martyn, M., Bejenaru, A., Brotherton, G., Gahleitner, S., Gunderson, C. and Rusu, H. (2011) *Violence, Exploitation and Trafficking: Service User Perspectives*, research report, Children, Young People and Families Research Centre, Newman University. Available online at www.newman.ac.uk/files/w3/Research/pdf/DAPHNE%202009-10%20E%20 version.pdf (accessed July 2012)

Walby, S. and Towers, J. (2012) 'Measuring the impact of cuts in public expenditure on the provision of services to prevent violence against women and girls', report, Trust for London, Department of Trade and Industry. Available online at www.trustforlondon.org.uk/VAWG%20Full%20report.pdf (accessed October 2012)

Wilcox, P. (2006) 'Communities, care and domestic violence', *Critical Social Policy*, 26(4): 722–747

Women's Aid Federation (2007) 'What is domestic violence?' Women's Aid website. Available online at www.womensaid.org.uk/domestic-violence-articles.asp?section=0001 0001002200410001&itemid=1272 (accessed July 2012)

10

YOUNG PEOPLE, DIGITAL MEDIA AND RISK

A problem of polarisation

Stephen Dixon

Introduction

In the wake of the 2011 UK riots, and disregarding the fact that more people used such tools to organise clean-up operations, David Cameron's first response was to propose a ban on the use of Facebook, Twitter and Blackberry Messenger. Two months later, Lissa Paul celebrated the fact that the riots and the Occupy Wall Street protests demonstrated that the young perpetrators 'know how to communicate very effectively and they also know very well how to use the power generated by their ability to communicate' (Paul 2011, p.8). Such reactions demonstrate the often confused debate around young people's use of digital technology – one that too often centres on the technology itself rather than its use, and one that can simultaneously invoke alarmist knee-jerk reactions and celebrations of emancipation.

This chapter will look at perceptions of risk with regard to young people's use of the internet and digital media, showing how much of the debate is polarised and emotive, portraying young people as either technologically savvy or extremely vulnerable. This polarisation is, it will be argued, unhelpful, echoing earlier moral panics in the popular media. Examining more recent policies and publications as well as internet safety initiatives and organisations, the chapter will examine contemporary responses to the debate, identifying common risks that young people face online.

It will be argued that to identify any perceived risks and issues of vulnerability they have to be contextualised against an understanding of technological development and its associated discourses in relation to young people, as well as a realistic examination of young people's use of digital media. As such, one could argue that the shift to so-called 'web 2.0' and 'media 2.0' tools (particularly social media and social networking sites) and the proliferation of access platforms has widened the scope of the debate beyond mere communication and access to encompass a wide range of 'traditional' media. For example, expressing concerns over the premature sexualisation of young people and in the wake of the furore surrounding the Rihana/Christine Aguilera routines on the 2010 final of *The X Factor*, David Cameron endorsed a report by Reg Bailey (Chief Executive of the Mothers' Union) that found Ofcom's controls on age-appropriateness too weak. This preoccupation with the traditional 9 p.m. watershed completely misunderstood the way that 'television' is now produced, distributed and watched. Traditional television content can now largely be viewed irrespective of time and place, the rise of video on demand services and proliferation of platforms meaning that people are not only watching at different times but viewing via PCs, phones and games consoles. The report betrays a misunderstanding of both the nature of technology and its use, and also utilises a model of media effects which, it will be seen, is now widely discredited.

Issues of e-safety education and the response to perceived risks in both school and home will also be discussed. For example, many school and local authority policies have historically advocated a restrictive, protectionist approach to technology through the use of 'walled garden' systems, censorship software and blocked or limited access to sites, and there has been a corresponding rise in home-use tools such as filtering software and parental controls. Set against this is the increasing realisation that such moves, as well as being often ineffective, may adversely magnify issues of vulnerability through restricting young people's opportunities, understanding and development. Whilst exploring examples of good practice and recommending an approach that both empowers young people and promotes a model of resilience, recent political developments are identified that potentially render such approaches problematic.

A question of context

To gain any understanding of the potential risk that young people face when using the internet and digital media, we first need to contextualise these against recent technological developments and the prevailing discourses that surround them. We are living in an era of often bewildering technological change and it will be seen that the development of digital media and the effects that these are seen to have on users have fundamentally changed ideas of childhood. Much of this can be seen as a *reaction* to technological development itself, as Green and Haddon illustrate:

> Every new medium with the potential to reach a mass audience has been a source of concern over its potential impact, and this has usually been conceptualised in negative terms. New media are seen as disrupting existing relations of communication between powerful and powerless, and so threatening existing hierarchies of power and control.
>
> *(2009, p.2)*

The web now has a myriad of tools and resources, each requiring different forms and levels of interaction and involvement. Much has been made of the relatively recent generation of 'web 2.0' tools (DiNucci 1999) available online: the proliferation of blogging sites, online video platforms such as YouTube, wikis (Wikipedia in particular) and social networking sites such as Bebo or Facebook have all been proclaimed as having either the potential to transform young people's education and lives in a positive manner or as both cause and symptom of a variety of generational ills. Undoubtedly there has been a fundamental shift in the way we both access and engage with technology and, potentially, since the common characteristic of the majority of web 2.0 tools is social, each other.

Some commentators – for example, Henry Jenkins (2006) – argue that recent technological developments have caused a cultural shift and that we are now living in a *convergence culture*. This has also caused a shift in the relationship between technologies: increasingly we are seeing a synergy amongst industries and creative practices – film, video games, literature, software development, television and radio – that were traditionally distinct. Consider, for example, how you can now download apps for specific literary texts and 'watch' webcasts of radio shows on your television. Similarly, we are also seeing a simultaneous proliferation of devices that can now access (and, importantly, allow the creation of) media content. Think of the myriad ways in which mobile phones are used, for example. Typically, modern mobile phone devices also have internet access capability and can be used for texting, playing games, web browsing, social networking, watching video content, tweeting, checking emails, taking photographs, making videos and listening to music – it would seem, actually, that making a phone call is one of the ways in which they are least used.

In parallel with these technological developments has been a proliferation of polarised discourses on the effects that new technologies and digital media have on young people. Many arguments focus on simple 'generational differences', and education has not been immune in this respect. In 2001 the American writer Marc Prensky published a short but provocative essay entitled 'Digital Natives, Digital Immigrants', arguing that education was dangerously out of step with the behaviour and philosophy of its student population, the 'digital natives'. Arguing that young people's lives were now immersed in technologies that were helping to redefine the very nature of social interaction, he argued that they were now separated from previous generations by their sophisticated technological skills and new cognitive abilities. Dixon and Sanders (2012, p.13) highlight some of the difficulties of this polarised view:

> [T]his persuasive discourse has proliferated over the last ten years, with Raines' (2002) 'Generation Y', Veen's (2004, p.3) 'Homo Zappiens', Oblinger and Oblinger's (2005, p.24) 'Milennials', Tapscott's (2008, p.3) 'Screenagers', and more recently, Palfrey and Gasser's (2008, p.3) 'Digital Settlers' and Rosen's (2010, p.20) 'Net Generation' and 'I-Generation'.

> Each … presupposes an innate affinity with digital constructs, and unquestioned high levels of media and digital literacy.

Other writers, whilst agreeing that the use of technology and social media is having a profound effect on young people, have focused on the perceived dangers, playing directly on generational fears. Looking more specifically at the impact on young children, Sue Palmer (2006) cites electronic media as a contributory factor towards what she terms 'toxic childhood', arguing that technology causes children to retreat into their own solitary virtual worlds and lose opportunities for 'real play'. For this she cites research from Japan, where the term *hikikomori* has been coined to describe individuals who increasingly withdraw from human contact, and only communicate through virtual or online means (2006, p.258). Similarly, an over-reliance on media-led activities is seen as being associated with poor eating habits (think of the online gamer who constantly snacks) and even a lack of sleep (children have too many digital distractions in their bedrooms). Arguing that the mind needs to 'slow down' in order to read, Palmer argues that technology is having a bad impact on literacy levels among young people because it speeds up the mind and facilitates 'quick-fix learning'. Ignoring the myriad number of ways that young people now communicate, Palmer seems fixated on the stereotypical view of the young lone gamer: 'The more they "play", the less socially adept they become' (Palmer 2006, p.258).

This sense of moral outrage is nothing new, however. Writing in 1993, the American media theorist Neil Postman warned that 'The uncontrolled growth of technology destroys the vital sources of our humanity. It creates a culture without a moral foundation. It undermines certain mental processes and social relations that make human life worth living' (Postman 1993, p.xiii). Palmer may have some valid concerns, and, to be fair, not all of her argument is pessimistic – 'technology can enrich their children's lives as much as it enriches the lives of most adults' (2006, p.267). However, a distinction does have to be drawn in that many of her fears refer not to the tools themselves but to their inappropriate or poorly devised educational use and to patterns of behaviour that are also observed in non-educational contexts.

Furthermore, in taking technology and social media as their starting point, one could argue that both Palmer and Prensky, whilst ideologically opposed, are making the same mistake: both coming from a *technological determinist* angle where the child is perceived as having no *agency*. Both are also using old-fashioned, widely discredited models that claim that media have simple direct and causal effects, rather than contextualising media use and taking into account a wide array of increasingly complex phenomenon. Furthermore, more recent research, such as that carried out by Plowman *et al.* (2010), highlight a disjunction between those warning of the toxic effects of technology and parents' own perceptions. Although many parents, having grown up pre-digitally, are seen as lacking an 'informing model' on technology use, most were seen as happy with the role of technology in their children's lives, even when aware of the 'toxic' concerns expressed in the popular media.

Other writers claim a more scientific approach. In sensationally titled articles such as 'Is Google making us stupid?' (2008) and his book, *The Shallows: How the internet is changing the way we think, read and remember* (2010), Nicholas Carr argues that the online environment promotes cursory reading, distracted thinking and superficial learning. Citing neurological and psychological research, he claims that online activity is chipping away at our capacity for concentration and contemplation. The UK scientist Susan Greenfield (2008) argues that excessive use of electronic media compromises learning and can cause selfishness and attention deficiency in young people. Citing that addictive game playing stimulates excessive dopamine production, she claims that this can lead to a loss of attention span and, more disturbingly, ultimately dysfunctional behaviour and a distorted perception of reality. Such arguments have been popular with much of the British press, both tabloid and broadsheet, leading to sensationalist headlines such as 'How Facebook Addiction is Damaging Your Child's Brain' (*Daily Mail*) and 'Facebook and Bebo risk "infantilising" the human mind' (*The Guardian*). Such coverage is symptomatic of much of the debate on young people's use of digital technology. Indeed, seemingly lone voices such as that of social researcher Paul Flatters (2012), who argues that the internet is a force for good for children and can improve their educational attainment and broaden their social networks in a positive way, tend to be drowned out in the cacophony of negative coverage.

Looking at these debates in the context of Green and Haddon's argument, many can be seen as knee-jerk reactions in a time of change – even Greenfield recognises the need for further research into the effects that computing and the use of electronic media have on the brain. And placed in a historical context, the arguments are not new. The Greek philosopher Plato (through his mouthpiece, Socrates) argued that technology would destroy human thinking processes as it lacked the flexibility of speech and would lead to human forgetfulness: the technology he was referring to was *writing*. The Roman writer Seneca also complained of the distractions of technology – caused by having too many books to read. Yet articles on the damaging impact of technology on young people proliferate in the popular press, where headlines are overwhelmingly negative except when they are about a precociously talented teenager making their first internet million or confounding their teachers with their app-building skills. Buckingham (2007, p.85) identifies this polarisation in the construction of the child, be it vulnerable and in need of protection, or liberated and empowered by technology, arguing that much of this stems from adults' sense of exclusion from children's digital culture.

Reflective Activity

Recently, there has been much in the popular media about the dangers of too much 'screen-time' for young people, be it their use of television, computers, hand-held devices or games consoles. For example, one recent report by the National Trust warned of the dangers of 'Nature Deficit

Disorder' in our nation's childhood. Have a look at the proliferation of discourses surrounding these ideas (a simple Google search will yield a wealth of material).

Do you think that the debate is balanced?
Is NDD (Nature Deficit Disorder) a recognised medical term?
Why do you think such language is being used?

The web, social media and risk

This polarisation, which is often emotive in nature, is really not helpful in any rational debate on young people's use of technology and issues of safety and, it could be argued, has led to enhanced public anxiety about perceived risks when children use the internet and social media. As Tanya Byron states in *Safer Children in a Digital World*, her review of the potential risks that children face when using the internet and video games (see below), 'panic and fear often drown out the evidence' (2008, p.1). If we again consider the popular press, barely a week goes by without media headlines proclaiming that the internet is an inappropriate or even dangerous place for learning to take place, encouraging antisocial and even self-destructive behaviour; they highlight the shortcomings of Wikipedia, the dangers of blogs that espouse strong opinions or contain offensive messages and the ample evidence in YouTube of internet misuse and abuse. A trawl of recent headlines reveals a bewildering array of the perceived dangers: dumbing down, grooming, computer viruses, happy slapping, pornography and inappropriate content, a lack of information skills, contact with paedophiles, cyberbullying, suicide sites, plagiarism, piracy and illegal downloading, erosion of traditional reading skills, brain re-wiring and even wi-fi cancers. The wide-ranging nature of these perceived risks shows how ubiquitous the web and social media have become and how new emotive terms (e.g. *happy slapping*) have entered our vocabulary to describe its dangers. As a result, there is little agreement on the level and nature of risk that young people are exposed to in their use of technology.

It could be argued that few of these perceived risks are new, but the medium of access and exposure is different. As early as 2005, in the early days of web 2.0, North and McKeown highlighted:

> There is a good chance that young people will access unsuitable materials. They have of course always been able to find print material which others might deem unsuitable. The difference with the web and email is that some of the material may come looking for them.
>
> *(2005, p.100)*

More recently, the advent of web 2.0 tools that allow for greater communication and collaboration across a range of different media have increased the propensity for connecting people together and, in consequence, the possibility of e-safety issues has arisen. This, to some extent, has been recognised by young people themselves: Tarapdar and Kellett (2011, p.8) show, for example, how 78 per cent of young people interviewed felt that levels of cyberbullying would increase due to the evolving nature of technology.

However, there is also the distinct possibility that the polarised debate is 'over-blowing' the hyped risks to the detriment of the 'rational risks' that young people face online on a daily basis. Again, this is nothing new – research from David Buckingham at the Institute of Education in 2004 warned of the danger that parental fears actually meant that children were not being given the information they need to behave safely and sensibly online, as awareness of risks extended only to those most frequently promoted by moral campaigners. In other words, fears that children are meeting murderers and being groomed online mean that the real and more frequent dangers of web and social media use are ignored. Children who haven't had adequate e-safety training worry about 'urban myths' such as bomb-making information and hackers taking control of their PCs. Indeed, Cranmer *et al.* (2009, p.136) highlight how young children's portrayal of potential risks (such as the health risks of being too close to hardware) are often exaggerated or even fantastical. For the pupils in their study, e-safety remains an abstract and poorly understood concept, and this is a cause for concern, notwithstanding that the same pupils clearly see e-safety as an issue that needs to be addressed in school.

More recently, a lot of work has been done in an attempt to formulate a rational classification of the risks that young people face when using the web and social media. Echoing much of the excellent work done by Livingstone *et al.* in their *Risks and safety on the internet: The perspective of European children* (2011a), Becta, the now sadly defunct UK government agency that promoted and advised on the use of new technologies in schools, identified the potential risks under four main headings, Content, Contact, Conduct and Commerce:

> **Content** – this may mean exposure to content that is unsuitable, potentially illegal, offensive or pirated, be it pornographic, racist, violent or inaccurate. The advent of web 2.0 tools and new means of sharing information give rise to questions about the motivations and authority of those who produce content and hence about its reliability. Furthermore, through, for example, social networking sites, young people are now producing their own content, which gives rise to possible issues of privacy and identity theft. There are also issues of intellectual property to consider – the ability to share content online has resulted in a growth of copyright theft, be it music or homework.
>
> **Contact** – this may be unwelcome or inappropriate contact, such as grooming or sexual contact. Many recent technological developments blur the boundary between public and private, providing new opportunities for self-expression and communication but also placing the user at risk. Issues can arise if inappropriate individuals are able to use technology to get in

touch with children or young people, for example via chatrooms, emails, social networking sites or text messaging.

Conduct – focusing on young people's online behaviour, this could be as a recipient or as an active participant – and involve, for example, giving out too much personal information or the bullying of another person.

Commerce – this could be 'phishing' or other methods of identity theft. Unscrupulous companies have been known to use mobile phones and the internet to promote or sell often largely worthless goods and services to children and young people, and in doing so extract valuable commercial information such as household income levels and expenditure patterns. Furthermore, new internet-based services provide significant opportunities for 'personalised' marketing and for gathering data about individual consumers, which may be less apparent than traditional forms of advertising.

(adapted from Becta 2010)

Such classification exercises are an essential first step in both *mapping out the territory* in order to understand the nature of online risks that young people face and providing a solid foundation for any effective e-safety educational programme. They have also allowed for more focused research into diverse and specific areas of perceived risk, such as CIBER's identification of a lack of information retrieval skills in young people (2008), or investigations of cyberbullying, an area of increasing concern. Cyberbullying can be defined as 'bullying that occurs through media and communication devices such as mobile phones, email, and the Internet (e.g. social networking sites, web pages and blogs)' (Rivers and Noret 2010, p.644), and can be a more pervasive threat than traditional forms of bullying. The use of technology means that the home no longer provides its traditional sanctuary and malicious material can be distributed to a much wider audience. In 2005, *Action for Children* found that 20 per cent of 770 young people surveyed had experienced some form of bullying through technology (Rivers and Noret 2010, p.645), and more recent studies highlight how this figure appears to be growing. For example, in their report *Young People's Voices on Cyberbullying: What Can Age Comparisons Tell Us?*, Tarapdar and Kellett (2011) recognise the continued growth of cyberbullying, often surpassing the speed of response and intervention. Although showing that most cyberbullying occurs in a non-persistent manner, their study identifies a disturbing 38 per cent of young people as being either victims of or witnesses to cyberbullying, with a greater number of older children at risk than younger children. The most common forms are seen to be abusive e-mails (26 per cent), abusive texts (24 per cent) and prank and silent calls (19 per cent) (2011, p.7). They rightly identify the scope for greater intervention and provide a number of key recommendations, many of which will be covered later in this chapter.

Some researchers have also identified varying levels of vulnerability amongst young people according to their social status or background. Much has been made in recent years of the so-called 'digital divide', a polarity which originally differentiated between those who had access to technology and those who did not.

Although obviously still an issue at an international level, web and social media use amongst young people in the UK can be seen as very much the norm – for example, in February 2012 the Office for National Statistics (ONS) (2012) estimated that 98.7 per cent of 16–24-year-olds used the internet on a regular basis, although figures for younger children are unavailable. A digital divide in terms of access seems very much predicated in terms of wealth – as recently as 2010, the E-Learning Foundation warned of an estimated 2 million children from poorer families not having internet access at home, and ONS figures still show a disturbing correlation between access and family income, with internet access for the children in families earning less than £200 per week dropping to 91.9 per cent. Discussing the link between wealth and access, Sue Palmer clearly makes her feelings known – children from the 'other side of the tracks' are, she argues, disadvantaged by a lack of access to worthwhile digital technology in the home, and 'too wide an access to junk TV and mindless computer games' (Palmer 2006, p.279). Such emotive language and use of sweeping generalisations is really not helpful to the debate.

Much of the digital divide debate has shifted from a polarisation of 'information-haves' and 'information-have-nots' to one that focuses more on the skills needed to use the web and social media more effectively – a shift to another polarisation of 'information-cans' and 'information-cannots'. However, any new differentiation between users could still be predicated on wealth – Woollard *et al.*, for example, in their discussion of e-safety materials, identify that:

> It is likely that the context of the activity and the individual child's characteristics will have a greater influence on the effects of the activity than the activity itself. For example, children from more deprived backgrounds may be more at risk online because of a lack of confidence with new technology or because their parents are less likely to be engaged with their children's use of the internet.
>
> *(2009, p.40)*

Such generational understandings of a digital divide echo Prensky's 'digital native' argument and are also highlighted by Byron (2008), who discusses how parents' concerns about their children's internet use are exacerbated by their ignorance of what these children are experiencing. Furthermore, Barber and Cooper (2012, p.22) claim that this divide can also potentially be applied to education, as seen in the relationship between the pupil and the teacher, particularly where the former is stereotypically seen as 'techno-savvy' and the latter lacking in confidence. Livingstone (2009, p.16) shows how this echoes the usual polarised view of young people's use of technology – that young people are vulnerable and the internet introduces potential dangers, or that young people are competent, media-savvy and probably know more about technology than their parents.

In their work on the *EU Kids Online* project, Livingstone *et al.* (2011b) identify how some minority groups amongst young people may face particular challenges online. Agreeing that some children may be disadvantaged by a lack of economic or cultural capital, they also highlight that some groups may also be disadvantaged through social or psychological vulnerability. A simplified and polarised view, however, does not help our understanding:

> [A]lthough the internet and online technologies afford an array of interlinked opportunities and risks, there is no necessary mapping of opportunities onto benefits or risks onto harms as experienced by children. Instead, what the internet makes available to children interacts with a range of individual and contextual factors to determine outcomes. These may be positive or negative in ways yet to be fully understood.
>
> *(Livingstone* et al. *2011a)*

In their final report (2011b), the authors do much to debunk many of the myths concerning young people's use of the web and social media, and their findings are interesting to map against Becta's classification of risk (above). Pointing out that myths about internet safety tend to exaggerate or oversimplify, as well as often being out of date, Livingstone *et al.* highlight the top ten myths:

1 Bullies are baddies
   Finding both bully and victim psychologically vulnerable, the project found that 40 per cent of online bullies had been bullied online themselves.

2 People you meet on the internet are strangers
   Only 9 per cent of respondents met offline someone they first met online – most (87 per cent) 11–16-year-olds are in touch online with people they know face to face.

3 Offline risks migrate online
   In part, the evidence is seen to support this (children who report more offline risks are more likely to report more risk encounters online), with the important proviso that we still don't know all the factors that account for online harm, and it is important to see risks in context.

4 Digital natives know it all
   This is exaggerated, and obscures children's need for support in developing digital skills. Only 36 per cent of 9–16-year-olds say it is 'very true' that 'I know more about the internet than my parents', with 31 per cent saying it is 'a bit true'.

5 Everyone is creating their own content now
   Whilst social networking allows for easy upload content, very few file-share, have avatars or write a blog – most children use the internet for ready-made, mass-produced content.

6 Under-13s can't use social networking sites so no worries
Many 'underage' users register with a false age, with 38 per cent of 9–12-year-olds having an SNS profile.

7 Everyone is watching porn online
Estimates are lower than anticipated – one-quarter saw sexual images in the past year online or offline, and one in seven saw them online, rising to a quarter of older teens. It seems that media hype over pornography is based on unrepresentative samples or just supposition.

8 Putting the PC in the living room will help
This is very out of date and does not reflect on the myriad ways we now go online – 53 per cent go online at a friend's house, 49 per cent in their bedroom and 33 per cent via a mobile phone or hand-held device.

9 Teaching digital skills will reduce online risk
Although more skills could reduce the harm that some children experience from online risk, paradoxically they are associated with more, not less, risk, as greater use leads to more skills, more skills lead to more opportunities and opportunities are linked to risk. Opportunities and risks are linked because children must explore and encounter some risk to learn and gain resilience.

10 Children can get around safety software
Although nearly a half think their parents' actions limit their online activities, only 28 per cent of 11–16-year-olds say they can change filter preferences.

Adapted from Livingstone *et al.* (2011b)

Their findings highlight a complex range of factors when considering young people's use of the web and social media, particularly in how their use cannot be reduced to an old-fashioned model of linear, one-way effects. Furthermore, as will be seen below, a polarised understanding does not help to inform either the debate or any effective policy.

Reflective Activity

Consider your own use of technology and your 'digital footprint'. How much information about yourself is freely available online? Have you ever Googled yourself? Do you have a social networking account, and if you do, have you looked at the security settings for this? Did you even read the user agreement when you signed up? Do you use the same password for a range of accounts? Do you use online banking? If you do, are you sure it is secure? A mere 30 minutes of reviewing your digital footprint can often yield some rather surprising results …

From polarity to policy

Early guidelines on safe internet use for young people tended to be brief and limited in scope. Publications for parents, such as Parry Aftab's *The Parent's Guide to Protecting Your Children in Cyberspace* (1999), or more educational guidelines, such as the charity Action for Children's publication *Get IT Safe* (2006), were well-intentioned but quickly dated, lacking a breadth of scope and failing to keep pace with rapid technological developments. In 2008, amid rising media panic over the perceived dangers of digital media, Professor Tanya Byron was commissioned by the then prime minister to carry out an independent review of the risks children face from the internet and video games. Byron initially commissioned three literature reviews on the effects of video games and the internet on children, children's brain development and child development. These reviews were used to inform the Byron Review (Byron 2008), a widely disseminated report with a strong evidence-based tone, generally well received by parenting groups and the media industry, as well as the UK education community. The Review considers aspects of e-safety with regard to 'content', 'contact' and 'conduct' (again echoing the findings of *EU Kids Online*) and very much advocates a dual approach that encourages both information and guidance, identifying the need to 'build children's resilience to the material to which they may be exposed so that they have the confidence and skills to navigate these new media waters more safely' (Byron 2008, p.8). The key findings of the Review are as follows:

- Internet and video games are very popular with children and young people and offer a range of opportunities for fun, learning and development.
- There are some concerns over potentially inappropriate material, which range from content (e.g. violence) through to contact and conduct of children in the digital world.
- Debates and research in this area can be highly polarised and charged with emotion.
- Need to move from a discussion about the media 'causing' harm to one which focuses on children and young people, what they bring to technology and how we can use our understanding of how they develop to empower them to manage risks and make the digital world safer.
- Generational digital divide means that parents often feel unequipped to help their children – can be compounded by a risk-averse culture which inclines us to keep our children 'indoors' despite their developmental needs to socialise and take risks.
- Children are confident with technology, but they are still developing critical evaluation skills and need our help to make decisions.
- Need a shared culture of responsibility, with families, industry, government and others all playing their part to reduce the availability of potentially harmful material, restrict access to it by children and increase children's resilience.

- Need for a national strategy for child internet safety which involves better self-regulation and better provision of information and education for children and families.

Adapted from Byron (2008, p.2)

Importantly, the Byron Review eschews the use of emotive language, which Selwyn (2011), amongst others, has also identified as problematic, citing that young people are adversely affected by exaggerated fears. The report does examine the potential harm to children caused by exposure to inappropriate materials, suggesting that there is a growing body of research pointing to a link between such exposure and negative beliefs and attitudes. Byron also highlights the fears that children do not yet have the necessary skills to recognise material that, for example, reinforces stereotypical or even negative images or which has inappropriate commercial content. Children are seen as lacking the necessary critical skills to interpret and judge, particularly as they are still attempting to establish these rules offline. Byron identifies a need for clear instruction and moral guidance, with adults simultaneously empowering young people 'to take responsibility for their own online behaviours' (Byron 2008, p.109). The Review also draws on child development literature, arguing that understanding the way children learn can be a useful guide to identifying and managing potential online risks, as well as arguing that perceptions of online risk are part of wider changes in social norms. There is a strong irony, for example, in the fact that in increasingly keeping our children at home (inherent in our so-called risk-averse culture) and allowing excessive use of new technologies we may be inadvertently exposing children to a greater potential of online risk.

The Review is wide reaching, ranging from a call for more public awareness of 'safe-search' options to recommending a review of the methods used for online age verification. The Review's scope allows Byron to look at the impact of a range of specific web tools and social media as well as young people's behaviour. On social networking, for example, the Review identifies the problem that social network sites 'group' children together, with no consideration for age – this can provide further avenues and potential risk for inappropriate contact and possibly cyberbullying. Byron reports on increasing evidence that people *change their behaviour* offline, often because of the lack of gatekeepers and visual cues that we use to moderate our interactions offline. As such, in many ways this can be seen as facilitating a less risk-averse approach in dealing with others online, the lack of contextual clues freeing social inhibition. Interestingly, on the subject of video game addiction (one of the areas least covered), Byron concludes that, although excessive time spent playing could be a cause for concern, very few children fit the criteria for true addiction and there is a lack of research evidence (particularly longitudinal) on the impact of video games on child development.

One of the recommendations of the Byron Review was the formation of the UK Council for Child Internet Safety, which was launched in September 2008. Comprised of more than 140 organisations and individuals, the Council includes government departments and agencies, law enforcement companies, charities, parenting groups and academics and sees itself 'as a partnership where responsible organisations involved with the internet and children's welfare come together to help children and young people enjoy the benefits of the internet whilst staying safe from the risks' (UKCCIS 2009). Complementing work done by CEOP (the Child Exploitation and Online Protection Centre) and building on local, national and international initiatives such as the Taskforce on Child Protection on the Internet and the EU Safer Internet Programme, the Council's 'Click Clever, Click Safe' code, seen as the first UK child internet safety strategy, was published in 2009.

The aims of the Council are threefold: the creation of a safer online environment, giving everybody the skills, knowledge and understanding to help children and young people stay safe online, and inspiring safe and responsible use and behaviour (UKCCIS 2009). These objectives are to be fulfilled through the use of campaigns, training, information and resources, with the intention that companies and providers are periodically reviewed against a code of practice. In terms of vulnerability, the strategy recognises that some children who may be more vulnerable to harm in the offline world – due, for example, to a disability or home-life issues – may also be more vulnerable online. Interestingly, it also identifies young people whose technical skills are very high as being potentially more vulnerable, as these skills may be 'ahead of their ability to judge sensibly' (UKCCIS 2009). One of the Council's specific aims is to understand and take account of the needs of vulnerable groups and look at issues of changing vulnerability as children develop.

Digital safety is now included in the definition of safeguarding that OFSTED uses to judge schools and, as a direct response to the Byron Review, it published *The safe use of new technologies* (OFSTED 2010). Much of this report advocates a shift in practice (see below), from protectionism to empowerment, and the promotion of a resilience model – requiring pupils to take responsibility themselves for using new technologies safely is seen as the way forward. Arguing that blanket restrictions on internet use leave children unprepared to deal with online risk, the report echoes the argument of Buckingham (2004) in finding that pupils whose schools use a prohibitive, heavily filtered network are ultimately more vulnerable, arguing that they lack the skills needed to protect themselves online, and that schools that use a 'managed system' are ultimately more successful in terms of e-safety: 'a child whose use of the internet is closely monitored at school will not necessarily develop the level of understanding required to use new technologies responsibly in other contexts' (OFSTED 2010). More recent research, such as that of Davies and Merchant (2009), has also advocated this approach, identifying how educational programmes are likely to be 'far more effective if real experience is provided rather than the alternative of applying blocks, filters and other controls' (Davies and Merchant 2009, p.112).

Highlighting this shift in approach, the report recommends that schools help pupils learn how to *manage* risk, arguing that to achieve this, schools need to be active in three main areas: e-safety curriculum development, the provision of training to enable all members of staff to support pupils, and helping families to keep their children safe. The report also highlights examples of what it considers good practice, describing how one secondary school, for example, provided an excellent e-safety curriculum through part of the personal, social and health education programme. In addition, both pupils and parents were able to access ten e-safety lessons on the school website from home. This latter facility is key, as the report recommends that schools need to work closely with families in promoting e-safety issues – other examples of good practice have included e-safety displays in areas which pupils' families are likely to visit, one-to-one meetings where advice is available from trained staff, and the provision of an online forum where families can share information on online safety. Bearing in mind disparities in access, however (see above), schools would need to consider how to provide this information to families who do not have an internet connection.

In a more recent report, and despite recognising that many children spend considerably more time online outside school, OFSTED has called for schools to continue to adopt a robust approach to managing safety and to keep policy and practice under continuous review (OFSTED 2011). Identifying that staff training around issues of e-safety is a relative weakness, particularly when responsibility for it has not been delegated or when plans have not been made to include it within training related to child protection or ICT, the report argues that the provision of training is often not systematic and its impact not monitored. However, many of OFSTED's recommendations focus very much on PC use at school and home, with little (if any) discussion of the use of digital and mobile devices or cultural issues of convergence. Furthermore, OFSTED advocates a multi-agency approach to development, arguing that schools need more support from the Department for Children, Schools and Families, BECTA, CEOP and local authorities. As will be seen, more recent political developments have rendered this approach problematic.

From policy to practice

Looked at historically, the use of the internet in education seems to be one of both protectionism and opportunity. Notwithstanding the recommendations of both the Byron Review and OFSTED, for example, there are still contrasting views on and strong disagreements over the use of the internet in schools. Woollard (2011, p.37) identifies a three-level approach:

1 there is the issue of harm (to others, and psychologically to the user);
2 the use of restrictions to reduce risk (such as that advocated by Livingstone);
3 education as the key to promoting online safety and appropriate behaviour (e.g. Byron).

Since the late 1990s, most schools and local authorities have advocated a protectionist approach, with the use of site-blocking software (many schools still block access to social networking and video-sharing sites, for example), filtering tools, and 'walled gardens' where pupils are only allowed access to an approved range of services and sites. However, many have now identified the shortcomings of this approach, from Buckingham's concurrence with OFSTED and Byron in arguing that 'the use of filtering software is both an ineffective response and a rather self-defeating constraint on students' ability to seek out information and to communicate' (Buckingham 2007, p.94) to Palmer's moral outrage at the unreliability of blocking and filtering services (Palmer 2006, p.259). More recently, Barber and Cooper (2012, p.27) have highlighted that the use of filtering systems, although offering some protection from potential harm, does not represent an all-encompassing solution to e-safety, as they 'can also restrict the opportunity for enquiry and collaboration, the very heart of web 2.0 potential'.

Many schools do take advantage of a range of internet initiatives aimed at promoting e-safety. Childnet International (www.childnet-int.org/) and its accompanying site Kid Smart (www.kidsmart.org.uk/), for example, include a range of excellent projects, education resources and online safety advice for schools, parents and children. Educanet (www.educanet2.ch/) is a European Union-funded programme that aims to teach children how to assess and reduce the risks of internet use, including taking a critical view of what they see online. The award-winning QUICK site – sadly now only available in an archived version – mirrored this approach. An acronym for QUality Information ChecKlist, this was an excellent site for teaching children how to judge the quality of internet information. Although laudable, use of these resources tended to be piecemeal and there is a lack of a coherent approach that all schools could learn from. Following the Byron Review and New Labour's acceptance of its recommendations, the UK Council for Child Internet Safety (UKCCIS) was established, charged with raising awareness of internet safety, and in 2009, an e-safety resource for primary school teachers, *Know IT All for Primary Schools*, was developed as part of the 'Click Clever, Click Safe' programme, and a copy sent to every primary school in England. UKCCIS now promotes an annual Safer Internet Day, and events such as Safer Internet Week in February 2010 (when even the BBC children's show *Newsround* became involved) and Get Safe Online week in November 2011 show how a more co-ordinated approach has moved up the policy agenda. This new approach, rather than being protectionist in nature, encompasses a more realistic model of technology use that promotes both empowerment and resilience. In February 2010, for example, UKCCIS launched 'Zip It, Block It, Flag It', a digital code for parents and children to help them stay safe online. As Byron (2010) highlights, for any approach to be realistic, e-safety issues have to be taught and discussed *online*, using the very tools that young people employ in online activity.

It could be argued that this approach is not new, however. Becta's very successful Websafe Crackerz, a range of micro-sites, online games and spoof pages (in the form of a narrative) aimed at helping young people make informed decisions about using online media, also utilised this approach. As part of a range of publications for the education sector, Becta also provided guidance for learners, learner providers, technical staff, curriculum managers, teachers and training staff. Recognising that schools need to take an institutional and holistic approach to e-safety and utilising a combination of effective **P**olicies and practice, a secure technology **I**nfrastructure and **E**ducation and training for both staff and learners, underpinned by **S**tandards and inspection, the PIES model was developed in 2010.

> Becta's PIES model is an effective framework for approaching safeguarding strategy across learning provision. It offers a simple way of mitigating against risk through a combination of effective policies and practice, a robust and secure technology infrastructure, and education and training for learners and employees alike, underpinned by standards and inspection.
>
> *(Becta 2010)*

Aimed at empowering users to manage risk in the school, workplace, home and beyond and advising institutions that this will only work if policy is considered across any potential partnerships, PIES provided guidelines on how to educate, inform and engage learners through the development of robust frameworks in three main strategic areas: the integration of e-safety into existing practice, the provision of a robust technological infrastructure, and the development of e-safety policies and procedures. Coupled with this was a 'resilience-model' approach to empowering young people, in that 'assessing and understanding risks as they apply to your learners, then taking mitigating action, and empowering learners to protect themselves are key to effective safeguarding in the digital environment' (Becta 2010). An outline of the PIES approach can be seen in the table below:

Integration	Infrastructure	Policy and procedures
Acceptable Use Policy	Firewall	Provision of clear and confident messages about working safely online
Learner course induction	Anti-virus	Educate learners and empower them to make informed choices
Teaching and learning processes	Filters	Equip staff with skills to support learners
Learner support arrangement (including anti-bullying and harassment policy)	Tracking and monitoring systems	Creation of clear lines of responsibility for online safeguarding
Staff development and training		Development of robust e-safety policies for training, monitoring, reporting, supporting and review arrangements

Adapted from Becta 2010

Many of these institutional recommendations are echoed in more recent research. Tarapdar and Kellett's recommendations on countering issues of cyber-bullying, for example, call for the fostering of a better understanding, building capacity and sustainability, maintaining and sharing good practice, and providing direct protection (2011, p.9).

The recommendations also allow schools to build on any current local-level practice, such as acceptable use policies (AUPs). These are user agreements covering issues such as security and behaviour, and in schools generally include rules such as:

- not sharing passwords with others;
- ensuring that any mobile devices used with school equipment do not have viruses;
- not to purposefully access sites that include unsuitable material;
- reporting any suspicious sites or suspicious behaviour witnessed online;
- not make any defamatory comments about others online.

However, even AUPs can be difficult to enforce if staff are not adequately trained or lack the experience or understanding to deal with possible infringements. This is not merely a pragmatic view – learning providers also have a legal responsibility to get this right. Under the Children Act 2004, teachers have the same responsibilities to learners when they are working online as when they are being taught face to face. Interestingly, in the same report, Tarapdar and Kellett (2011, p.6) show how young people themselves recognise the need for e-safety issues to be taught in school, identifying that 99 per cent of young people feel 'safe and secure' at school, and that 94 per cent feel that the school is the most effective place for education and deterrence.

The Byron Review acknowledges the need for monitoring the ICT understanding of teachers and originally recommended that the Training and Development Agency (set to become the Teaching Agency in April 2012) include questions around e-safety in their annual surveys (Byron 2008, pp.8–9). Despite e-safety issues now being firmly embedded in the National Curriculum at key stages 3 and 4, with a growing wealth of material available for key stages 1 and 2, e-safety provision, as OFSTED recognises, can still be patchy in schools. CEOP, for example, which provides information and resources related to e-safety, now has a dedicated area on its site for teacher development called 'Think U Know'. As a growing number of schools adopt web 2.0 tools and social media for use in teaching and learning, these materials are becoming increasingly important, not just in terms of education but for their own practice. Yet there also appears to be a growing confidence in teachers' ability to deal with e-safety issues. In their study on the use of web 2.0 tools in schools, for example, Davies and Merchant claim that 'plenty of guidance is now available and the vast majority of teachers are well aware of how they might deal with issues of exposure to inappropriate material and child protection in online environments' (2009, p.109). Similarly, in *Do We Have*

Safer Children in a Digital World? (2010), Byron claims that 70 per cent of teachers feel that they have necessary knowledge of digital safety and 74 per cent feel they can use this understanding in their teaching. She also reports progress of teacher training through the inclusion of an ICT test for newly qualified teachers (Byron 2010, p.18). There is, however, much progress still to be made: in their research on e-safety in teacher training, Woollard *et al.* (2009) identify in particular that initial teacher training programmes have a full curriculum and difficulty in fitting in 'extra' content. Identifying that the needs of trainees are different to those of practising teachers and utilising (amongst other resources) the *Jenny's Story* DVD, Woollard *et al.* recommend the use of mass lectures to deliver generic e-safety content, followed by group sessions to allow for discussion of issues. A prescriptive approach is very much advocated, highlighting that trainee teachers lack both the time and experience in determining suitable resources for a particular curriculum, class or school context.

Interestingly, Woollard *et al.* also highlight how teacher trainees feel that there is no correlation between e-safety issues and subject specialism, particularly ICT (2009, p.192). Similarly, the Becta guidelines move beyond the idea that e-safety is merely an IT issue, advocating a much more holistic approach. Indeed, if e-safety is added as a 'bolt-on' to ICT or Citizenship lessons, there is a danger it may be perceived as a 'dampener' by pupils – a view echoed by Byron's call for digital safety and digital literacy skills to be embedded across the curriculum (2010). Others from outside the education sector have also called for an approach that moves beyond merely educating children and young people as to the risks in using the web and social media (necessary though this is), to one that advocates empowerment and a sense of trust that young people, given the right tools, will be able to deal with situations they may find themselves in online. Speaking at the Empowering Children and Young People in a Digital World conference in 2010, Ann-Marie Born of the East Riding Safeguarding Children Board argues that e-safety issues do not rest with steering groups or IT departments in schools but with *all* practitioners. Although the primary focus of Local Safeguarding Children Boards (LSCBs) is the 'staying safe' outcome, other functions include communication and raising awareness through informing, enabling, educating and encouraging partners, agencies, parents and carers. For this reason, the development, publicising and delivery of a range of training programmes, as well as practices and procedures, is advocated, recognising that LSCBs will need to include e-safety as an everyday part of their core business – although this is only likely to come about if e-safety becomes a National Indicator (Born 2010).

Reflective Activity

Think back to your own use of technology in school. Did your school have an Acceptable Use Policy? Did you have your own username and password?

Were there limits on what you could access online? Were e-safety issues discussed, or even formally taught? Were you taught how to 'safe-search'? Did your school have a cyberbullying policy? If it did, how might this have been improved?

Moving away from the moral panic

Stanley Cohen first brought the term 'moral panic' into widespread discussion in 1972, in his now classic book, *Folk Devils and Moral Panics* (Cohen 2011), showing how both the media and those with political power define a social group or condition as a threat to perceived social values. Some of the common themes he discusses include how popular culture is seen as damaging, new cultural forms and technologies as dangerous, young people as most at risk (or the biggest 'threat') and how the 'innocence' of childhood must be protected. These themes are often cyclical in nature, emerging from the search for explanation in public discourse, a need to attribute blame, demands for action and a disregarding or even ridiculing of research that contradicts popular assumptions. Consider, for example, the following damning indictments of a popular pastime: 'It wastes thousands of hours in the misapplication of time', it is 'dangerous and habit-forming' and it creates an 'insatiable craving for novelty'. These are not modern newspaper headlines on young people's use of digital media, nor even the impact of television or the 'dangers' of rock and roll, but contemporary fears over women's reading habits in the eighteenth and nineteenth centuries (Pearson 1999). Cohen shows how these often hysterical discourses quickly become part of the popular imagination, whilst simultaneously inhibiting any rational debate.

Byron (2010) recognises that child digital safety is becoming more embedded within public consciousness and the education system, as well as there being increased media debate around the issue. However, reporting is still seen to predominantly focus on the extreme and tragic, and she urges those reporting 'to take a proportionate and balanced view to ensure that they represent the needs of all children and young people who engage with the digital world' (Byron 2010). Canadian studies have also identified the need for this approach. Arguing that young people's growing engagement with media warrants a reworking of critical pedagogy in the context of a risk society, Kline *et al.* (2006, p.141) identify that 'media literacy programmes can reduce risks associated with children's media use' and are in fact essential in enabling learners to become useful, intelligent and responsible citizens. This, then, is very much a cultural issue, and if we are to teach young people how to manage online risk, we first need to understand online behaviour – not just the context (and indeed content) of online communication but how online behaviour may differ from that offline – in order to offer guidance on appropriate use of social media and suitable strategies for challenging inappropriate behaviour.

It can be seen that much of the moral panic around young people's use of digital and social media is technologically deterministic in nature and hence is starting from the wrong viewpoint. In 2007, Vint Cerf, one of the founders of Google, argued that the internet was merely a reflection of society, as most of the content was contributed by users: 'When you have a problem in the mirror you do not fix the mirror, you fix that which is reflected in the mirror' (BBC News 2007). Any successful media literacy programme that encompasses e-safety would need to avoid a technologically deterministic approach whilst simultaneously engaging young people at a realistic level. As Byron (2010) highlights, it is the same funda-mental attributes of the internet and online sources that both create potential risks and simultaneously empower young people and allow for personal development. Yet as Buckingham (2007) shows, there is a gap between internet and digital media use inside and outside school, one being often quite limited and the other allowing for a great deal of communication and entertainment. In arguing for schools to help develop children's critical and creative capabilities with regard to new media – a form of 'digital media literacy' (2007, p.144), Buckingham highlights the dangers of this approach, labelling it the 'new digital divide'. This is similarly labelled by Selwyn as the 'digital disconnect' (2011, p.29), and, in an argument that echoes that of OFSTED, he identifies how schools' 'risk-averse' ICT policies are actually hindering expansive uses of new technology.

Some commentators, such as Woollard, have called for a more centralised approach, identifying 'the need to establish the requirements as well as values of e-safety awareness through the Professional Standards and "statutory and non-statutory curricular frameworks" including the UK National Curriculum, the common core of skills, and the UK Children's [sic] Act' (Woollard et al. 2009, p.198). Such an argument makes perfect sense and also allows practitioners to build on policy which is already in place. In terms of cyberbullying, for example, the Education and Inspections Act of 2006 already 'gives headteachers the ability to ensure that pupils behave when they are not on school premises or under the lawful control of school staff' (Department for Education 2011). Recent political developments, however, have delivered potentially serious blows to such an approach. As stated above, and despite excellent work in promoting the use of technology (including issues of e-safety) in schools, the Coalition government deemed Becta an unnecessary 'quango' and cut its funding in April 2011. Similarly, and notwithstanding its recommendation as the host of a one-stop-shop for child digital safety information by UKCCIS, the announcement in 2010 that CEOP will be merged with the Serious and Organised Crime Agency (SOCA) and UK Border Agency in 2013 has led to fears of loss of valuable work done to support victims and develop educational resources. Citing the ensuing resignation of CEOP's chief executive as symptomatic of the sense of betrayal felt by many child safety organisations, child protection consultants have bemoaned the potential risk to e-safety programmes: 'You cannot approach child protection with a "crime-only" police unit. We need a proactive child protection centre, not just a reactive police approach' (Booth 2010).

Conclusion

In tackling issues of vulnerability and young people's use of digital media, there is a need for an informed and consultative dialogue between partners and an approach that encapsulates realistic notions of risk. A risk-free childhood is no childhood. This is not to belittle the potential dangers that young people face whilst engaging with online media but, as Livingstone highlights, 'learning to take calculated risks, and to cope with the consequences, is central to adolescence' (2009, p.155). Awareness of internet risks and the presence of risk taking are developmental factors, not just in terms of digital media literacy, but in allowing young people to define themselves in terms of social status – facing anxieties, developing maturity and experimenting online with identity and relationships. As such, in equipping young people with the skills and knowledge they need to use digital media safely and responsibly there is also a need to focus on a model of empowerment, one that listens to young people's views and, as Byron advocates, promotes a model of resilience. Other educators (for example, Alexander 2008) are also calling for a shift away from alarmist views to a cultural construct of childhood in which children are empowered, identifying the danger that the most strongly stated childhood concerns come not from young people but from parents. As many identify (Livingstone 2009; Cranmer *et al.* 2009) there is a need for a young person-centred approach to e-safety, one that recognises personal experiences whilst simultaneously situating 'ICT practices within accounts of the changing conditions of childhood and youth' (Cranmer *et al.* 2009, p.130). E-safety discourses need to be re-orientated to focus on likely risks before more extreme issues are discussed, and embedded within digital media literacy programmes in which pupils are encouraged to participate, using the very tools that generate such emotive discourse. It is only by moving away from polarised, simplistic (and confused) understandings that allow us to calm the moral panic. As Byron (2008, p.2) claims:

> Children and young people need to be empowered to keep themselves safe – this isn't just about a top-down approach. Children will be children – pushing boundaries and taking risks. At a public swimming pool we have gates, put up signs, have lifeguards and shallow ends, but we also teach children how to swim.

References

Action for Children (2006) 'Get IT Safe'. Available online at: http://www.google.co.uk/url?sa=t&rct=j&q=&esrc=s&frm=1&source=web&cd=2&cad=rja&ved=0CDcQFjAB&url=http%3A%2F%2Fimage.guardian.co.uk%2Fsys-files%2FEducation%2Fdocuments%2F2006%2F07%2F17%2FNCHreport.pdf&ei=N76IUanKEc3EPdLUgaAM&usg=AFQjCNEgKXaMSyt0-wVaTK6lhVzZ8tRS8Q&sig2=_lFMY2lekpmECWZs4gCA2g (accessed 7th May 2013)

Aftab, P. (1999) *The Parent's Guide to Protecting Your Children in Cyberspace*, Maidenhead: McGraw Hill

Alexander, R. (2008) 'The Cambridge Primary Review: emerging perspectives on childhood', *Conference on Childhood, Wellbeing and Primary Education*, London, 17 March. Available online at: www.primaryreview.org.uk/downloads/Childhood_lecture_2.pdf (accessed 28 March 2012)

Barber, D. and Cooper, L. (2012) *Using New Web Tools in the Primary Classroom: a practical guide for enhancing teaching and learning*, Abingdon: Routledge

BBC News (2007) 'Call to regulate the net rejected', BBC News [online], 29 August. Available at: http://news.bbc.co.uk/1/hi/technology/6968322.stm (accessed 20 January 2012)

Becta (2010) *Safeguarding in a Digital World: guidance for learning providers*. Available online at: http://webarchive.nationalarchives.gov.uk/20110130111510/http://publications.becta.org.uk/download.cfm?resID=42310 (accessed 6 February 2012)

Booth, R. (2010) 'Child Exploitation and Online Protection Centre row deepens', *The Guardian*, 5 October. Available online at: www.guardian.co.uk/society/2010/oct/05/ceop-row-deepens-more-resignations?INTCMP=SRCH (accessed 28 March 2012)

Born, A. (2010) *The Young People's Challenge from the Local Safeguarding Board Perspective*. Available online at: http://webcache.googleusercontent.com/search?q=cache:ww-gfS p6EbkJ:webarchive.nationalarchives.gov.uk/20101102103654/events.becta.org.uk/con tent_files/corporate/resources/events/2010/feb/ann_marie_born_erscb.odp+becta+empo wering+children+and+young+people+in+a+digital+world+2010&cd=18&hl=en&ct=cl nk&gl=uk (accessed 6 March 2012)

Buckingham, D. (2004) *The Media Literacy of Children and Young People: A review of the literature on behalf of Ofcom*. Available online at: www.google.co.uk/url?sa=t&rct= j&q=ioe% 202004%20internet&source=web&cd=3&ved=0CDgQFjAC&url=http%3A%2F%2Freprints. ioe.ac.uk%2F145%2F1%2FBuckinghammedialiteracy.pdf&ei=HiBfT8ChGIu18QP-1IDG Bw&usg=AFQjCNEmDs4NYQR7uIBxp1aH4zYeTUsbCQ&cad=rja (accessed 13 March 2012)

——(2007) *Beyond Technology: children's learning in the age of digital culture*, Cambridge: Polity

Byron, T. (2008) *Safer Children in a Digital World: the Report of the Byron Review*, Nottingham: DCSF Publications. Available online at: http://media.education.gov.uk/assets/files/pdf/s/ safer%20children%20in%20a%20digital%20world%20the%202008%20byron%20review.pdf (accessed 6 February 2012)

——(2010) *Do we have safer children in a digital world? A review of progress since the 2008 Byron Review*, Department for Education guidance. Available online at: http://media.education. gov.uk/assets/files/pdf/d/do%20we%20have%20safer%20children%20in%20a%20digital% 20world%202010%20byron%20review.pdf (accessed 5 March 2012)

Carr, N. (2008) 'Is Google making us stupid?', *Atlantic Magazine*, July/August. Available online at: www.theatlantic.com/magazine/archive/2008/07/is-google-making-us-stupid/ 6868/ (accessed 22 January 2012)

——(2010) *The Shallows: How the internet is changing the way we think, read and remember*, London: Atlantic Books

CIBER (2008) *Information behaviour of the researcher of the future*, CIBER briefing paper. Available online at: www.ucl.ac.uk/slais/research/ciber/downloads/ggexecutive.pdf (accessed 13 March 2012)

Cohen, S. (2011) *Folk Devils and Moral Panics*, Abingdon: Routledge

Cranmer, S., Selwyn, N. and Potter, J. (2009) 'Exploring primary pupils' experiences and understandings of "e-safety"', *Journal of Educational Information Technology*, 14, pp. 127-142

Davies, J. and Merchant, G. (2009) *Web 2.0 for Schools: Learning and Social Participation*, New York: Peter Lang

Department for Education (2011) *Preventing and Tackling Bullying: what does the law say and what do I have to do?* Departmental advice. Available online at: www.education.gov.uk/ schools/pupilsupport/behaviour/bullying/f0076899/preventing-and-tackling-bullying/what-does-the-law-say-and-what-do-i-have-to-do (accessed 14 February 2012)

DiNucci, D. (1999) 'Fragmented future', *Print*, 53 (4), p.32. Available online at: http:// darcyd.com/fragmented_future.pdf (accessed 12 March 2012)

Dixon, S. and Sanders, R. (2012) 'Dangerous assumptions: what our media students have taught us', *Media Education Research Journal*, 2 (2), pp.12-25

Flatters, P. (2012) 'Viewpoint: Children have never had it so good', *BBC News Magazine* [online]. Available at: www.bbc.co.uk/news/magazine-16409882 (accessed 6 January 2012)

Green, N. and Haddon, L. (2009) *Mobile Communications*, Oxford: Berg

Greenfield, S. (2008) *The Quest for Identity in the 21st Century*, London: Sceptre

Jenkins, H. (2006) *Convergence Culture: When Old and New Media Collide*, New York: New York University Press

Kline, S., Stewart, K. and Murphy, D. (2006) 'Media literacy in the risk society: toward a risk reduction strategy', *Canadian Journal of Education*, 29 (1), pp.131–153

Livingstone, S. (2009) *Children and the Internet*, Cambridge: Polity Press.

Livingstone, S., Haddon, L., Görzig, A. and Ólafsson, K. (2011a) *Risks and safety on the internet: The perspective of European children, full findings*. LSE, London: EU Kids Online.

——(2011b) *EU Kids Online, final report*. Available online at: www2.lse.ac.uk/media@lse/research/EUKidsOnline/EU%20Kids%20II%20(2009-11)/EUKidsOnlineIIReports/Final%20report.pdf (accessed 5 March 2012)

North, M. and McKeown, S. (2005) *Meeting SEN in the Curriculum – ICT*, London: David Fulton

Office for National Statistics (2012) *Internet Access Quarterly Update 2011 Q4*. Available online at: www.ons.gov.uk/ons/dcp171766_256200.pdf (accessed 13 March 2012)

OFSTED (2010) *The safe use of new technologies*. Available online at: www.ofsted.gov.uk/sites/default/files/documents/surveys-and-good-practice/t/The%20safe%20use%20of%20new%20technologies.pdf (accessed 6 January 2012)

——(2011) *ICT in Schools 2008–11: An evaluation of information and technology education in schools in England 2008–11*. Available online at: www.ofsted.gov.uk/sites/default/files/documents/surveys-and-good-practice/i/ICT%20in%20schools%202008-2011.pdf (accessed 6 January 2012)

Palmer, S. (2006) *Toxic Childhood: how the world is damaging our children and what we can do about it*, London: Orion

Paul, L. (2011) 'history.child.book.shop.2.0.', *Book 2.0*, 1 (1), pp.7-20

Pearson, J. (1999) *Women's Reading in Britain 1750–1835: A Dangerous Recreation*, Cambridge: Cambridge University Press

Plowman, L., McPake, J. and Stephen, C. (2010) 'The technologisation of childhood? Young children and technology in the home', *Children and Society*, 24 (1), pp.63–74

Postman, N. (1993) *Technopoly: the surrender of culture to technology*, New York: Vintage Books

Prensky, M. (2001). 'Digital Natives, Digital Immigrants', *On the Horizon*, 9 (5). Available online at: www.albertomattiacci.it/docs/did/Digital_Natives_Digital_Immigrants.pdf (accessed 12 March 2012)

Rivers, I. and Noret, N. (2010) 'I h8 u: findings from a five-year study of text and email bullying', *British Educational Research Journal*, 36 (4), pp.643–671

Selwyn, N. (2011) *Schools and Schooling in the Digital Age: a critical analysis*, Abingdon: Routledge

Tarapdar, S. and Kellett, M. (2011) *Young People's Voices on Cyberbullying: what can age comparisons tell us?* Available online at: http://childrens-research-centre.open.ac.uk/research/Cyberbullying%20-%20Young%20Peoples%20Voices%20Report.pdf (accessed 5 February 2012)

UKCCIS (2009) *Click Clever, Click Safe – The First UK Child Internet Safety Strategy*. Available online at: http://media.education.gov.uk/assets/files/pdf/c/click%20clever%20click%20safe%20ukccis%20strategy%202009.pdf (accessed 5 March 2012)

Woollard, J. (2011) *Psychology for the Classroom: E-Learning*, Abingdon: Routledge

Woollard, J., Wickens, C., Powell, K. and Russell, T. (2009) 'Evaluation of e-safety materials for initial teacher training: can Jenny's story make a difference?', *Technology, Pedagogy and Education*, 18 (2), pp.187-200

11

CONCLUSION

Working with vulnerability?

Graham Brotherton and Mark Cronin

The central argument of this book has been that vulnerability needs to be acknowledged as a complex set of issues rather than simply a process of individual weakness or limitation. In this short final chapter we will seek to summarise key aspects of this argument and its implications. In the first section of the book we sought to locate vulnerability in its theoretical (psychological and sociological) and policy context. Key themes from this section are as follows.

- Vulnerability needs to be located in the context of a complex series of changes in both socio-political thinking and consequent policy changes.
- At the heart of this has been the dominance of neo-liberal thinking and the changing relationship between individuals and families, the state and the private sector.
- A consequence of this has been the 'individualisation' of vulnerability and the construction of vulnerable individuals and groups as needing to 'take responsibility' for their own circumstances, regardless of the appropriateness of this model.

As discussed in Chapter 1, key changes in sociological thinking have included and increased the emphasis on both reflexivity and risk. Anthony Giddens made the link between the sense of vulnerability that comes from perceiving oneself as being at risk from a range of social and economic factors and the passivity that can result from being overwhelmed by this sense of being at risk. For Giddens the solution lies in creating ways of enabling individuals to be reflexive about this risk and take greater ownership of their own personal circumstances by creating a more positive self-narrative. Whilst it is clear that this is a helpful model in terms of helping us think how vulnerability is constructed, the next stage of the argument is rather more problematic.

It is our contention that this analysis has been subsequently imbued with elements of the neo-liberal critique of the state as too big, too bureaucratic and too expensive and that ideas about promoting independence have been used as a way of seeking to reduce the role of the state in both providing protection where required and actively promoting supportive services which promote independence (or perhaps more accurately, support interdependence). The consequence has been the conflation of two separate issues into a discourse which has a number of problematic aspects. These are summarised below.

- The need to provide support in ways which respond flexibly and imaginatively to individuals or groups whose circumstances make them vulnerable has become conflated with the consumerist, privatising aspects of neo-liberalism.
- The rhetoric of the need to reduce public spending following the banking crisis of 2008 has been linked to the notion of promoting 'independence' and used as a justification to reduce services to a number of highly marginalised groups.
- As a consequence of this, some vulnerable groups have been framed as inherently problematic – 'to blame' for their own circumstances because of poor lifestyle choices.

In the second part of the book the contributors sought to examine how these issues 'play out' in the context of particular individuals and groups and the consequences this might have. It is not the intention of this book to seek to prescribe particular ways of working, not least because an inevitable conclusion of the argument we have tried to make is that practice needs to be aware of the micro context and place a premium on flexible, negotiated strategies rather than seeking to impose pre-set models.

Vulnerability and evidence-based practice

One of the drivers of current policy is the notion of 'evidence-based' practice, and perhaps the most explicit reference to this is found in the Allen Report on early intervention which emphasises funding evidence-based interventions through social impact bonds, as discussed in Chapter 3. At this point it is worth exploring the increased centrality of evidence-based practice in the debate about vulnerability. The Department for Education website uses the definition of evidence-based practice provided by Eva Lloyd (1999, cited by Department for Education 2012): 'Finding out what works, and ensuring that the interventions we and others make in children's lives are as good as they possibly can be'.

It would be difficult to argue with this as a statement; however, the question of how we judge it is a complex one, with significant implications for the vulnerability debate. In the same article on the website it is claimed that:

> Randomised control trials (RCTs) are considered by many to be the most robust way of determining whether an intervention is effective. As the name

implies, RCTs are conducted by randomly assigning participants to a 'treatment' and a 'control' or comparison group. Thus, one group receives the treatment under investigation and the other receives no additional support other than what they would normally be given. This random assignment is done to ensure that any potential biases are evenly distributed across both groups.

Participants from both groups are then asked to complete measures that are given to them prior to the intervention and then once again afterwards. Change is then measured for both groups. If the treatment group demonstrates a measurable improvement and this is substantially greater than the comparison group, it is assumed that the treatment has had a significant effect.

(Department for Education 2012)

Several significant points can be drawn from this. The references to measurable change and treatment are both important, especially in the context of a move towards services which are funded in a way which requires the demonstration of quantifiable outcomes. 'Treatment' is an interesting way to conceptualise services (especially as this is a quote from the Department for Education) but it does clearly suggest that practitioners are expected to follow definable trajectories in their work, leading ideally to a defined set of outcomes. This raises questions about the nature of the relationship between the practitioner and the 'service user', whether they are an ATOS assessor, a social worker, or a youth worker. In particular it raises questions about the nature of the power relationship and whether these ways of working are compatible with the sort of reflexive approach outlined elsewhere in this book. This is not of course an argument against services 'which work' but rather an argument for services which take a more nuanced approach to what counts as evidence and a much greater emphasis not on 'top-down' measurement but on negotiated notions of 'success'.

Vulnerability and human need

In seeking to conclude this chapter we wish to suggest a model which we believe has the capacity to provide a useful starting point for a discussion of how to respond to the 'problem' of vulnerability. This is the work of Martha Nussbaum (originally through a collaboration with Amartya Sen), who suggests that there are ten 'central functional human capabilities' which need to be acquired in order to live a 'dignified' life, thus providing a non-monetary way of thinking about welfare (here being used in the full sense of the promotion of well-being). These capabilities are:

- life as in a 'normal' lifespan;
- bodily health – able to be healthy, with access to the necessities which support health (food, shelter, etc.);

- bodily integrity – including freedom of movement, being secure against all forms of violence and assault, the ability to express sexuality;
- senses, imagination and thought – encompassing literacy and freedom of expression (creatively, politically and spiritually);
- emotions – the ability to love and care for others and to have this reciprocated;
- practical reason – the ability to reflect upon and be involved in the planning of one's own life;
- affiliation – the ability to live with and associate with others (including support for the social and political institutions which protect this capability);
- other species – living with and showing concern for other species;
- play – being able to laugh and enjoy recreation;
- control over one's political (both micro and macro) and material environments.

(Nussbaum 2000 adapted by Brotherton 2008)

For Nussbaum and others advocating a capabilities-based approach, the key issue is the focus that this places on particular approaches to vulnerability. Crucially, the notion of capabilities can help in evaluating practice through its emphasis on the necessity of supportive intervention which acknowledges that not all groups or individuals are equally placed to take advantage of opportunities 'available' to them. As Carpenter (2009) suggests, the capabilities approach takes account of 'the fact that the playing field is bumpier for some groups than others, and offers ways of reconciling principles of equality and diversity in social justice' (p.356).

Some critics have suggested that this focus on what appears to be a rather subjective and individualist understanding simply creates another set of problems. However, it is our contention that the capabilities approach provides a useful way of applying a broader perspective to the notion of vulnerability. The limited research that exists on perceptions of well-being – such as that undertaken by the New Economics Foundation (Seaford 2010) – does suggest that people's subjective definitions of well-being are very similar to the capabilities expressed by Nussbaum. Furthermore, they suggest that inequalities are a significant barrier to achieving a sense of well-being.

Reflexivity revisited

We started this book with a discussion of reflexivity and the role it plays in both conceptualising and working with vulnerability, and in this final chapter we need to reflect on this. Giddens argues that reflexivity is crucial to maintaining a positive identity in the rapidly changing, fluid circumstances in which we now live. Central to this complexity are notions of risk and how we perceive ourselves as positioned against the risks that we face. Several chapters in this book have sought to lay out the risk environment in relation to particular issues – in the context, for example, of violence within personal relationships, becoming homeless or experiencing the 'looked-after' system.

In seeking to conclude we need to return to how the risk environment impacts on our day-to-day experience of being or perceiving others as vulnerable and how this is mediated through reflexivity. Looking at this first from the perspective of those who may require support as a result of becoming vulnerable, it means working with an understanding of the need to support people in making reflexive decisions about themselves and therefore helping them decide how to respond to the circumstances they find themselves in. It also requires approaches which 'go with the grain' of their experiences and support them in making positive choices when responding to their circumstances. There is always a danger that constructing the argument in this way seems platitudinous but, as the various chapters in this book have sought to demonstrate, effective responses to vulnerability need to recognise that:

- Vulnerability is often the result of significant changes in circumstances which may be experienced as personal but are also the consequence of social policy and/or economic change. For example, the experience of being a survivor of domestic violence or the partner or child of a prisoner are deeply personal but are also profoundly shaped by dominant social attitudes and the policies which result from them.
- These experiences take place in a context which increasingly takes a particular moral perspective influenced by neo-liberalism; this seeks to categorise those who may need support as at 'fault' because of their circumstances and therefore as needing to take responsibility for themselves by changing their behaviour and (it is argued) thereby being able to change their circumstances.

In this context a particular challenge for practitioners is to respond in constructive ways to the fact that the overall climate of opinion around support has changed markedly over the last 25 years or so. As an example of this, the British Social Attitudes Survey, which has tracked opinion on a range of issues, includes the question, 'How much do you agree or disagree that ... if welfare benefits weren't so generous, people would learn to stand on their own two feet?' In 1987 around 33 per cent agreed or strongly agreed with the statement, with 46 per cent disagreeing or disagreeing strongly; by 2011 55 per cent agreed, with only 21 per cent disagreeing (British Social Attitudes 2012). A climate where public attitudes to supporting vulnerable individuals, groups and families are increasingly hostile and where budgets are increasingly tight presents a major challenge. An interesting explanation for this significant change in social attitudes is offered by Lister (2008) and Killeen (2008), who observe the emergence of 'povertyism', described by them as the process by which the poor or vulnerable are 'othered' and subsequently labelled as 'inferior or of lesser value' and constructed 'as a source of moral contamination, a threat, an undeserving economic burden', which fits well with the themes in this book. In this context the arguments for programmes which deliver demonstrable results against pre-determined outcomes can look overwhelming. However, if we seek to apply the insights of sociological or psychological understandings of vulnerability we can also argue that the need for services to demonstrate flexibility and an ability to respond to particular circumstances is a prerequisite for providing effective support and creating the circumstances in which people can in an actual rather than rhetorical sense take ownership of their situation.

It is our contention that it is not possible to develop a simplistic overarching model of working with vulnerable individuals, groups or families but that all services need to identify the extent to which they can genuinely claim to be working in a way which supports the development of people's capacity to be active partners in seeking solutions that are appropriate for their own circumstances. This means an emphasis on actively promoting people's reflexive capacity in a safe and supportive way. There are many examples of services which are responding to this challenge but much more needs to be done in creating a policy framework which actually facilitates it. Understanding the economic foundations of policy is central, but attention also needs to be paid to policy consequences in terms of access to the resources necessary for what Nussbaum calls 'dignified life'.

References

British Social Attitudes Survey (2012) *British Social Attitudes Information System*. Available online at www.britsocat.com/Home (accessed October 2012).

Brotherton, G. (2008) 'Planning and Managing Care' in Brotherton, G. and Parker, S. *Your Foundation in Health and Social Care*, London: Sage.

Carpenter, M. (2009) 'The capabilities approach and critical social policy: lessons from the majority world?', *Critical Social Policy*, 29 (3), p.351–373.

Department for Education (2012) *Evidence Based Practice*. Available online at www.education. gov.uk/childrenandyoungpeople/families/b00203759/evidence-based-practice (accessed October 2012).

Killeen, D. (2008) *Is poverty in the UK a denial of people's human rights?*, York: Joseph Rowntree Foundation.

Lister, R. (2008) 'Povertyism and "othering": why they matter', *Challenging Povertyism: TUC Conference*, London, 17 October.

Seaford, C. (2010) *Well-being: Human well-being and priorities for economic policy-makers*, New Economics Foundation working paper. Available online at www.neweconomics.org/ sites/neweconomics.org/files/Well-being_Human_well-being_and_priorities_for_economic _policy-makers.pdf (accessed November 2012)

INDEX

Page numbers in **bold** indicate reference to a table. Page numbers in *italics* indicate text within a figure.